The Challenge
of Incompetence
and Poverty

J. McVicker Hunt

UNIVERSITY OF ILLINOIS PRESS
Urbana   Chicago   London

The Challenge
of Incompetence
and Poverty

Papers on the
Role of Early Education

To J. P. Guilford

the teacher who introduced me to psychology,
who invited me to make my career in the field,
and who expressed pleasure whenever any of his
students came forth with a new idea

Preface

Incompetence and poverty are interrelated. As a characteristic of individual persons, incompetence results in poverty. And, the poverty of one generation becomes, by virtue of the circumstances which hamper the development of abilities and motives, a basis for the incompetence of the next generation. As the burgeoning role of technology in our society calls for higher and higher levels of competence in larger and larger supply, those without at least fairly high levels of competence find it harder and harder to earn their way in the marketplace and to participate in the affluence deriving from our technology. Also, since the Supreme Court ruled that separate facilities for the races cannot be equal, the problems of race and social class have become intertwined because a large proportion of black people have been condemned to limited competence by their long history in slavery and then in poverty.

The papers which follow are concerned with our changing conceptions of the basis for competence. These changing conceptions concern the origins of both intelligence and motivation. The last two of these papers are concerned directly with the implications of these changing conceptions for the challenge of incompetence and poverty. It is no longer tenable to regard the poor as just naturally inept, lazy, and untrustworthy. The poor, be they black or white, typically do an inadequate job of teaching their children the abilities and motives needed to cope with schooling even though they love their children as much as any parents do. A new role for education is emerging in early childhood. Such education, as illustrated by Project Head Start, is compensatory. It attempts to make up during their fifth year what children missed during their first four years. Such education may also take the form of a deliberate effort to help parents learn how to arrange circumstances for their young children the better to foster from birth on the sensorimotor, attitudinal, and linguistic bases for the abilities, the attitudes, the motives, and the values which must be acquired later if the child is to become able to cope with school and later to participate in the mainstream of our increasingly technological culture.

Early childhood education will not alone, of course, solve the problems of incompetence and poverty. Where these problems are a product of the limited opportunities afforded black people by racial discrimination, that discrimination must go. Where lack of competence in those now adults or approaching adulthood makes them nearly unemployable, our society must provide training and make available jobs appropriate to their existing level of competence. Where housing in the slums has become ugly and unhealthy, our society must help those living there to have adequate housing without destroying the social structure of neighborhoods or denying developing children the opportunities to observe and to imitate adults in work-a-day roles. All such programs are necessary, and they must be provided in a way that encourages rather than discourages individual initiative. Early childhood education can never be the sole response to the challenge of poverty and the problem of our inner cities, but if our society is to prevent that incompetence which makes for the poverty of individuals, early childhood education is a highly important part of what is needed in our response to the challenge of incompetence and poverty.

The seven papers included in this book represent an evolving progress report of my grasp of the new evidence calling for changes in our conceptions about the origins of intelligence and motivation and the implications for our response to this challenge. Because the papers were originally prepared individually without any expectation or intention of making a book, they overlap considerably. Certains points are made redundantly, perhaps far too redundantly. Each of the chapter-papers can be read separately without loss of continuity, yet a transition exists between the early and the late chapters. The earlier ones emphasize changing theoretical beliefs which provide a rationale for early childhood education. The later ones emphasize the investigative characteristics of children from families in poverty and the nature of the circumstances which these children face. They also present, at least in outline, ways to help these children develop the required abilities and motives and values through compensatory education or to help their families prevent that incompetence so commonly associated with being reared in poverty.

These papers were originally prepared for audiences of professional people from the behavioral and educational sciences or from the educational and helping professions. The points I make are heavily documented with evidence, and references are provided which will lead those who wish to examine that evidence to the relevant investigative literature. Even though these papers were originally prepared for professional people, a high proportion of those requesting reprints, especially of the earlier papers, are from outside the behavioral and educational and helping professions. Even so, I should never have considered putting these papers together as a book had Mrs. James P. Rich—a friendly summer neighbor in Estes Park, Colorado, and the program chairman for the Parent-Teachers Association at Nyack, New York—not wondered aloud as to why such papers should remain in scientific journals, unavailable to her and other interested readers like her. Since others with whom I have consulted have agreed with Mrs. Rich, I am emboldened to make these papers available by collecting them between the covers of this book.

It needs noting that danger, as well as potential value, lurks in the idea of early childhood education. Damage can be done by overly ambitious parents who insist that their child keep up behaviorally and academically with the proverbial Jones child. Parents can make their children exceedingly unhappy by demanding of them performances outside their interests and beyond their competence. Serious damage may result when parents make their acceptance and love contingent upon accomplishments beyond the limits of their children's existing competence. Unhappiness and even danger lurks when parents merely provide models too complex for their children's competence if they implicitly demand imitation. Such threads of damage can readily be avoided, however, if enriching circumstances are always presented in such a way that the infant or child can take them or leave them as he wishes. No damage will occur if parents will heed the behavioral signs of distress and let up, or the behavioral signs of interests and wishes and proceed accordingly, and if decisions for action and choice are made in the course of mutual communication and consideration of both the wishes of all and the potential outcomes.

Many are my debts in this enterprise. If the overlap among the papers included here proves to be annoying to the reader, it is but a minuscule fraction of the repetitiousness of my discussions with my wife, Esther. She has endured them patiently, and even managed to lend encouragement when something new appeared in the discourse. I am highly indebted to Cynthia and Martin Deutsch of the Institute for Developmental Studies at New York University for inviting me to give the first of these seven papers at the Arden House Conference on Preschool Enrichment of Socially Disadvantaged Children in December of 1962. Although my book, *Intelligence and Experience* (1961), was relevant so far as the scientific evidence was concerned, the paper now constituting the first chapter of this book was really my first on the topic of early childhood education. I am indebted to Dr. Donald Young and to the Russell Sage Foundation for the support that enabled me to have several summers in Estes Park, Colorado, for uninterrupted scholarly effort on the implications of the evidence available in the behavioral and social sciences literature for what we believe about child rearing and early childhood education. The effort is reflected in these papers. Also reflected is the work supported by the Commonwealth Fund and the Carnegie Corporation. The actual writing of these papers, however, has been done with the support of Grant Nos.

MH-K6-18567 and MH No. 11321 from the United States Public Health Service.

The repetition of both content and structure in these papers is less than it might have been had I not had the skillful editorial counsel of Mrs. Gay Menges of the University of Illinois Press. Finally, I am especially indebted to the secretaries who have helped me in the preparation of these papers and in the process of assembling the bibliography from the separate papers into one for this volume. It was Mrs. Sharon Ferguson who worked with me so helpfully on the papers which constitute here Chapters 1 and 3. It was she who also devised for me a cumulative bibliography that has saved tremendous hours of time in the preparation of the bibliography of each new paper as I write it. It was Mrs. Bonnie Stone and Mrs. Merle Thorne who skillfully transcribed my dictation of the other five papers in their original form and who assembled the bibliographies of these several papers into a single one. Mrs. Suzanne Chapple has transcribed the revisions and seen the manuscript to press. To all these people I am grateful.

Urbana, Illinois
23 November 1968
J. McV. Hunt

Contents

1 The Psychological Basis for Using Preschool Enrichment as an Antidote for Cultural Deprivation 1

2 The Evolution of Current Concepts of Intelligence and Intellectual Development 48

3 Traditional Personality Theory in the Light of Recent Evidence 76

4 The Epigenesis of Intrinsic Motivation and the Fostering of Early Cognitive Development 94

5 Political and Social Implications of the Role of Experience in the Development of Competence 112

6 Toward the Prevention of Incompetence 142

7 Poverty Versus Equality of Opportunity 190

References 235

Author Index 265

Subject Index 277

1

The Psychological Basis for Using Preschool Enrichment as an Antidote for Cultural Deprivation

The task of maximizing the competence of our children has acquired new urgency. Two of the top challenges of our day lie behind this urgency. First, the rapidly expanding role of technology, now taking the form of automation, decreases the demand and the opportunity for persons of limited competence and skills while it increases the demand and opportunity for those competent particularly in the use of written language, in mathematics, in problem-solving, and in willingness to accept responsibility. Second, the challenge of eliminating racial discrimination requires not only equality of employment opportunity and social recognition for persons of equal competence, but also an equalization of the opportunity to develop that intellectual capacity, those skills, and those motivational systems upon which competence is based (from Hunt, 1964).

During most of the past century anyone who entertained the idea of increasing the "natural" competence of human beings was regarded as an unrealistic "do-gooder." Individuals, classes, and races were considered to be what they were because either God or their inheritance made them that way. In the light of the challenge of our changing ecology, it is very exciting to me to encounter people who are generally considered sensible plan-

Originally prepared for the Arden House Conference on Preschool Enrichment of Socially Disadvantaged Children (December, 1962). Reprinted from *The Merrill-Palmer Quarterly*, 10 (July, 1964), 209-248.

ning to utilize preschool experiences as an antidote for what we
are now calling cultural deprivation and social disadvantage.
The group at the Child Welfare Research Station at the University of Iowa, under the leadership of George D. Stoddard
(see Stoddard & Wellman, 1940), described effects of their
nursery school which they considered evidence justifying just
such a use of these schools. This was about 25 years ago. Their
work, however, was picked to pieces by critics and, in the
process, lost much of the suggestive value it was justified in
having. Many of you will recall the ridicule that was heaped
upon the "wandering IQ" (Simpson, 1939) and the way in
which many people (e.g., Florence Goodenough, 1939) derided
in print the idea of a group of 13 "feeble-minded" infants being
brought within the range of normal intelligence through training by moron nursemaids in a State School for the Mentally
Retarded (referring to the work of Skeels & Dye (1939) to
which I shall return). The fact that such compensatory educational use of nursery schools is now being seriously planned
by sensible people with widespread approval means that something has changed.

The change, of course, is not in the nature of man or in the
nature of his development; it is rather in our conceptions of
man's nature and of his development. Some of our most important beliefs about man and his development have changed or
are in the process of changing. It is these changes in belief
which have freed us to try as demonstrative experiments what
only as recently as World War II would have been considered
a stupid waste of effort and time. It is also these changes in
theoretical belief about man and his development which provide my topic, namely, the psychological basis for using preschool enrichment as an antidote for cultural deprivation.

I number these changing beliefs as six. Let me state them in
their prechange form, in the form that has so much hampered
the sort of enterprise in which this group is about to engage:
1. a belief in fixed intelligence; 2. a belief in predetermined development; 3. a belief in the fixed and static, telephone-switch-
board nature of brain function; 4. a belief that experience during the early years, and particularly before the development of

speech, is unimportant; 5. a belief that whatever experience does affect later development is a matter of emotional reactions based on the fate of instinctual needs; 6. a belief that learning must be motivated by homeostatic need, by painful stimulation, or by acquired drives based on these.

Let me discuss the evidential and conceptual bases for the change which has been taking place since World War II in these hampering beliefs, one by one. Then I shall close by trying to justify the sort of enterprise you propose, and by indicating how the largely forgotten work of Maria Montessori may well contain practical suggestions concerning the way to go about the enterprise.

The Belief in Fixed Intelligence

Almost every idea has roots in both communicated conceptual history and observed evidence. The notion of fixed intelligence has conceptual roots in Darwin's (1859) theory of evolution and in the intense emotional controversy that surrounded it. You will recall that Darwin believed that evolution took place, not by changes wrought through the use or disuse as Lamarck (1809) had thought, but by changes resulting from variations in the progeny of every species or strain which are then selected by the condition under which they live. Their selection is a matter of which variations survive to reproduce so that the variations are passed on into the successive generations. The change is conceived thus to be one that comes via the survival of a variation in a strain through reproduction. Implicit in this notion was the assumption that the characteristics of any organism are predetermined by the genetic constitution with which the organism comes into being as a fertilized ovum. Probably this implicit assumption would never have caught on with anywhere near the force it did, had it not been for two outstanding figures in the history of relatively recent thought. The first of these is Sir Francis Galton, Charles Darwin's younger cousin. You will remember that it was Galton who made the assumption of hereditary determination of variations in adult characteristics explicit. Galton reasoned, furthermore, that if his cousin were correct, it would mean that the hope of improving the lot of man does not lie in *euthenics,* or in trying to change him through education; rather, such hope lies in *eugenics,* or in the selection of those superior persons who should survive. Secondly, he saw that if decisions were to be made as to which human beings were to survive and reproduce, it would be necessary to have some criteria for survival. So he founded his anthropometric laboratory for the measurement of man, with the hope that by means of tests he could determine those individuals who should survive. Note that he was not deciding merely who should be selected for jobs in a given industry, but who should survive to reproduce. This was his concern. Because of the abhorrence which such a plan met, Galton talked and wrote relatively little about it. However, the combination of the context of his life-work with the few remarks he did make on the subject gives these remarks convincing significance (see Hunt, 1961).

Galton had a pupil who was very influential in bringing such conceptions into the stream of American thought. This was J. McKeen Cattell, who brought Galton's tests to America and, beginning in 1890, gave them to college students, first at the University of Pennsylvania and then at Columbia University. Because Cattell was also an influential teacher at both Penn and Columbia, his influence spread through the many students he had before World War I—when his sympathies with Germany led to a painful separation from Columbia.

A second psychologist who was almost equally influential in bringing the stream of thought supporting fixed intelligence into American thought is G. Stanley Hall. Hall did not personally know Galton; neither did he personally know Darwin, but he read about evolution while still a college student, and, as he has written in his autobiography, "it struck me like a light; this was the thing for me." Hall's importance lies in that he communicated a strong attachment to the notion of fixed intelligence to his students at Clark University, of which he was the first president, and these students became leaders of the new psychology in America (see Boring, 1929, p. 534). Among them were three of the most illustrious leaders of the testing movement. One was Henry H. Goddard, who first translated the

Binet tests into English for use at the Vineland Training School and also wrote the story of the Kallikak family (1912). Another was F. Kuhlmann, who was also an early translator and reviser of the Binet tests and who, with Rose G. Anderson, adapted them for use with preschool children. The third was Lewis Terman, who is the author of the Stanford-Binet revision, the most widely known version of the Binet tests in America. These three communicated their faith in fixed intelligence to a major share of those who spread the testing movement in America.

So much for the conceptual roots of the belief in fixed intelligence that come by way of communication in the history of thought.

The assumption of fixed intelligence also had an empirical basis. Not only did test-retest reliabilities show that the positions of individuals in a group remained fairly constant, but also the tests showed some capacity to predict such criterion performances as school success, success as officers in World War I, etc. All such evidence concerned children of school age for whom the experiences to which they were exposed is at least to some degree standardized (see Hunt, 1961). When investigators began to examine the constancy of the DQ (developmental quotient) or IQ in preschool children, the degree of constancy proved to be very much lower. You will recall some of the very interesting interpretations of this lack of constancy in the preschool DQ (see Hunt, 1961, p. 311ff). Anderson argued that since the tests at successive ages involved different functions, constancy could not be expected. But an epigenesis of man's intellectual functions is inherent in the nature of his development, and the implications of this fact were apparently missed by these critics of the findings from the infant tests. While they knew that the basic structure of intelligence changes in its early phases of development just as the structures of the body change in the embryological phase of morphological development, they appear not to have noted that it is thus inevitable that the infant tests must involve differing content and functions at successive ages.

It was Woodworth (1941) who argued, after examining the evidence from the studies of twins, that there might be some difference in IQ due to the environment but that which exists among individuals in our culture is largely due to the genes. In the context of cultural deprivation, I believe Woodworth asked the wrong question. He might better have asked: What would be the difference in the IQ of a pair of identical twins at age six if one were reared as Myrtle McGraw (1935) reared the trained twin, Johnny (so that he was swimming at four months, roller-skating at 11 months, and developing various skills at about one-half to one-fourth the age that people usually develop them), and if the other twin were reared in an orphanage, like the one described by Wayne Dennis (1960) in Tehran, where 60 per cent of the infants two years of age are still not sitting up alone and where 85 per cent of those four years of age are still not walking alone? Although observations of this kind come from varied sources and lack the force of controlled experimentation, they suggest strongly that lack of constancy is the rule for either IQ or DQ during the preschool years and that the IQ is not at all fixed unless the culture of the school fixes the program of environmental encounters. Cross-sectional validity may be substantial, with predictive validity being little above zero (see Hunt, 1961). In fact, trying to predict what the IQ of an individual child will be at age 18 from a DQ obtained during his first or second year is much like trying to predict how fast a feather might fall in a hurricane. The law of falling bodies holds only under the specified and controlled conditions of a vacuum. Similarly, any laws concerning the rate of intellectual growth must take into account the series of environmental encounters which constitute the conditions of that growth.

The Belief in Predetermined Development

The belief in predetermined development has been no less hampering, for a serious consideration of preschool enrichment as an antidote for cultural deprivation, than that in fixed intelligence. This belief also has historical roots in Darwin's theory of evolution. It got communicated into the main stream of psychological thought about the development by G. Stanley Hall (see Pruette, 1926). Hall gave special emphasis to the belief in predetermined development by making central in his version of the theory of evolution the conception of recapitulation. This is the notion that the development of an individual shows in summary form the development of the species. Hall managed to communicate many valuable points about psychological development by means of his parables based on the concept of biological recapitulation. One of the most famous of these is his parable of the tadpole's tail. To Hall also goes a very large share of the responsibility for the shape of investigation in child and developmental psychology during the first half of this century. This shape was the study of normative development, or the description of what is typical or average. It was, moreover, Arnold Gesell (see, e.g., 1945, 1954), another student of G. Stanley Hall, whose life's work concerned the normative description of children's behavioral development. Gesell took over Hall's faith in predetermined development in his own notion that development is governed by what he has termed "intrinsic growth." It should be noted that once one believes in "intrinsic growth," the normative picture of development is not only a description of the process but an explanation of it as well. Thus, whenever little Johnny does something "bad," the behavior can be explained by noting that it is just a stage he is going through. Moreover, following Hall's parable of the tadpole's tail—in which the hind legs fail to develop if the tail is amputated— Johnny's unwanted behavior must not be hampered lest some desirable future characteristic should fail to appear.

This notion of predetermined development has also an empirical basis, for the evidence from various early studies of behavioral development in both lower animals and in children was readily seen as consonant with it. Among these are Coghill's (1929) studies of behavioral development in amblystoma. These demonstrated that behavioral development, like anatomical development, starts at the head and proceeds tailward, starts from the inside and proceeds outward, and consists of a progressive differentiation of more specific units from general units. From such evidence Coghill and others inferred the special additional notion that behavior unfolds automatically as the anatomical basis for behavior matures. From such a background came the differentiation of the process of learning from the process of maturation.

Among the early studies of behavioral development are those of Carmichael (1926, 1927, 1928), also with amblystoma and frogs, which appeared to show that the circumstances in which development takes place are of little consequence. You will recall that Carmichael divided batches of amblystoma and frog eggs. One of these batches he chloretoned to inhibit their activity; another batch he kept in tap water on an ordinary table; and a third group he kept in tap water on a work bench, where they received extra stimulation. Those kept in tap water on an ordinary table swam as early as did those that got the extra stimulation from the work bench. Moreover, even though those that were chloretoned had been prevented from activity through five days, they appeared to be as adept at swimming within half an hour after the chloretone was washed out as were either of the two batches reared in tap water. Although Carmichael himself was very careful in interpreting these results, they have commonly been interpreted to mean that development is almost entirely a function of maturation and that learning, as represented in practice, is of little consequence.

Such an interpretation got further support from early studies of the effects of practice. In one such study of a pair of identical twins by Gesell & Thompson (1929), the untrained twin became as adept at tower-building and stair-climbing after a week of practice as was the trained twin who had been given practice in tower-building and stair-climbing over many weeks. In another such study by Josephine Hilgard (1932), a group of ten preschool children were given practice cutting with scissors, climbing a ladder, and buttoning over a period of 12 weeks; yet they retained superiority over the control group, which had received no special practice, for only a short time. One week of practice in those skills by the control group brought their performance up to a level which was no longer significantly inferior to that of the experimental group from a statistical standpoint. Later work by two other investigators appeared to lend further support. Dennis & Dennis (1940) found that the children of Hopi Indians raised on cradleboards, which inhibited the movements of their legs and arms during waking hours, walked at the same age as did Hopi children reared freely, in the typical white man's manner. Moreover, Dennis & Dennis (1935, 1938, 1941) found the usual sequence of autogenic behavior items in a pair of fraternal twins reared under conditions of "restricted practice and minimal social stimulation." Many such studies appeared to yield results which could be readily seen as consonant with the notion that practice has little effect on the rate of development and that the amount of effort to be got from practice is a function of the level of maturation present when the practice occurs.

It was just such a notion and just such evidence that led Watson (1928) to argue in his book, *The Psychological Care of the Infant and Child,* that experience is unimportant during the preschool years because nothing useful can be learned until the child has matured sufficiently. Thus, he advised that the best thing possible is to leave the child alone to grow. Then when the child has "lain and grown," when the response repertoire has properly matured, those in charge of his care can introduce learning. He conceived that learning could "get in its licks" tying these responses to proper stimuli, via the conditioning principle, and by linking them together in chains to produce complex skills. I suspect that the use of B. F. Skinner's baby-box, with controlled temperature, humidity, etc., may be based upon just such assumptions of predetermined development and of an automatic unfolding of a basic behavioral repertoire with anatomical maturation.

It should be noted that the animal evidence cited here comes from amblystoma and frogs, which are well down the evolutionary scale. They have brains in which the ratio of those portions concerned with association or intrinsic processes to the portions concerned directly with input and output is small; i.e., the A/S ratio, as formulated by Hebb (1949), is small. When organisms with higher A/S ratios were studied, in somewhat the fashion in which Coghill and Carmichael studied the behavioral development of amblystoma and frogs, the evidence yielded has been highly dissonant with the implications of predetermined development. When Cruze (1935, 1938) found that the number of pecking errors per 25 trials decreased through the first five days, even though the chicks were kept in the dark—a result consonant with the notion of predeterminism—he also found facts pointing in a contrary direction. For instance, chicks kept in the dark for 20 consecutive days, and given an opportunity to see light and have pecking experience only during the daily tests, *failed* to attain a high level of accuracy in pecking and exhibited almost no improvement in the striking-seizing-swallowing sequence.

Similarly, Kuo's (see Hunt, 1961) wonderful behavioral observations on the embryological development of chicks in the egg indicate that the responses comprising the pecking and locomotor patterns have been "well-practiced" long before hatching. The "practice" for pecking seems to start with head-bobbing, which is among the first embryonic movements to be observed. The practice for the locomotor patterns begins with vibratory motions of the wing-buds and leg-buds; these movements become flexion and extension as the limbs lengthen and joints appear. At about the eleventh day of incubation, the yolk sac characteristically moves over to the ventral side of the embryo. This movement of the yolk sac forces the legs to fold on the breast and to be held there. From this point on, the legs cannot be fully extended. They are forced henceforth to hatching to remain in this folded position with extensive thrusts only against the yolk sac. Kuo argues that this condition establishes a fixed resting posture for the legs, and prepares them for lifting of the chick's body in standing and locomotion. Moreover, his interpretation gets some support from "an experiment of nature." In the 7,000 embryos that he observed, nearly 200 crippled chicks appeared. These crippled chicks could neither stand nor walk after hatching. Neither could they sit in the roosting position, because their legs were deformed. Over 80 per cent of those with deformed legs occurred in those instances in which the yolk sac failed for some reason, still unknown, to move over to the ventral side of the embryo.

Such observations suggest that the mammalian advent of increasingly long uterine control of embryological and fetal environment in phylogeny reflects the fact that environmental cir-

cumstances become more and more important for early development as the central nervous system control becomes more predominant. It should be noted, moreover, that as central nervous
system control becomes more predominant, capacity for re-
generation decreases. Perhaps this implies a waning of the relative potency of the chemical predeterminers of development as
one goes up the phylogenetic scale.

Perhaps even more exciting in this connection is the work of
Austin Riesen (see 1958), Brattgård (1952), and others. Riesen
undertook the rearing of chimpanzees in darkness in order to
test some of Hebb's (1949) hypotheses of the importance of
primary learning in the development of perception. What he
appears to have discovered—along with Brattgård (1952);
Liberman (1962); Rasch, Swift, Riesen, & Chow (1961); and
Weiskrantz (1958)—is that even certain anatomical structures
of the retina require light stimulation for proper development.
The chimpanzee babies who were kept in the dark for a year-
and-a-half have atypical retinas; and, even after they are brought
into the light, the subsequent development of their retinas goes
awry and they become permanently blind. The result of such
prolonged stimulus deprivation during infancy appears to be
an irreversible process that does not occur when the chimpanzee
infant is kept in darkness for only something like seven months.
Inasmuch as Weiskrantz (1958) has found a scarcity of Mueller
fibers in the retinas of kittens reared in the dark, and since other
investigators (especially Brattgård, 1952) have found the retinal-
ganglion cells of animals reared in the dark to be deficient in the
production of ribonucleic acid (RNA), these studies of rearing
under conditions of sensory deprivation appear to be lending
support to Hydén's (1959, 1960) hypothesis. This reasons that
the effects of experience may be stored as RNA within the glial
component of retinal tissue and, perhaps, of brain tissue as well.

For our present purposes, it is enough to note that such
studies are bringing evidence that even the anatomical structures
of the central nervous system are affected in their development
by experience. This lends credence to Piaget's (1936) aphorism
that "use is the ailment of a schema."

Consider another study of the effects of early experience. This is a study by Thompson & Heron (1954), comparing the adult problem-solving ability of Scotty pups which were reared as pets in human homes from the time of weaning until they were eight months of age with that of their littermates reared in isolation in laboratory cages for the same period. The adult tests were made when the animals were 18 months old, after they had been together in the dog pasture for a period of ten months. Adult problem-solving was measured by means of the Hebb-Williams (1946) test of animal intelligence. In one of these tests, the dog is brought into a room while hungry. After being allowed to smell and see a bowl of food, the dog is permitted to watch as this food is removed and put behind a screen in one of the opposite corners of the room. Both pet-reared and cage-reared dogs go immediately to the spot where the food disappeared. After the same procedure has been repeated several times, the food is then placed, while the animal watches, behind a screen in another opposite corner of the room. In order to see this clearly, think of the first screen being in the corner to the dog's right, the second in the corner to the dog's left. Now, when the dog is released, if he is pet-reared he goes immediately to the screen in the left corner for food. But, if he was cage-reared, he is more likely to go to the screen in the right corner where he had previously found food. In his tests of object permanence, Piaget (1936) describes behavior of children about nine months old resembling that of the cage-reared pups, and of children about 14 months old resembling that of the pet-reared pups.

It is interesting to compare the results of this study by Thompson & Heron (1954), in which dogs were the subjects, with the results of various studies of the effects of early experiences on adult problem-solving in which rats were subjects (see Hebb, 1947; Gauron & Becker, 1959; Wolf, 1943). Whereas the effects of early experience on the problem-solving of dogs appear to be both large and persistent, they appear to be both less marked and less permanent in the rat. Such a comparison lends further credence to the proposition that the importance of the effects of early experience increases as the associative or intrinsic portions of the cerebrum increase in proportion, as reflected in Hebb's notion of the A/S ratio.

But what about the fact that practice appears to have little or no effect on the development of a skill in young children? How can one square the absence of the effects of practice with the tremendous apathy and retardation commonly to be found in children reared in orphanages? In the case of the orphanage in Tehran reported on by Dennis (1960), the retardation in locomotor function is so great, as I have already noted, that 60 per cent fail to sit up alone at two years of age, even though nearly all children ordinarily sit up at ten months of age; and 85 per cent still fail to walk alone at four years of age, even though children typically walk at about 14 or 15 months of age and nearly all are walking before they are two years of age. I believe the two sets of results can be squared by taking into account the epigenesis in the structure of behavior that occurs during the earliest years. The investigators of the effects of practice neglected this epigenesis. They sought the effects of experience only in practice of the function or schema to be observed and measured. The existence of an epigenesis of intellectual function implies that the experimental roots of a given schema will lie in antecedent activities quite different in structure from the schema to be observed and measured. Thus, antecedent practice at tower-building and buttoning may be relatively unimportant for the development of skill in these activities; but an unhampered antecedent opportunity to throw objects and to manipulate them in a variety of situations, and an even earlier opportunity to have seen a variety of sights and to have heard a variety of sounds, may be of tremendous importance in determining both the age at which tower-building and buttoning will occur and the degree of skill that the child will manifest. I shall return to this topic.

Brain Function Conceived as a Static Switchboard

One cannot blame Darwin for the conception of brain function as static, like that in a telephone switchboard. The origin of the ferment leading to these conceptions, however, does derive from Darwin's (1872) shift of attention from the evolution of the body to the evolution of mind. This he began in his

book, *The Expressions of the Emotions in Man and Animals.*
It was thus Darwin who provided the stimulus for what was
later to be called *comparative psychology.* The original purpose
was to show that there is a gradual transition from the lower
animals to man in the various faculties of the mind. It was
Romanes (1882, 1883) who took up this task in an attempt to
show the manner in which intelligence has evolved. Romanes'
method was to show through anecdotes that animals are capable
of intelligent behavior, albeit at a level of complexity inferior to
man's. It was C. Lloyd Morgan (1894) who said that it was
reasoning by very loose analogy to impute to dogs, cats, and the
like, the same kind of conscious processes and faculties that man
can report. It was Morgan who applied Ockham's "razor of
parsimony" to the various mental faculties. Then, shortly, Thorndike & Woodworth (1901) knocked out such old-fashioned
faculties as memory with their studies showing that such forms
of practice as daily memorizing poetry do not improve a person's capacity to memorize other types of material, and that
being taught mathematics and Latin does not improve performance on reasoning tests.

It was still obvious, however, that animals do learn and that
they do solve problems. Morgan (1894) saw this occurring by
a process of trial and error. According to this conception, as
Hull (1943) later elaborated it, an organism comes to any given
situation with a ready-made hierarchy of responses. When those
at the top of the hierarchy fail to achieve satisfaction, they are
supposed to be weakened (extinguished). Other responses lower
in the hierarchy then take their places and become connected
with stimuli from the situation. Or, as Thorndike (1913) put
it earlier, new S-R bonds are established. Complex behavior was
explained by assuming that one response can be the stimulus
for another, so that S-R chains could be formed. The role of the
brain in such learning also needed explanation. Here the telephone was the dramatic, new invention supplying a mechanical
model for a conception of the brain's role. Inasmuch as the reflex arc was conceived to be both the anatomical and the functional unit of the nervous system, the role of the brain in learning could readily be conceived to be analogous to that of a

telephone switchboard. Thus, the head was emptied of active functions, and the brain, which filled it, came to be viewed as the focus of a variety of static connections.

All this led to what I fear is a basic confusion in psychological thought, one which has been prominent for at least the last 35 or 40 years. This is a confusion between S-R methodology on the one hand, and S-R theory on the other. We cannot escape S-R methodology. The best one can possibly do empirically is to note the situations in which organisms behave and to observe what they do there. But there is no reason why one should not relate the S-R relationships, the empirical relationships one observes between stimulus and response, to whatever the neurophysiologist can tell us about inner brain function and to whatever the endocrinologists can tell us. The broader one makes his nomological net, the better, in that the more nearly his resulting conceptions will approach those of the imaginary, all-seeing eye of deity.

Stimulus-Response (S-R) methodology appeared at first to imply the notion of the empty organism. It is interesting to recall, however, that very shortly after the concept of mental faculties had been eliminated, Walter Hunter (1912, 1918) discovered that various animals could delay their responses to stimuli and also learn double alteration. Both achievements implied that there must be some kind of symbolic process intervening between stimulus and response. It was to explain just such behavior, moreover, that Hull (1931) promulgated the notion of the pure-stimulus act. This became in turn the response-produced cues and the response-produced drives of Miller & Dollard. When Miller & Dollard (1941, p. 59) began conceiving of the responses which serve as stimuli occurring within the brain, traditional S-R theory with its implicit peripherality of both stimulus and response began to fade. The demise of peripheral S-R theory became nearly complete when Osgood (1952) turned these response-produced cues and drives into central mediating processes. It is interesting to note in this connection that it is evidence from S-R methodology which has undone traditional peripheral S-R theory, and it is these observations which are now demanding that brain function be conceived in terms of active processes.

The theoretical need for active brain processes, however, has been both stimulated by and got much of its form from cybernetics (Wiener, 1948). Such investigators as Newell, Shaw, & Simon (1958), in the process of programming computers to solve problems, and especially logical problems, have been clarifying the general nature of what is required for solving such problems. They have described three major kinds of requirements: (1) memories or information stored somewhere, and presumably in the brain; (2) operations of a logical sort which are of the order of actions that deal with the information in the memories; and (3) hierarchial arrangements of these operations and memories in programs. Thus, the electronic computer has been replacing the telephone as the mechanical model for brain function.

Such a notion of memories and, even more, the notion of operations of a logical sort as actions, and the notion of hierarchial arrangements of these operations—these notions differ markedly from the notion of reflexes being hitched to each other. Moreover, ablation studies have been showing that it is not communication across the cortex from sensory-input regions to motor-output regions that is important for behavior. The cortex can be diced into very small parts without serious damage to behavioral function; but if the fibers, composed of white matter, under an area of the gray matter cortex are cut, behavior is damaged seriously. Thus, the notion of trans-cortical association gives way to communication back and forth from the center to the periphery of the brain (see Pribram, 1960). With such changes in conception of brain function being dictated by their own observations, when neuropsychologists become familiar with what is required in programming computers to solve logical problems, it is not surprising that they ask themselves where one might find a locus for the various requirements of computer function—i.e., for the memories, the operations, and the hierarchial arrangements of them. Karl Pribram (1960) has reviewed the clinical and experimental findings concerning the functional consequences of injuring various portions of the brain, and he has come up with a provisional answer. The brain appears to be divided into intrinsic portions and extrinsic portions.

This is the terminology of Rose & Woolsey (1949), and here the term *intrinsic* is used because this portion has no direct connections with either incoming sensory fibers or outgoing motor fibers. The extrinsic portion is so called because it does have such direct peripheral connections. What Pribram suggests is that these components of what is required for the various kinds of information processing and of decision-making may well reside in these intrinsic portions of the brain.

There are two intrinsic portions: one is the frontal portion of the cortex, with its connections to the dorsal frontal nuclei of the thalamus; the other, the nonsensory portions of the parietal, occipital, and temporal lobes with their connections with the pulvenar or the posterial dorsal nucleus of the thalamus. Injury to the frontal system disrupts executive functions and thereby suggests that it is the locus of the central, neural mechanism for plans. Injury to the posterior intrinsic system results in damage to recognitive functions, which suggests that it may be the locus of the central, neural mechanisms for information processing per se. The intrinsic portions of the cerebrum appear to become relatively larger and larger as one samples organisms up the phylogenetic scale. Perhaps what Hebb (1949) has called the A/S ratio might better be called the I/E ratio—for "Intrinsic/Extrinsic."

From such studies, one can readily conceive the function of early experience to be one of "programming" these intrinsic portions of the cerebrum so that they can later function effectively in learning and problem-solving.

Preverbal Experience Unimportant

Early experience, particularly preverbal experience, however, has historically been considered to be relatively unimportant. It has been argued that such experience can hardly have any effect on adult behavior, because it is not remembered. There have been, of course, a few relatively isolated thinkers who have given at least lip service to the importance of early experience in the development of the personality. Plato is one who thought that the rearing and education of children was too important a function to be carried out by mere amateur parents. But when he described the rearing that children should have in his *Republic*, he described only experiences for youngsters already talking.[1] Rousseau (1762) gave somewhat more than lip service in *Emile* to the importance of early experience. Moreover, at least implicitly, he attributed importance to preverbal experience with his prescription that the child, Emile, should very early be exposed to pain and cold in order that he might be toughened.

An even earlier example is to me somewhat embarrassing. I thought that I had invented the notion of split-litter technique for determining the effects of infant feeding-frustration in rats— but later I found, in reading Plutarch's *Lives*, that Lycurgus, the Law-Giver of the Spartans, took puppies from the same litter and reared them in diverse ways, so that some became greedy and mischievous curs while others became followers of the scent and hunters. He exhibited these pups before his contemporaries, saying, "Men of Sparta, of a truth, habit and training and teaching and guidance in living are a great influence toward engendering excellence, and I will make this evident to you at once." Thereupon, he produced the dogs with diverse rearing. Perhaps it is from the stories of the Spartans that Rousseau got his notion that Emile should be toughened. Such followers of Rousseau as Pestalozzi and Froebel certainly saw childhood experience as important, but as educators they were concerned with the experiences of children who had already learned to verbalize. So far as I can tell, the notion that preverbal experience is seriously important for adult personal characteristics comes from Freud (1905) and his theory of psychosexual development.

UNIMPORTANCE OF PSYCHOSEXUAL DEVELOPMENT

Freud not only attributed importance to preverbal experience; he also proposed an hypothesis concerning the nature of the kinds of experience important for later development. These were

[1] Since I wrote this, I have become indebted to Richard Kobler for pointing out to me that in the opening pages of Book VII of the *Laws*, Plato gave extended consideration to the importance of preverbal experience.

the experiences deriving from the fate of instinctive impulses arising out of homeostatic need, painful stimulation, and especially, the pleasure-striving which he saw as sexual in nature (Freud, 1905). If one examines the objective studies of the effects of the various kinds of factors deemed to be important from the standpoint of their theory of psychosexual development, one has a very hard time finding clear evidence that they are important (see Hunt, 1945, 1956; Orlansky, 1949). For every study that appears to show an effect of some given psychosexual factor in early history, there is another study to be matched with it that fails to show an effect. Furthermore, the more carefully the various studies appear to be controlled, the more nearly the results tend to be consonant with the null hypothesis. The upshot of all this is that it looks very much as if the kinds of factors to which Freud attributed importance in his theory of psychosexual development are not very important.

It was commonly believed before World War II that early experience was important for emotional development and for the development of personality characteristics, but unimportant for the development of intellect or intelligence. Some of the animal studies of early experience were widely quoted to support this belief. One of these was my own study of the effects of infant feeding-frustration upon adult hoarding in rats (Hunt, 1941). Actually, the effects of the infantile feeding-frustration were exhibited in both eating rate and hoarding, and exhibited in the eating rate more regularly than in the hoarding. Rats do not always hoard as a consequence of infantile feeding-frustration, although they do regularly eat faster than littermates without such experience. Yet, the feeding or drinking frustration need not occur in infancy to get the effect of speeded eating or speeded drinking (Freedman, 1957). In the case of the work of my colleague and myself, much of it still unpublished, various kinds of effects that should, theoretically, have followed did not occur. The upshot of all this, I now believe, is that our theoretical expectations were wrong. I also believe that the general notion that the emotional characteristics of persons are most influenced by early experience while the intellectual characteristics are not influenced is also quite wrong.

IMPORTANCE OF PREVERBAL EXPERIENCE FOR COMPETENCE

I am prompted to change my belief because the approach to the study of the effects of early experience suggested by Donald Hebb's theorizing about cerebral functioning has regularly yielded results confirming his hypothesis. According to Hebb's (1949) theory, firing systems, which he terms "cell assemblies" and "phase sequences," must be built into the cerebrum through what he has termed "primary learning." This may be seen as another way of expressing the idea that the intrinsic regions of the cerebrum must be properly programmed by preverbal experience if the mammalian organism is later to function effectively as a problem-solver. Most of this "primary learning" Hebb (1949) presumed, moreover, to be based upon early perceptual experience. It is in this presumption that he broke most radically with the traditional emphasis on the response side in learning (a point to which I shall return).

It was this conception which led Hebb (1947) early to compare the problem-solving ability in adulthood of those rats which had their perceptual experience limited by cage-rearing, with that of rats that had their perceptual experience limited by pet-rearing. As I have already noted in connection with my comments on the notion of predetermined development, the problem-solving ability of the cage-reared rats was inferior to that of the pet-reared rats. The theory, as encouraged by these exploratory results, led then to a series of studies in which various kinds of early perceptual experiences were provided for one sample of rats and not for an otherwise comparable sample. Thus, the difference between the groups in later problem-solving or maze-learning provided an index of both the presence and the degree of effect. Such studies have regularly yielded substantial effects for various kinds of early perceptual experience. These studies, moreover, appear to be clearly reproducible (Hunt & Luria, 1956). Furthermore, as I have already noted in connection with my remarks on predetermined development, these effects of early perceptual experience on adult problem-solving appear to become more and more marked up the phylogenetic scale as the intrinsic portions come to constitute a higher and higher proportion of the cerebrum. It looks now as though early experience may be even more important for the perceptual, cognitive, and problem-solving functions than it is for the emotional and temperamental functions.

CHANGE IN THE CONCEPTION OF TRAUMA

The investigations of the effects of early experience in animals appear to be calling for still further changes in our conception of the nature of the most important kinds of early experience. Freud (1900, 1915, 1926) had various theories of anxiety. But in his later theorizing about it he not only relied upon the notion of association but also conceived of painful stimulation, either through excessive homeostatic need or an overflow of excitement, as a basis for trauma. He also presumed that organisms which had experienced high levels of such traumatic excitement during infancy were made more prone to be anxious and neurotic later in life.

With the goal of demonstrating just such effects, Levine, Chevalier, & Korchin (1956) undertook the experiment in which they shocked rats daily for two minutes, keeping them squealing frantically throughout this period, on each of the first 20 days of their lives. A second sample of rats were picked up and brought to the grid-box, where they were put down without being shocked. Those of a third group were left unmolested in the maternal nest. One of the adult tests (at 60 days of age) involved defecation and urination in an unfamiliar situation. This is the test of so-called emotionality invented by Hall (1934). Those animals that had been shocked during infancy did not defecate and urinate more than those handled or than those left unmolested in the nest, as would be expected from trauma theory. On the contrary, the shocked animals defecated less on the average. The difference in this experiment fell short of statistical significance; but various subsequent experiments by both Levine and Denenberg (see Denenberg, 1962) yielded results showing that rats shocked in infancy defecated and urinated significantly less than those left unmolested in the maternal nest. Levine, Chevalier, & Korchin (1956) also found that the animals shocked in infancy and the animals handled in infancy both learned to avoid shock, by learning to respond to a signal before the onset of shock, in fewer trials than did those animals which had remained unmolested in the maternal nest. Confirming results have been obtained by Denenberg (1962).

Other evidence has come from the work of my own students. Goldman (1964) has shown that the intensity of shock required to move a rat over a barrier, from one end of a runway to the other end, is greater for rats that have been shocked during their preweaning stage in infancy than it is for those which have been left unmolested in the warm maternal nest. Salama (Salama & Hunt, 1964), has repeated the Farber (1948) study, in which rats shocked just past the choice point in a T-maze became "rigid" about giving up the place where they had got food, even after food had ceased to appear there. Salama compared the number of trials required to bring about such a shift in goal-box by animals shocked in infancy, by animals merely picked up in infancy, by animals petted in infancy, and by animals left unmolested in the maternal nest. While animals shocked in infancy require more trials (nine, on the average) to make the shift from the "fixated" arm and goal-box to the other arm of the T-maze than do animals which have not been shocked at the choice point (an average of 2.8 trials), they require substantially fewer than do animals handled or left unmolested in the maternal nest before weaning (an average of 20.7) or than do those petted (an average of 21.4 trials). Thus, the experience of having been shocked regularly before weaning appears actually to diminish the capacity of shock either to motivate behavior or to fixate a response.

Such evidence appears to call for a revision of the trauma theory. I find this evidence from animal studies especially interesting, moreover, because there is a study of human children with results which are consonant. This is a study by Holmes (1935) in which fear scores for children of a day-care center proved to be much lower than those for children of a nursery school. These results have seldom been cited in the secondary literature, perhaps because they were troublesomely dissonant with the dominant theoretical expectations. The dominant expectation would be that the opposite should have prevailed, because the children of day-care centers came from the lower class where painful experience and hunger (i.e., traumatizing experiences) were common, whereas the children of the nursery schools came from the upper class where such presumably traumatizing experiences are relatively rare. I believe this is an item of evidence from human subjects to indicate that children as well as infant animals, who have been through a great many painful circumstances are not as fearful in strange or unfamiliar situations as are children who have not experienced such painful circumstances. This evidence lends support to the recommendations that Rousseau made for Emile, and it helps to clarify how the Spartan culture could have survived for something like 500 years even though it practiced what has sometimes been seen as "infant torture."

It now looks as if there may be two quite different kinds of effect of early infantile experience. One is that just described, in which the effect of painful experience is one of reducing the aversiveness of later painful or strange circumstances. Although the evidence is not clear yet, that from Salama's experiment indicates that such other kinds of experience as mere picking up or petting do not have this effect. The other kind of effect is one increasing the capacity of an organism to learn. I have already mentioned that both the shocked rats and the handled rats in the study by Levine, Chevalier, & Korchin (1956) learned to respond to a signal to avoid shock more rapidly than did the rats that remained unmolested in the maternal nest. This is adaptive. Denenberg (see 1962) has shown that even shocking animals once on the second day of life will decrease the number of trials they require to learn an avoidance response, as compared with those left unmolested in the maternal nest. This kind of effect appears to result not only from shock during the preweaning phase of development but also from handling and petting. It looks very much as if any increase in the variation of circumstances encountered during those first three weeks of life will facilitate later learning, not only in the avoidance situation but also in such problem-solving situations as those to be found in the Hebb-Williams (1946) tests of animal intelligence.

CHANGE IN CONCEPTION OF THE RELATIVE IMPORTANCE OF THE SENSORY AND THE MOTOR

Yet another belief about what is important in early experience appears to need correction. G. Stanley Hall was fond of the aphorism that "the mind of man is handmade" (Pruette, 1926). Watson (1919) and the other behaviorists have believed that it is the motor side, rather than the sensory side, that is important in learning. Dewey (1902) gave emphasis to the motor side also in his belief that the child learns chiefly by doing. Dewey went even further to emphasize that the things that the child should be encouraged to do are the things that he would later be called upon to do in taking his place in society. More recently, Osgood (1952) has conceived that the central processes which mediate meanings are the residues of past responses. I am simply trying to document my assertion that in the dominant theory of the origin or of central mediating processes, these have been conceived to be based upon the residues from past responses.

Hebb's (1949) theorizing, as I have already noted, took sharp issue with this dominant theoretical position. He has conceived the basis for primary learning to be chiefly on the sensory side. Riesen (1958) began his experiments on the effects of rearing chimpanzees in darkness with what he called S-S, or stimulus-stimulus relations. Piaget (1936) although he has emphasized "activity as the aliment of a schema," has conceived of *looking* and *listening*, both of which are typically viewed as sensory input channels, as existing among the schemata ready-made at birth. Moreover, it is looking and listening to which he attributes key importance during the first phases of intellectual development. This emphasis is registered in his aphorism that "the more a child has seen and heard, the more he wants to see and hear" (Piaget, 1936, p. 276).

Evidence requiring this correction of belief comes from more than just the studies of the effects of early perceptual experience on the later problem-solving capacity of animals. It also comes from comparing the effects of the cradling practice on the age of onset of walking in Hopi children, with the effects of the homogeneous auditory and visual stimulation on the age of onset of walking in the children in a Tehran orphanage. The cradling practice inhibits actions of an infant's legs and arms during his waking hours through most of the first year of his life. Yet, the mean and standard deviation of the age of walking for those cradled proved to be the same as that for those Hopi children reared with free use of the legs and arms (Dennis & Dennis, 1940). Contrariwise, 85 per cent of the children in the Tehran orphanage were still not walking alone at four years of age—and here the factor in which the circumstances of these children most differ from those of most young infants was probably the continuous homogeneity of auditory and visual experience (Dennis, 1960). The children of the Tehran orphanage had full use of the motor function of their legs and arms. The Hopi children reared with the cradling practice did not have free use of their legs and arms—but they were exposed, by virtue of their being carried around on their mothers' backs, to a very rich variety of auditory and visual inputs.

Perhaps this emphasis on the motor side is erroneous only as another example of failure to take into account the epigenesis of behavioral and intellectual functions. While it may be true that education by doing is best for children of kindergarten and primary-school age, it appears that having a variety of things to listen to and look at may be most important for development especially during the first half year of life [2] (see also Fiske & Maddi, 1961).

All Behavior and All Learning Is Motivated by Painful Stimulation or Homeostatic Need

The fact that both apathy and retardation have been regularly noted in orphanage-reared children who typically live under conditions of homogeneous circumstances (especially marked of the children observed by Dennis (1960) in the Tehran orphanage) suggests that homogeneous stimulation some-

[2] Since this was written, it has become clear to me that this statement neglects the influence of very early phases of that motivation inherent in information processing (see p. 37), for evidence from my own laboratory has shown that responsiveness of circumstances to an infant's actions may become a factor as early as two months of age (Uzgiris & Hunt, 1969).

how reduces motivation. This suggestion brings me to yet another major change of theoretical belief.

It is common to state that "all behavior is motivated." But to make this statement specific, it must be completed with the complelx phrase, "by homeostatic need, painful stimulation, or by innocuous stimuli which have previously been associated with these." This has been the dominant conception of motivation for most of the last half-century—dominant because it has been held both by academic behavior theorists (e.g., Dashiell, 1928; Freeman, 1934; Guthrie, 1938; Holt, 1931; Hull, 1943; Melton, 1941; Miller & Dollard, 1941; Mowrer, 1960) and by psychoanalysts (e.g., Fenichel, 1945; Freud, 1915).

This notion implies that organisms should become quiescent in the absence of painful stimulation, homeostatic need, or the acquired drives based upon them. Since World War II, evidence has accumulated to indicate quite clearly that neither animals nor children actually do become quiescent in the absence of such motivating conditions (see Hunt, 1963a). Bühler (1928) noted earlier that the playful activity of children is most evident in the absence of such motivating conditions, and Beach (1945) has reviewed evidence to show that animals are most likely to show playful activity when they are well-fed, well-watered, and in comfortable circumstances. Harlow, Harlow, & Meyer (1950) have found that monkeys learn to disassemble puzzles with no other motivation than the privilege of disassembling them. Similarly, Harlow (1950) found that two monkeys worked repeatedly at disassembling a six-device puzzle for ten continuous hours even though they were quite free of painful stimulation and homeostatic need. Moreover, as he notes, at their tenth hour of testing they were still "showing enthusiasm for their work."

In an important series of studies beginning in 1950, Berlyne (see 1960) found that comfortable and satiated rats will explore areas new to them if only given an opportunity, and that the more varied the objects in the region to be explored, the more persistent are the rats' explorations. In a similar vein, Montgomery (1952) has found that the spontaneous tendency for rats to go alternately to the opposite goal-boxes in a T- or Y-maze is no matter of fatigue for the most recently given response, as Hull (1943) contended, but it is one of avoiding the place which the animals have most recently experienced. The choice of place is for the one of lesser familiarity (Montgomery, 1953), and rats learn merely in order to get an opportunity to explore an unfamiliar area (Montgomery, 1955; Montgomery & Segall, 1955). In this same vein, Butler (1953) has observed that monkeys will learn discriminations merely to obtain the privilege of peeking through a window in the walls of their cages, or (Butler, 1958) of listening to sounds from a tape recorder. All of these activities appear to be most evident in the absence of painful stimulation, homeostatic need, and cues which have previously been associated with such motivating stimuli. It is these findings which call for a change in the traditionally dominant theoretical conception of motivation.

Some of the directions of change in beliefs show in the modes of theoretical significance given to such evidence. One of these ways is drive-naming. Thus, in reecnt years, we have been hearing of a manipulatory drive, an exploratory drive, a curiosity drive, etc. This form of theoretical recognition, which is logically circular, appears to be revisiting McDougall's (1908) theory of instincts.

A second mode of theoretical recognition is naming what appears to be the telic significance of an activity. This is what Ives Hendrick (1943) has done in conceiving of the delight which children take in their new-found accomplishments as evidence of an "urge to mastery." This is also what White (1959) has done in his excellent review of such evidence by attributing the various activities observed to "competence motivation." Such terms of telic significance may be helpful as classificatory and mnemonic devices, but they provide few implications of antecedent-consequent relationships to be investigated.

A third mode of theoretical recognition has consisted in postulating *spontaneous activity*. I have been guilty of this (Hunt, 1960) and so also have Hebb (1949), Miller, Galanter, & Pribram (1960), and Taylor (1960). When my good colleague, Lawrence I. O'Kelly, pointed out that the notion of spontaneous activity may be just as malevolently circular as drive- and instinct-naming, however, I could readily see the force of his argument. But I could also see that I had begun to discern at least the outlines of a mechanism of what I have termed "intrinsic motivation" or "motivation inherent in information processing and action" (Hunt, 1963a).

INTRINSIC MOTIVATION

The outlines of the nature of this mechanism of intrinsic motivation are to be discerned from the evidence which has called for a change in the conception of the functional unit of the nervous system from that of the reflex arc to that of the feedback loop. The concept of the reflex was first formulated by Hall (1893). However, it was developed and popularized by Sherrington (1906) who clearly recognized, in spite of the anatomical evidence for the reflex arc, that the reflex was a logical construct rather than the obvious and palpable reality. It must be noted that the anatomical evidence for the notion of a reflex arc is based on an overgeneralization of the Bell-Magendie Law, which states that the dorsal roots of the spinal nerve are composed entirely of incoming sensory fibers and that the ventral roots are composed entirely of outgoing motor fibers. The statement is untrue. It is clear from recent neurophysiological investigation that the dorsal roots contain sensory as well as motor fibers (see Hunt, 1963a). Illustrative evidence for the first portion of this new statement comes from such observations as the cessation of the firing associated with the onset of a tone or a buzzer in the cochlear nucleus of a cat when the cat is shown a mouse in a bell jar (Hernandez-Peon, Scherrer, & Jouvet, 1956). Evidence for the second portion may be illustrated by the observation that eye-movements can be elicited by electrical stimulation of any portion of the visual receptive area in the occipital lobes of monkeys (Walker & Weaver, 1940). Such evidence makes way and calls for the concept of the feedback loop.

The notion of the feedback loop provides, in turn, the basis for a new answer to the motivational question concerning what starts and stops behavior. So long as the reflex served as the conception of the functional unit of neural function, any given kind of behavior was presumed to be started by the onset of a

drive stimulus and to be stopped by its cessation. As the feedback loop takes the place of the reflex, the onset of behavior
becomes a matter of incongruity between the input from a set of
circumstances and some standard within the organism. Miller,
Galanter, & Pribram (1960) have termed this the Test-Operate-
Test-Exit (TOTE) unit (see Fig. 1).

This TOTE unit is, in principle, not unlike the thermostat
which controls the temperature of a room. In such a case, the
standard is the temperature at which the thermostat is set.
When the temperature falls below this standard, the "test"
yields an incongruity which sets the furnace into operation (see
the arrow connecting the "test" to the "operate"). The furnace
continues to operate until the temperature in the room has been
raised to the standard. This congruity stops the operation, and
this particular motive system can be said to "exit."

Figure 1. Diagram of the TOTE unit. After Miller, Galanter, & Pribram (1960,
p. 26).

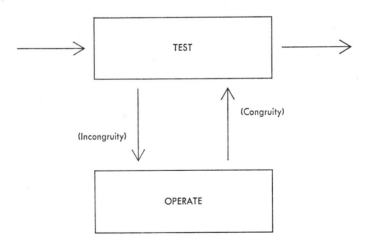

One can base a taxonomy of incongruities upon the various
kinds of standards existing within organisms. One class of in-

congruities may be based on the "comfort standard." While no one would have invented the TOTE unit to account for pain avoidance, conceiving of a "comfort standard" brings the facts of pain avoidance into a consonant relationship with the notion of the TOTE unit. A second class of incongruities may be conceived to be based on what Pribram (1960) has termed the "biased homeostats of the hypothalamus." Organisms have standards, for the most part innately established, for such things as the concentrations of blood-sugar or of sodium ions in the blood stream. When, for instance, the blood-sugar concentration falls below a certain level, the receptors along the third ventricle are activated. At one level of incongruity, they serve to release glycogen from the liver; but at a higher level, they prime the receptors to respond to the signs of food, the organism follows them with avid excitement, and the hunger motive is said to be activated. It is not easy to make the sex system consonant with such a scheme.

On the other hand, a variety of standards can be found within an organism's informational interaction with its circumstances. Perhaps the most primitive of such informational standards is the ongoing input of the moment. Whenever there is change from this standard, an organism exhibits what the Russians have termed the "orienting reflex" (see Berlyne, 1960; Razran, 1961). The operation elicited by such incongruity consists of an orientation toward the source of the change in input and arousal, as registered by the classical expressive indicators of emotion or by the electroencephalogram. A second kind of informational incongruity is based upon a standard of expectations, where the expectations are based on information stored in the course of previous encounters with the same object, person, or place. Such systems of expectations as the self-concept appear to take on special importance in motivation (Hilgard, 1949). Aesthetic standards appear to be another variation of expectations.

Another category of standards appears to be comprised of ends or goals. These are what Miller, Galanter, & Pribram (1960) have termed "plans." Some plans are tied to painful stimulation or to homeostatic needs, but others are quite independent of these. Piaget (1936) has described how an infant will make holding onto an interesting input, or retaining it, a goal. Typically, inputs have become interesting through repeated encounters by becoming recognizable. It would appear that emerging recognition can make objects, persons, and places attractive. Later it is a novelty which is attractive. The full range of the various kinds of standards that emerge in the course of a child's informational interaction with his circumstances during the process of psychological development has never been described. At adolescence, however, an important variety of standards consists of ideals. This kind of standard appears to emerge with the development of what Piaget (1947) has termed "formal operations." With the emergence of these operations, the adolescent can imagine a world more desirable than the one he encounters, and the incongruity between the world observed and the imagined ideal can instigate plans for social reforms. These same formal operations enable the adolescent to formulate "theories" of how various aspects of the world operate, and incongruities between observed realities and these theoretical creations instigate inquiry. Thus, one may view scientific work as but a professionalization of a form of cognitive motivation inherent in the human organism's informational interaction with circumstances.

INCONGRUITY AND THE DIRECTION-HEDONIC QUESTION

The concept of incongruity also provides a tentative, hypothetical answer to the puzzling direction-hedonic question—the question of what it is that determines whether an organism will approach or withdraw from the source of incongruous or novel information (see also Schneirla, 1959). This is also an answer to the hedonic question, because approach presumably indicates a positive hedonic value in the source of stimulation, and withdrawal presumably indicates a negative hedonic value.

The evidence that incongruous or novel information will instigate approach to its source and that it has positive hedonic value derives from several sources. In an early study by Nissen (1930)—which has never got into the textbooks, apparently because it was far too dissonant with the dominant beliefs—it was shown that rats will suffer the pain of electric shocks from a

Warden obstruction apparatus in order to get from empty cages into a Dashiell maze filled with novel objects. Once the animals have discovered the fact that such a maze exists at the end of the runway beyond the obstruction apparatus, they will endure the pain of the crossing in order to achieve the opportunity to explore this "interesting place" and to manipulate the "interesting objects." The behavior of the rats in this study of Nissen's resembles in many ways that of Butler's (1953) monkeys, which would undertake the learning of discriminations in order to peek through the window at students passing the hall beyond. In fact, most of the evidence cited show that animals and children do not become quiescent in the absence of homeostatic need and painful stimulation may be arranged to support the notion that a certain degree of incongruity is appealing, and that too little is boring and unappealing.

Perhaps the more convincing are the results from the studies of so-called "stimulus deprivation" in the McGill laboratory by Bexton, Heron, & Scott (1954). You will recall that the McGill students who served as subjects in these experiments were paid $20 a day to lie on a cot in a room with temperature and humidity controlled to provide an optimum of comfort, with translucent glasses on that provided for light to reach the eyes but did not permit pattern vision, with sound vibration attenuated as much as possible, and with movement inhibited by the padded cardboard sleeves for arms and legs. Yet they could seldom endure such homogeneous circumstances for longer than two or three days, even for such a liberal monetary reward. The strength of the tendency to withdraw from such homogeneity of circumstances and to approach any source of stimulation that would provide some variety is dramatized by the word-of-mouth story of a student with "high-brow" musical tastes who, several times an hour, pressed a key that brought the playing of a scratchy, well-worn recording of "country music." This makes it look as if it were a case of, to paraphrase the seaman's aphorism, "any port of relative incongruity in a storm of homogeneous circumstances."

Withdrawal from the source of incongruous information also occurs, this when the degree of incongruity between the incoming information and that already stored in the memory from previous experience is too great. Here the evidence comes largely from the work of Hebb (1946b). His studies of fear in chimpanzees were designed to call into question Watson's notion that emotional reactions to innocuous stimuli are based upon their having been associated with earlier painful stimulation (see Watson & Rayner, 1920). This traditional conception of fear met with sharply dissonant evidence, when Hebb & Riesen (1943) noted that fear of strangers does not appear in chimpanzee infants reared in the nursery of the Yerkes Primate Laboratory until these infants approach about four months of age. The fact that the histories of these infants were fully recorded made it possible to know with certainty that these strangers had not been associated with previous painful stimulation. Later, Hebb (1946b) found that even intense panic reactions could be induced in adult chimpanzees reared in this laboratory merely by showing them the sculptured head of a chimp or human being, or by showing them an anesthetized infant chimpanzee. Such figures were clearly familiar but definitely without previous association with painful or other fearful stimuli. The fact that an infant chimpanzee, which had been a pet, withdrew in fear upon seeing its beloved experimenter-master in a Halloween mask or even in the coat of an equally familiar "keeper" suggested that the basis for the fearful withdrawal resided in seeing a "familiar figure in an unfamiliar guise." Thus, the absence of the expected remainder of the body in the case of the sculptured head of a chimpanzee or human being, and the absence of the expected motions and customary postures in the case of the anesthetized infant chimpanzee, provide "the unfamiliarity of guise"—or the discrepancy between what is expected on the basis of past experience and what is observed, that I am calling incongruity.

Puzzling emotional disturbances in children and pets become readily understandable in these terms. It was, for instance, fear of the dark and fear of solitude in the human child that puzzled Freud (1926) and made him unhappy with even his later theory of anxiety, and it was such behavior in the chimpanzee that puzzled Köhler (1925, p. 251). These can be readily seen as incongruity which results from the presence of unaccustomed receptor inputs or from the absence of accustomed receptor inputs within any given context. Still other examples are that of the child who becomes disturbed when a familiar nursery rhyme is altered in the reading; that of a pet dog that barks excitedly and whines when he observes his young master walking on his hands; and that of the cat that runs frantically to hide at the sight of his child-mistress being hoisted onto the shoulders of a familiar neighbor. Although Piaget (1936) was without special concern about the point, he noted in his observations that his children showed emotional distress in seeing altered versions of things with which they had become familiar.

The fact that incongruous information can elicit both an approach to its source and a withdrawal from its source may be puzzling, until one notes that this implies that there is an optimum of incongruity (see Hunt, 1963a). Hebb (1949) first gave at least implicit recognition to the notion of an optimum of incongruity in his theory of the nature of pleasure. In this theory he noted that organisms tend to be preoccupied with "what is new but not too new" in any situation. This suggests that controlling intrinsic motivation is a matter of providing an organism with circumstances that provide a proper level of incongruity—that is, incongruity with the residues of previous encounters with such circumstances that the organism has stored in his memory. This is what I find myself calling "the problem of the match" between the incoming information and that already stored (Hunt, 1961, p. 267ff).

Relevant experiments in this area are difficult to find; but one by Dember, Earl, & Paradise (1957) is particularly interesting. Incongruity can be a matter of discrepancy between the level of complexity encountered and the level of complexity with which an organism has become accustomed. The efforts to keep an optimum of incongruity, or discrepancy and complexity, provide a kind of explanation for the sort of "growth motivation" which Froebel (1826) postulated and which Dewey (1900) later appears to have borrowed from Froebel. What Dember, Earl, & Paradise (1957) did in their experiment was to present rats placed in a figure-eight maze with a choice between two levels of complexity. In the two mazes used, the walls of one loop were painted in a solid color and those of the other loop in black-and-white horizontal stripes, or the walls of one loop had horizontal stripes and the other had vertical stripes. On the basis of theorizing similar to that presented here, these experimenters made no attempt to predict which loop would be preferred immediately by any given rat because they had no knowledge concerning the degree of incongruity to which the rats had become accustomed. They did, however, predict that any animal registering a change of choice of loop between his first and second exposures to this choice would make a change toward the more complex loop. This would mean that they would expect no changes in preference from the striped loop to the one painted a solid color, but would rather expect all changes to occur in the opposite direction. This prediction was confirmed. In a total of 13 animals making such spontaneous changes of choice, 12 were clearly in the predicted direction. Such experiments need to be repeated and elaborated. In the light of such considerations, the problem for a teacher endeavoring to keep children interested in intellectual growth is one of providing circumstances so matched, or mis-matched, to those with which her pupils are already familiar that an interesting and attractive challenge is continually provided.

EPIGENESIS OF INTRINSIC MOTIVATION

In the traditionally dominant theory of motivation, the basic structure of the motivational system is essentially performed. Learning is conceived to operate only by way of the conditioning principle, wherein previously innocuous circumstances acquire motivational significance by virtue of being associated with either painful stimuli or homeostatic needs. The fact that Piaget's observations indicate so clearly that there is an epigenesis in the structure of intelligence and in the construction of such aspects of reality as the object, causality, space, and time suggests that there may also be a hitherto unnoted epigenesis in the structure of what I am calling "intrinsic motivation." Piaget has been unconcerned with motivation; he has narrowed his field of concern largely to intelligence and to the development of knowledge about the world. Nevertheless, many of his observations and certain of his aphorisms have implications which provide at least a hypothetical picture of an epigenesis of intrinsic motivation (see Hunt, 1963b). Such is the case with the aphorism that "the more a child has seen and heard, the more he wants to see and hear" (Piaget, 1936, p. 276).

Three phases appear to characterize this epigenesis of intrinsic motivation. These phases, or stages, may well characterize the organism's progressive relationships to any completely new set of circumstances (Harvey, Hunt, & Schroeder, 1961). They may appear as phases of infantile development only because the infant is encountering various sets of completely new circumstances almost simultaneously during his first two years of life.

During the first phase, the child is, of course, motivated by homeostatic need and painful stimulation, as O. C. Irwin's (1930) classic studies have shown. Studies of the Russian investigators (see Berlyne, 1960; Razran, 1961) have shown that the orienting reaction is also ready-made at birth in all mammals including the human being. During this first phase, which lasts from birth to something like four or five or six months of age, the child is chiefly a responsive organism, responding to the short-term incongruities of change in characteristics of the on-going input. Thus, the relatively sudden dimming of a light or the sudden disappearance of a sound which has been present for some time will instigate a young infant's orienting responses or attention to bring about physiological evidences of arousal. During this first phase, the ready-made schemata of sucking, of looking, of listening, of vocalizing, of grasping, and of wiggling each change by something like the traditional conditioning process, in which various new kinds of change in stimulation acquire the capacity to evoke the schemata consistently. Thus, something heard becomes something to look at, something to look at becomes something to grasp, and something to grasp becomes something to suck. This phase terminates with a "landmark of transition" in which the child comes gradually to try actively to retain situations or circumstances or forms of input which he has encountered repeatedly (see Hunt, 1963b; Piaget, 1936).

The second phase begins with this "landmark of transition" in which the infant manifests intentional interest in what may be characterized as the newly familiar. The newly familiar is, of course, some circumstance or situation which has been encountered repeatedly. Presumably, this course of encounters has gradually constructed and stored somewhere within the intrinsic system of the cerebrum some kind of template which provides a basis of recognition for the circumstance when it recurs. One evidence for such recognition comes in the infant's smile. Rene Spitz (1946c) has conceived of this smiling response as social in nature. But Piaget's (1936) observations indicate that recognition of the parental face is but a special case of a more general tendency to smile in the presence of a variety of repeatedly encountered situations—which include the toys over an infant's crib, Piaget's newspaper laid repeatedly on the hood over his son's bassinette, and the child's own hands and feet. Such behavior may properly be described as intentional, because it occurs when the situation disappears and the child's efforts clearly imply an anticipation of the circumstances of spectacle to be regained. Moreover, inability to get the newly recognized circumstance or spectacle to return commonly brings on frustrative distress. Separation anxiety and separation grief appear to be special cases of the emotional distress that follow inability to restore the recognized circumstance or spectacle. This consideration suggests that the process of repeated encounters leading to recognition may in itself be a source of emotional gratification and pleasure which may be at least one basis for the reinforcement important in the early emotional attachments of cathexes—which Freud (1904) attributed to the libido, and which Hull (1943) and Miller & Dollard (1941) have attributed to drive reduction, and which Harlow (1958) has recently attributed to the softness of the surrogate mothers of infant chimpanzees in his experiments. This second phase in the epigenesis of motivation terminates when repeated encounters with familiar objects have led gradually to something like the boredom that comes with too little incongruity, and when this boredom provides the basis for an interest in novel variations in the familiar.

This interest in the newly familiar may well account for such autogenic activities as the repetitious babbling commonly appearing in the second, third, and fourth months, and the persistent hand-watching and foot-watching commonly beginning in the latter part of the fourth month and possibly persisting well into the sixth month. It would appear to be in the process of babbling that the infant brings his vocalizing schema under the control of his listening schema. It would appear to be in the course of hand-watching, and sometimes foot-watching, that the infant establishes his eye-hand, and eye-foot, coordinations. This second phase terminates when, with repeated encounters with various situations, boredom ensues and the infant comes to be interested in what is new and novel within the familiar stituation (see Hunt, 1963b).

The third phase begins with the appearance of this interest in novelty. Typically, this begins at about the end of the first year of life, or perhaps somewhat earlier. Piaget (1936) describes its beginnings with the appearance of the throwing schema. In the course of this throwing, the child's attention shifts from the act of throwing to observing the trajectory of the object thrown. It shows also an interest not only in familiar ways of achieving ends but also in the development of new means through a process of groping. It shows in the child's attempts to imitate not only those schemata, vocal and otherwise, which he has already developed, but also new schemata. This development of interest in the novel is accompanied by a marked increase in the variety of the infant's interests and actions. He learns in this way new phones within the vocalization schema, and these become symbols for the images he has already developed, and pseudo-words make their appearance (see Hunt, 1961, 1963b; Piaget, 1945).

With the development of interest in novelty, the child has achieved the basis for the "growth motivation" already illustrated in the intriguing experiment of Dember, Earl, & Paradise (1957).

Applications of Such Evidence and Theorizing for the Development of an Antidote for Cultural Deprivation

It remains for me to examine some applications of the theoretical fabric that I have been weaving from recent lines of evidence to the development of a preschool enrichment program for the culturally deprived. First of all, cultural deprivation may be seen as a failure to provide an opportunity for infants and young children to encounter the circumstances required for adequate development of those semi-autonomous central processes demanded for acquiring skill in the use of linguistic and mathematical symbols and for the ability and motivation to analyze causal relationships. The difference between the culturally deprived and the culturally privileged is, for children, analogous to the difference between cage-reared and pet-reared rats and dogs. At the present time, this notion of cultural deprivation or of social disadvantage is gross and undifferentiated, indeed. On the basis of the evidence and conceptions I have summarized, however, I believe the concept points in a very promising direction. It should be possible to arrange institutional settings where children now culturally deprived by the accident of socioeconomic class of their parents can be supplied with a set of encounters with circumstances which will provide an antidote for what they may have missed.

The important study of Skeels & Dye (1939), that met with such a derisive reception when it first appeared, is highly relevant in this context. This study was based on a "clinical surprise." Two infants, one aged 13 months with a Kuhlman IQ of 46 and the other aged 16 months with an IQ of 35, after residence in the relatively homogeneous circumstances of a state orphanage, were committed to a state institution for the feebleminded. Some six months later, a psychologist visiting the wards noted with surprise that these infants had shown a remarkable degree of development. No longer did they show either the apathy or the locomotor retardation that had characterized them when they were committed. When they were again tested with the Kuhlman scale, moreover, the younger had an IQ of 77 and the older an IQ of 87—improvements of 31 and 52 points respectively, and within half a year. You will also remember that in the experiment which followed this clinical surprise, every one of a group of 13 children showed a substantial gain in IQ upon being transferred from the orphanage to the institution for the feebleminded. These gains ranged between 7 points and 58 points of IQ. On the other hand, 12 other youngsters, within the same age range but with a somewhat higher mean IQ, were left in the orphanage. When these children were retested after periods varying between 21 and 43 months, all had shown a substantial decrease in IQ, ranging between 8 and 45 points of IQ, with five of these decreases exceeding 35 points.

In the last year-and-a-half, Harold Skeels has been engaged in a following-up study of the individuals involved in these two groups. With about three-fourths of the individuals found, he has yet to find one of the group transferred from the orphanage to the institution for the feebleminded who is not now maintaining himself effectively in society. Contrariwise, he had not yet found any one of the group remaining in the orphanage who is not now living with institutional support (personal communication). Although the question of the permanence of the effects of experiential deprivation during infancy is far from answered, such evidence as I have been able to find, and as I have summarized here, would indicate that if the experiential deprivation does not persist too long, it is reversible to a substantial degree. If this be true, the idea of enriching the cognitive fare in day-care centers and in nursery schools for the culturally deprived looks very promising.

PROBABLE NATURE OF THE DEFICIT FROM CULTURAL DEPRIVATION

The fact that cultural deprivation is such a global and un-differentiated conception at present invites at least speculative attempts to construe the nature of the deficit and to see wherein and when the infant of the poor and lower-class parents is most likely to be experientially deprived.

One of the important features of lower-class life in poverty is crowding. Many persons live in little space. Crowding, however, may be no handicap for a human infant during most of his first year of life. Although there is no certainty of this, it is conceivable that being a young infant among a large number of people living within a room may actually serve to provide such wide variations of visual and auditory inputs that it will facilitate development more than will the conditions typical of the culturally privileged during most of the first year.[3]

During the second year, on the other hand, living under crowded conditions could well be highly hampering. As the infant begins to throw things and as he begins to develop his own methods of locomotion, he is likely to find himself getting in the way of adults already made ill-tempered by their own discomforts and by the fact that they are getting in each other's way. Such considerations are dramatized in Lewis' (1961) *The Children of Sanchez*, an anthropological study of life in poverty. In such a crowded atmosphere, the activities in which the child must indulge for the development of his own interests and skills must almost inevitably be sharply curbed.

Beginning in the third year, moreover, imitation of novel patterns should presumably be well-established, and should supply a mechanism for learning vocal language. The variety of linguistic patterns available for imitation in the models provided by lower-class adults is both highly limited and wrong for the standards of later schooling. Furthermore, when the infant has developed a number of pseudo-words and has achieved the "learning set" that "things have names" and begins asking "what's that?" he is all too unlikely to get answers. Or, the answers he gets are all too likely to be so punishing that they inhibit such questioning. The fact that his parents are preoccupied with the problems associated with their poverty and their crowded living conditions leaves them with little capacity to be concerned with what they conceive to be the senseless questions of a prattling infant. With things to play with and room to play in highly limited, the circumstances of the crowded lower class offer little opportunity for the kinds of environmental encounters required to keep a two-year-old youngster developing at all,

[3] In the light of more recent evidence and theoretical considerations, this appears to have been a bad guess. Continual or too-often repeated encounters with loud voices can apparently lead to an habituation, an habituation that leaves the child inattentive to vocal imputs later (see Deutsch, 1964, and Hunt, 1966, pp. 103ff).

and certainly not at an optimal rate and not in the direction demanded for adaptation in a highly technological culture.

If this armchair analysis has any validity, it suggests that the infant developing in the crowded circumstances of lower-class poverty may develop well through the first year; begin to show retardation during the second year; and show even more retardation during the third, fourth, and fifth years. Presumably, that retardation which occurs during the second year, and even that during the third year, can probably be reversed to a considerable degree by supplying proper circumstances in either a nursery school or a day-care center for children of four or five—but I suspect it would be preferable to start with children at three years of age. The analysis made here, which is based largely upon what I have learned from Piaget (1936) and from my own observations of development during the preschool years, could be tested. The scales of psychological development in infancy, apparently ordinal in character, which Dr. Ina C. Uzgiris and I have developed should be helpful in such testing (Uzgiris & Hunt, 1970).

PRESCHOOL ENRICHMENT AND THE PROBLEM OF THE MATCH

Our traditional conceptions of school, with its emphasis on reading, writing, and arithmetic, and of kindergarten and nursery school, with their emphases on free play, can well lead us astray in our attempts to develop an appropriate program of preschool enrichment to compensate for the consequences of cultural deprivation. The trick is to capture each child's interest by making the circumstances which he encounters in the program relevant to the information he already has in his storage and to the skills he has already developed. The problem is to adapt the program to the child instead of waiting for the child to attain readiness for the program. If the hierarchial conception of psychological development is correct, this means providing progressive combinations of circumstances not commonly thought of. If Piaget's (1936, 1945) observations are correct, even spoken language can have little symbolic value until after images, or the central processes representing objects, persons, events, and relationships, have been developed through concrete perceptual encounters with those objects, persons, events, and relationships. The fact that chimpanzees show clearly the capacity to dissemble their own purposes even though they lack language (Hebb & Thompson, 1954) lends support to these observations from evolutional comparisons to this generalization of Piaget's. We have probably been overemphasizing the importance of the motor side in learning—in learning language as well as other things. You have undoubtedly heard that O. K. Moore, of Yale, has been teaching children of three and four years of age to read with the aid of an electric typewriter hooked up to an electronic system of storing and retrieving information. He has noted that once children have learned to recognize letters, by pressing the proper keys of a typewriter to produce them while hearing them pronounced, they are enabled to discover spontaneously that they can draw these letters on a blackboard or on paper. Moreover, Moore has observed that the quality of the muscular control of young children who have presumably acquired solid imagery of the letters from their experience with the electric typewriter corresponds to that typical of seven- or eight-year-olds (personal communication). Motor control appears from such suggested evidence to come with the imagery of what is to be drawn.

What appears to be especially important for compensatory, preschool enrichment programs is to foster the coordination of the imagery of objects, persons, qualities, and relatively abstract relationships with the spoken language symbolizing them. This calls for providing perceptual encounters with them which are sufficiently concrete to build the relevant imagery along with hearing and using the language symbolizing them. Such considerations suggest that preschool enrichments should provide children with a wide variety of objects and of models of actions and relationships among objects and actions where language with appropriate syntax accompanies the perceptual encounters. They suggest also that, as the symbolic and syntactical aspects of standard language are mastered, the children should be involved in problem-solving communication about the objects, actions, and relationships with which they have become clearly familiar.[4] The danger of attempting to prescribe materials and models at this stage of knowledge, however, is that the prescriptions may well fail to provide a proper match with what children already have acquired in the way of images and skills. The fact that most teachers have their expectations based on experience with culturally privileged children makes this problem of the match especially dangerous and vexing in work with the culturally deprived.

REVISITING MONTESSORI'S CONTRIBUTION

In view of the dangers of attempting prescriptions of enrichments for preschool children, it may be well to re-examine the educational contributions of Maria Montessori. Her contributions have been largely forgotten in America. In fact, until this past August (1962), I could have identified Maria Montessori only by saying that she had developed some kind of kindergarten and was an educational faddist who had made quite a splash about the turn of the century. I was, thus, really introduced to her work by Dr. Jan Smedslund, a Norwegian psychologist, who remarked to me, during a conference at the University of Colorado, that Maria Montessori had provided a practical answer to what I have called "the problem of the match" (Hunt, 1961, p. 276ff).

When I examined the library for materials on Maria Montessori, I discovered that the novelist, Dorothy Canfield Fisher, had spent the winter of 1910-1911 at the Casa di Bambini in Rome and that she had returned to write a book on Montessori's work. This book, entitled *A Montessori Mother* (1912), may still be the best initial introduction to Montessori's work. Books by E. M. Standing (1957) and Nancy Rambusch (1962) have brought the record up to date, and the book by Rambusch contains a bibliography of the materials in the English language concerning Montessori's work assembled by Gilbert E. Donahue.

Montessori's contribution is especially interesting to me because she based her methods of teaching upon the spontaneous

[4] The original version of these two paragraphs has been revised here to put more emphasis on coordinating language with perceptual encounters on the basis of valid criticism of my previous formulation for which I am indebted to Carl Bereiter.

interest of children in learning, i.e., upon what I am calling "intrinsic motivation." Moreover, she put great stress upon teachers observing the children under their care to discover what kinds of things foster their individual interests and growth. Furthermore, she put great stress on the training of what she called sensory processes, but what we might more appropriately call information processes today. The fact that she placed strong emphasis upon the training of sensory processes may well be one of the major reasons why her work dropped out of the main stream of educational thought and practice in America before World War I. This emphasis was too dissonant with the dominant American emphasis in learning upon the motor response, rather than upon the sensory input or information processes. It was Montessori's concern to observe carefully what interested a child that led her to discover a wide variety of materials in which she found children showing strong spontaneous interest.

Secondly, Montessori broke the lockstep in the education of young children. Her schools made no effort to keep all the children doing the same thing at the same time. Rather, each child was free to examine and to work with whatever happened to interest him. This meant that he was free to persist in a given concern as long as he cared to, and also free to change from one concern to another whenever a change appeared appropriate to him. In this connection, one of the very interesting observations made by Dorothy Canfield Fisher concerns the prolonged duration that children remain interested in given activities under such circumstances. Whereas the lore about preschoolers holds that the nature of the activity in a nursery school must be changed every 10 or 15 minutes, Mrs. Fisher described children typically remaining engrossed in such activities as the buttoning and unbuttoning of a row of buttons for two or more hours at a time.

Thirdly, Montessori's method consisted in having children aged from three through six years old together. As I see it, from taking into account the epigenesis of intellectual development, such a scheme has the advantage of providing the younger children with a wide variety of models for imitation. Moreover, it supplies the older children with an opportunity to help and teach the younger. Helping and teaching contain many of their own rewards.

Perhaps the chief advantage of Montessori's method lies in the fact that it gives the individual child an opportunity to find the circumstances which match his own particular interests and stage of development. This carries with it the corollary advantage of making learning fun.

There may be yet another advantage, one in which those financing preschool enrichment will be hardly concerned. Montessori's first teacher was a teen-age girl, the daughter of the superintendent of the apartment house in the slums of Rome where the first of the Casa di Bambini was established in 1907. In that school this one young woman successfully taught, or should we say, set the stage for the learning of, between 50 and 60 children ranging in age from three to six years old. I say "successfully" because, as Dorothy Canfield Fisher (1912) reports, a substantial proportion of these children learned to read by the time they were five years old. Moreover, they had learned it spontaneously through their own intrinsic motivation, and they appeared to enjoy the process. This observation hints that Montessori's contribution may also contain suggestions of importance economically.[5]

Summary

I began by saying that it was very exciting for me to encounter people, who are generally considered sensible, to be in the process of planning to utilize preschool experience as an antidote for the effects of cultural deprivation. I have tried to summarize the basis in psychological theory and in the evidence from psychological research for such a use of preschool enrichment. I have tried to summarize the evidence showing: (1) that the belief in fixed intelligence is no longer tenable; (2) that

[5] Since this was written, various bits of evidence have indicated to me that the standard program of the Montessori schools with which I have become acquainted puts too little emphasis on spoken language to enable them to compensate well for the language deficit in the culturally deprived children of the United States.

development is far from completely predetermined; (3) that what goes on between the ears is much less like the static switchboard of the telephone than it is like the active information processes programmed into electronic computers to enable them to solve problems; (4) that experience is the programmer of the human brain-computer, and thus Freud was correct about the importance of the experience which comes before the advent of language; (5) that, nonetheless, Freud was wrong about the nature of the experience which is important, since an opportunity to see and hear a variety of things appears to be more important than the fate of instinctual needs and impulses; and, finally, (6) that learning need not be motivated by painful stimulation, homeostatic need, or the acquired drives based upon these, for there is a kind of intrinsic motivation which is inherent in information processing and action.

In applying these various lines of evidence and these various changes in conception, I have viewed the effects of cultural deprivation as analogous to the experimentally found effects of experiential deprivation in infancy. I have pointed out the importance and the dangers of deriving from "the problem of the match" in attempting to prescribe from existing knowledge a program of circumstantial encounters for the purpose of enriching the experience of culturally deprived preschool children. In this connection, I have suggested that we re-examine the work of Maria Montessori for suggestions about how to proceed. For she successfully based her teaching method on the spontaneous interest of children in learning, and answered the problem of the match with careful observation of what interests children and by giving them individual freedom to choose which of the various circumstances made available they would encounter at any given time.

2

The Evolution of Current
Concepts of Intelligence
and Intellectual Development

History is as complex as life. If one is to write about it, one must limit and choose among both domains and kinds of focus. My domain for this paper was at least partially chosen by the topic assigned. Within any domain, one can focus on the changes in theoretical belief or the changes in practice. One can focus on the lives of men who have proposed the new theories and invented the new practices. One can focus on the various lines of evidence and the ecological conditions (social and technological) that force the changes of beliefs and practice. One can attempt to trace the various lines of influence, conceptual and evidential and ecological, and document carefully each one. Finally, one can concoct any combination of these that one can manage—and manage in the time allowed.

In the time allowed me, I shall focus synoptically on some of the main changes in the theoretical interpretation of the development of intelligence and the roles of heredity and environment therein. In this statement, *development* is a word almost as important as *intelligence,* so, first of all, I shall try to synopsize the main views of development. Second, I shall note the changes in belief about the structural nature of intelligence with their

Originally prepared for a symposium on the History of Conceptions of Heredity and Environment in Developmental Psychology organized by Charles D. Smock for the meetings of the Society for Research in Child Development in New York City, March, 1967.

interpreted relations to heredity and environment. Third, I shall examine the changing interpretation of order in the development of abilities. Fourth, I shall take a look at what I hope is the changing nature of practice. Fifth, I shall examine the changing views of differential fertility, and sixth, the social implication of these changes of view. For none of these dare I try to do more than provide allusions to the evidence and to the changes in human conditions which appear to have produced the changes.

Conceptions of Development

Development has been a troublesome concept throughout history. Although changes are obvious in both body and behavior with age, it is no easy matter to conceptualize the nature of these changes. Moreover, in the development of fowls and mammals, and even of insects, a major portion of the changes that constitute development—those occurring during the embryonic and fetal phases—take place out of sight. Thus, the debates about the early concepts of development belong to the history of embryology (see Needham, 1959).

The main conceptions of development can be subsumed under *preformationism, predeterminism,* and *interactionism.* The first two of these conceptions can readily be seen as applications of standard positions on the philosophical problems of appearance and reality to the phenomena of development.

Preformationism dominated thought about embryological development for at least 2,000 years. It persisted for a century after Leeuwenhock's invention of the compound microscope. Like object-permanence and the constancy of size and color in perception, preformationism appears to have rested upon a naïve notion that what is now must always have existed. Apparently this faith must have dominated perception through a microscope in the various reports of homunculi seen in both sperm cells and ova. Preformationism endured into the eighteenth century when, after a century of argument, Wolff's clearly depicted epigenesis of the circulatory system and the intestine in chick embryos disposed of the notion in so far as the development of body structure is concerned (see Needham, 1959). Yet, it was not until well into the nineteenth century that artists caught the changing ratios of the size of the head to the rest of the body in their paintings of babies and young children. Moreover, a kind of preformationism persisted in psychology throughout the nineteenth century and into the twentieth century in the notion of faculties that change only in power with age and development. Finally, it has been the contemporary merit of Piaget (1936, 1937) to show that our conceptions of such Kantian domains of reality as causality, space, and time go through a kind of epigenesis in their early development.

From preformationism to predeterminism. In his debate with von Haller, Wolff substituted for preformationism Leibniz's idea of a monad developing into an organism by means of its own inherent force, and thereby gave birth to a precursor of the idea of predetermined epigenesis. The notion of the predeterminers has changed. The monad notion is not too different from religious predestination in which God is the predeterminer. As the influence of the chemists gained in the early nineteenth century, this suggested that the monads might be chemical in nature. Although Charles Darwin never committed himself completely, his influence tended to attribute the predetermining forces to heredity. As the notion of genes came into being, first as logical constructs, then as entities seen through the electron microscope, the predetermining force was attributed to them, and it has remained within the domain of chemistry ever since. Now it is presumed to reside within the DNA molecules as information which programs the course of development.

Hereditary predeterminism got a tremendous boost in importance from the contributions of Francis Galton in England and G. Stanley Hall in the United States. For Galton, the dominating role of heredity appeared to be implicit in the theory of his cousin, Charles Darwin, that animals have evolved through a process in which chance variations and mutations which were inherited permitted them to survive and to reproduce their kind. He bolstered his deduction with his studies of *Hereditary Genius* (1869), and the *Inquiries into Human Faculty* (Galton, 1883) that launched the study of individual differences, and also his work on fingerprinting. His applications of these notions to the welfare of man appear in his founding of the eugenics movement.

The notion of predetermined development in general appears to have had part of its origin in the *Zeitgeist* deriving from Darwin's influence on psychological thought in America, but it came most significantly through the influence of G. Stanley Hall. The notion that "ontogeny recapitulates phylogeny" was central in Hall's theorizing. The tremendous impact of his work derives in considerable part because it was he who taught the leaders of the intelligence-testing movement in America: H. H. Goddard, F. Kuhlmann, and L. M. Terman. Hall's students also include Arnold Gesell who fastened the normative approach on study of the development of child behavior for at least 30 years.

It was clear that predeterminism could not be the whole story. In consequence, heredity and environment were each given a domain of influence in development. The domain of heredity was maturation. The domain of environment was learning. The two were so separated conceptually that, like Kipling's east and west, "never the twain shall meet." Implicitly, even such environmentalists as Watson appear to have assumed that heredity dominates completely the early phases of development until the various reflexes, those basic units of repertoire, have matured. Then, learning gets in its licks by way of conditioning and trial-and-error learning. Or, in current parlance, by way of classical and operant conditioning.

Interactionism is the third conception of development. This notion appears to have had its origins in the work of the Danish geneticist, Johannsen (1903, 1909). It was Johannsen, whom geneticists now rank with Mendel as a father of scientific genetics (see Sinnot, Dunn, & Dobzhansky, 1958; Srb & Owen, 1957), who discovered that altitude has differing effects upon chrysanthemums deriving from differing seeds, and who distinguished the *genotype* from the *phenotype*. By the genotype, Johannsen meant any constellation of genes that an organism receives from its progenitors. By the phenotype, he meant any characteristic of an organism or plant that can be observed and measured at any given point in its development. Johannsen also pointed out that the genotype can only be inferred from its effects on observable phenotypes. In America, the textbooks in genetics generally tended through the 1930's to emphasize the work of Mendel and to omit the work of Johannsen. The work of Mendel tended to emphasize the predeterministic aspects of genetics. To be sure, this predeterministic aspect has some evident validity. One does not, for instance, get elephants by breeding rats. Neither is one likely to get a winner of the Kentucky Derby in the offspring of such breeds of horses as Shires and Percherons, no matter whom he hires for trainer.

The interactionism of Johannsen was slow of recognition in American genetics, and even slower in American psychology. Although a few textbooks in genetics described some of the environmental effects on Mendelian traits, and although a few biologists such as Herbert Spencer Jennings (1930) emphasized what he called the interplay between genes and environment, the ideas of Johannsen (his distinction between the genotype and the phenotype, and his notion of development as an ongoing interaction between the genotype and the environmental circumstances encountered) did not become prevalent in American textbooks of genetics until the 1940's, and they are still not prevalent in the textbooks of psychology. In fact, I know of only three books in psychology that mention Johannsen and describe this combination of notions. We in psychology have not yet fully absorbed the implications of a concept of interactionism. Yet, some of the work on experimental embryology coupled with that on the role of maternal diet and with that concerning the effects of early experience are providing the basis for hypotheses which, when investigated experimentally, should lead to a growing understanding of these implications.

Conceptions of the Structural Nature of Intelligence

Investigations of intelligence and its relations to heredity and environment can probably be said to have begun with Galton's (1869) study of *Hereditary Genius*. Here the criterion was having achieved the reputation and distinction necessary to get into Britain's *Who's Who*. This criterion was silent with respect to the structure of intelligence. Investigations of the structure of intelligence can probably be said to have begun with Galton's (1883) *Inquiries into Human Faculty*. These inquiries were made in Galton's laboratory for anthropometric measurement. In his life's program, Galton appears to have seen the ultimate place for his "anthropometric measures" in the function of improving the human race. Strictly speaking, he had not yet constructed the concept of intelligence when he devised his many tests of simple sensory and motor functions. The sensory tests included such threshold measures as the number of vibrations required to be heard as a tone, the amount of pressure necessary to produce pain, the separation of two lines in visual angle required if the lines are to be seen as two, and the degree to which two points touching the skin must be separated in order to be felt as two. His motor tests included the number of taps an individual can make in half a minute, measures of the reaction time required for an individual to respond to the onset of a sound, a light, or a touch on the skin. As a measure of immediate memory, he used the number of letters, words, or names of objects that an individual can repeat after one hearing. Had Galton's tests proved efficient in differentiating those who achieve with distinction from those who do not, the idea of using them to determine those who would reproduce themselves would have been but a short step. When Galton invented the statistical technique of correlation, however, it served to discover little relationship among performances on his various tests and little relationship with such independent estimates of intelligence as teachers' ratings and academic grades. Thus, in a sense the search for a structure of intelligence in simple sensory motor tasks had failed even before the concept of intelligence itself had been constructed.

As early as 1895, Binet and Henri posed what have become two of the main problems for differential psychology, namely to determine the nature and extent of individual differences in psychological processes, and to discover the interrelationships of mental processes within the individual. In their criticism of Galton's tests as being too largely sensory and motor, and too simple, and in their suggestion that the measurement of more complex functions, such as imagination, comprehension, and aesthetic appreciation, would be of more importance for practical life, they suggested the first conception of the structure of intelligence as a single but complex faculty. It was just a decade later, and just a year after the French Minister of Public Instruction had appointed Binet (in 1904) to a commission to study the problem of retardation among the children in the public schools of Paris, that Binet & Simon (1905) published their first scale "to assess the intelligence." Later, Binet & Simon (1916) wrote, "It seems to us that in the intelligence there is a fundamental faculty, the alteration or lack of which is of utmost importance in practical life. This faculty is judgment, otherwise called good sense, practical sense, initiative, the faculty of adapting oneself to circumstances. To judge well, to comprehend well, to read well, these are the essential activities of the intelligence . . . indeed the rest of the intellectual faculties seem to be of little importance in comparison with the intelligence . . ." (p. 42).

This "fundamental faculty" came, in America, to be seen as an innately fixed dimension of human functional capacity. Such a view was quite contrary to that of Binet himself. After nearly two decades of work on intelligence, Binet (1909) deplored the fact that ". . . some recent philosophers appear to have given their moral support to the deplorable verdict that the intelligence of an individual is a fixed quantity . . . we must protest and act against this brutal pessimism . . . a child's mind is like a field for which an expert farmer has advised a change in the method of cultivating, with the result that in the place of desert land, we now have a harvest. It is in this particular sense, the one which is significant, that we say that the intelligence of children may be increased. One increases that which constitutes the intelligence of a school child, namely the capacity to learn, with instruction" (pp. 54-55).

When it was Binet's complex tests that turned out to be the ones that best predict which persons will achieve well and which poorly, how did it happen that, by 1934, Burt *et al.* could write: "By intelligence, the psychologist understands inborn, all-around, intellectual ability. It is inherited, or at least innate, not due to teaching or training; it is intellectual, not emotional or moral, and remains uninfluenced by industry or zeal; it is general, not specific, i.e., it is not limited to any particular kind of work, but enters into all we do, or say, or think. Of all our mental qualities, it is the most far-reaching; fortunately, it can be measured with accuracy and with ease" (pp. 28-29). Probably the answer lies in part in the fact that it was J. McKeen Cattell, a student of Galton, who coined the term "mental tests" and who brought them to America. Perhaps part of the reason lies in the fact that it was Goddard (1910) who translated the Binet-Simon scale into English and used it in his studies of the mentally retarded at the Vineland Training School. Goddard, the author of the well-known study of the Juke and Kallikak families, published in 1912, was a student of G. Stanley Hall and an ardent hereditarian. In addition, the scientific pride of the psychologists in their measurement tools may have resulted in semantics which lent support to the conception of intelligence as fixed. Intelligence has commonly been termed a *dimension*. The tests of intelligence have been termed *scales*. Such terminology derives from the physical sciences where objects are constant and where the systems of relationship among them are closed. This application of such terms as *dimension* and *scale* tends at once to carry their meaning in the physical world over into the world of organismic behavior and to imply that the concept of constancy and dimensions is being generalized from static objects to nonstatic persons and their behavior. At any rate, the complex tests of Binet came to be seen as reflecting intelligence with the structure of a single fixed dimension.

In passing, one needs to note that the concept of the intelligence quotient, or IQ, is that of rate. The notion of a constant IQ fits nicely with the notion of intelligence as a dimension that develops in power at a predetermined and constant rate. It is also worth noting in passing, too, that this notion of the faculty of intelligence as a dimension, one which does not change in nature or structure, with development that takes place at a constant rate, was a throwback to preformationism.

CHANGES OF CONCEPTION WITH CORRELATIONAL ANALYSIS

Galton's invention of the coefficient of correlation brought into being the method of correlational analysis. This method has undergone continuous modification from its simplest form to the various complex systems of factor analysis. From the methods of correlational analysis have come new theories of the structure of intelligence, and with each of these theories has come also a conception of the relation of the structure to heredity and environment. None of these theories has been unanimously accepted. Moreover, from the period before and after World War I to the present, one can see what is essentially a reversal of dominant opinion.

The historical course of investigation typically has not been a nice singular, sequential line. In one approach, the question has concerned the proportion of intelligence attributable to heredity and the portion attributable to environment. From the standpoint of this approach, intelligence has been seen largely as a single dimension as measured by the Binet-derived scales. One of the subcategories of approach to this question has consisted in comparing the size of the correlations between the scores for pairs of people of varying degrees of genetic relationship. The view that intelligence is mainly inherited got support from the fact that these correlations have typically run as follows: for identical twins, who presumably share the same set of genes, about $+.9$; for siblings, about $+.5$; for parents and their children, about $+.5$; for cousins, about $+.25$; for grandparent-grandchild, about $+.15$; and for unrelated children about $.00$ (see Hunt, 1961, p. 18). Various other attempts were made by way of statistical manipulations to estimate the proportion of the variants in the intelligence dimension attributable to the genotype and to the environment. Leahy (1935), for instance, correlated the IQ's of foster children with the IQ's of their foster parents. This correlation was $+.2$. By squaring it, Leahy was led to estimate that the home environment should have credit for about 4 per cent of the variance in intelligence. In another approach, R. B. Cattell (1950a) drew from the fact that the variance in IQ's for identical twins is about a fifth that for the population at large the implication that genetic inheritance must account for approximately 80 per cent of the population variance in IQ. Such an estimate had come earlier from the work of Barbara Burks (1928), and several of the general textbooks of psychology published before World War II gave currency to the conclusion that heredity accounts for about 80 per cent of the population variance in IQ, while environment accounts for only about 20 per cent of it.

It is a truism that the genotype sets limits on the development of capacity. No one has taught a rat to talk, and one can be confident that no one will. Man, moreover, cannot respond in microseconds no matter how he is reared. But this truism is essentially meaningless from a scientific standpoint. It is impossible, for instance, to measure the variations in the limits of capacity in individuals. To be sure, the genotype can greatly influence the nature of the consequences of encountering any given environment, as Johannsen made clear. Such genetic influences are illustrated regularly these days by the sex differences appearing in experiment after experiment with human infants. Differences in the consequences of encountering given sets of circumstances need not mean differing limits of capacity, however, for they may indicate differing ways of learning or differing routes to limits.

The question concerning what proportion of variance in test scores should be attributed to heredity and what proportion to environment is intrinsically unanswerable in any general sense (see Hunt, 1961, pp. 324-329). From the position of interactionism, both heredity and environment are *all*-important. Moreover, from the findings of changes of as much as 60 points in the IQ's of infants and young children (see Jones, 1954) and from the finding of differences of as much as 70 points in mean IQ on the Goodenough Draw-a-Man Test for typical samples of seven- and eight-year-old children from some 50 cultures (Dennis, 1966), one gathers that, at the extremes at least, gross variations in the circumstances under which children develop may produce variations in the IQ as measured by existing tests which are as large as the variations due to the genotype. This proportionality question has been considered essential for educational policy. I believe it is the wrong question. With man's cultures becoming increasingly technological, the demand for strong backs and weak minds decreases radically while the demand increases for higher and higher proportions of people with high-level competence in the manipulations of symbols in problem-solving, and it becomes more and more important to determine the degree to which existing genotypic potential permits increasing competence and intellectual capacity.

Spearman's g and s. The notion of intelligence as a unitary faculty or dimension of mind may be said to have statistical underpinnings from the work of Spearman (1904). It was obvious even to the most superficial observer that abilities are imperfectly correlated. Spearman's tetrad-difference method of treating the intercorrelations among test scores led him to his two-factor theory of intelligence. Spearman's subjects were children aged between six and ten years. He found the measures of performance on all tests to be positively correlated. These positive correlations he accounted for with the g-factor constituting the statistical bases for the unitary faculty. The imperfections of the intercorrelations, and they were substantial, he accounted for with a series of s-factors, or specific factors. These specific factors served to account for the special abilities of children on each of the tests and therefore to explain the imperfections of the intercorrelations. In Spearman's (1923, 1927) theory, the g-factor was considered to represent the individual's level of mental energy. This mental energy he presumed to be inherited. On the other hand, each child's special abilities were attributed to his past experience. It is worth noting, parenthetically, that Keith Hayes' (1962) recent attribution of individual differences in tested intelligence to inherited differences in motivation revisits this early view of Spearman's.

Although one can say that Spearman's work provided statistical underpinnings for the ancient notion of a unitary faculty, the existence of s-factors of substantial size can also be said to have called into question the notion of intelligence as a unitary faculty or dimension, and to have opened the way for other conceptions.

Group factors. The work of American investigators utilizing correlational techniques served definitely to change this picture of structure and intelligence. Part of the change derived from the ages of the subjects. While Spearman had worked almost entirely with children of the elementary school aged from six to ten, Truman Kelley (1928) and Thurstone (1938) worked chiefly with college students. Both Kelley and Thurstone found the variance in the scores of college students on tests better accounted for by factors intermediate between g and s. These are the so-called *group* factors. Kelley (1928) argued that g is of relatively minor importance. He attributed it to the heterogeneity of the subjects employed by Spearman and to the verbal nature of Spearman's tests. Using college students eliminated at least the lower half of the ability range all right, but it is hard to see why the *group* factors found in the intercorrelations from the attenuated range of ability should minimize the importance of the general factor that Spearman found in the full range of ability, unless, perhaps, college students are selected more on the basis of the g-factor than on the basis of the s-factor or *group* factors by our educational system. On the importance of the verbal nature of the tests employed, Kelly was wrong, for both g and s factors are also found by the tetrad-difference method from intercorrelating the scores of children on Raven's (1938) matrices.

It was on the basis of the same sort of evidence of *group* factors from intercorrelations among the scores made by college students on a variety of tests that Thurstone (1938) proposed his "primary mental abilities." These primary abilities, which have received repeated corroboration from the factor analyses of other investigators, include the following: V—Verbal Comprehension; W—Work Fluency; N—Number, which consists chiefly of speed and accuracy of simple arithmetic computations; S—Spatial Relations; M—Associative Memory; P—Perceptual Speed; and I—Induction.

The meaning of these group factors was a matter of dispute. Some factor analysts contended that the method uncovers genuine causal entities, genuine ability entities. These included Cattell (1952), Guilford (1940), Holzinger (1937), and Thurstone (1935). Some, e.g., Cattell (1937, 1950b), conceived of these ability entities as largely predetermined and fixed by heredity. Other factor analytic investigators conceived of the factors only as *descriptive categories*. These included Burt (1940), Thompson (1939), Tryon (1935), and Vernon (1961). So far as I can determine, none of these factor analysts of this early day conceived of factors as reflecting the consequences of learning. Although Burt (1940) was unwilling to view factors as fixed causal entities of ability, he (Burt *et al.*, 1934) nevertheless considered intelligence as inborn intellectual ability. This was clearly the dominant view through World War II.

Evidence dissonant with this dominant view came from various sources. One source was the study of twins. Differences of 15, 17, 19, and 24 points were found in four of the 19 pairs of identical twins, reared apart, investigated by Newman, Freeman, & Holzinger (1937). Moreover, the size of the discrepancy of IQ between the twins in these 19 pairs correlated $+.79$ with the judged discrepancies in educational advantage. Those holding the dominant view, however, attributed these large discrepancies largely to error of measurement. A second source of evidence dissonant with the dominant view were the test-retest correlations. These tended to drop rapidly with time between testings especially in young children. Thus, when Bayley (1940) combined the scores from the California preschool schedules obtained with her infant subjects at ages of seven, eight, and nine months, and correlated these combined scores with such scores obtained three months later, the correlation was $+.81$; at 22 months later it was only $+.39$; at 30 months later it was down to $+.22$; and by five years later it had dropped to approximately 0. This lack of longitudinal predictive validity was blamed on the nature of the baby tests by Anderson (1940). Because the behavioral elements in the infant tests have little in common with those in later tests, Anderson reasoned that one could hardly expect good prediction. In retrospect, this change in the behavioral elements appears to be an inevitable consequence of the epigenesis in intellectual structures described by Piaget (1936). Moreover, later investigations have shown that size of the correlations of the sources from an original test with the scores of later retestings vary with the age of the examinees at the time of the original test and with the amount of time between that test and the subsequent retestings. The longer the time between testings, and the younger the examinees at the time of the original test, the lower is the correlation between any two distributions of scores (see Humphreys, 1962a). Complete matrices of the intercorrelations among the scores from tests and retestings follow Guttman's symplex pattern wherein the highest correlations in a table are adjacent to, and the lowest correlations are furthest from, the principal diagonal of the matrix (Humphreys, 1960). Thus what appeared originally to be an exception to the rule has turned out with further investigation to be the rule.

A third line of dissonant evidence came from the studies of the effects of practice on the factor structure of a given group of test measures. In the studies by Anastasi (1936), Fleishman & Hempel (1954), and Woodrow (1938, 1939) factor structures were clearly altered by practice. Thus, the factors of intelligence could not properly be considered to be immutable elements in a structure of intelligence fixed, once and for all, by heredity.

With the work of Ferguson (1954, 1956, 1959) and Humphreys (1959), the emphasis in the relationship of the structure of intelligence to heredity and environment becomes exactly the reverse of that in the view dominant before World War II. Ferguson (1954, 1956) has based his logical analysis upon a scrutiny of the terms *ability* and *transfer*. The term *ability* refers, first, to measures of performance which, subject to error, locate individuals on an underlying latent variable; second, in the case of factor analysis, to the weighted additive sum of measures of performance on separate tasks which imply a latent factor variable; and third, to some attribute of the organism of person. Ferguson (1954) assumes that the various ability factors which have achieved stability have done so through overlearning and are approaching a crude limit beyond which no systemic improvement is likely to come with further practice. The term *transfer*, defined after the mathematical concept of function (Ferguson, 1956, 1959), "implies change in performance on one task is a function of change resulting from practice on another." Ferguson thereby explains a general factor of ability and the considerable degree of positive correlation found among psychological tests in terms of positive transfer, and he explains the group factors of ability which emerge in the performance of adults in any culture in terms of those abilities which tend to facilitate rather than to inhibit one another. Humphreys (1959, 1962b) extended the analysis to include the manner whereby the experimental manipulations which had traditionally been used to study the transfer of training could well account for the obtained correlations among abilities. Thus, where the traditional view saw g and the various group factors as basic causal entities of genotypic origin, the interpretations of Ferguson and Humphreys attribute these factors to transfer of training.

Although this new interpretation can hardly be said to have become the dominant one, its acceptance has been growing rapidly. Guilford (1940, 1956, 1957, 1959) has uncovered progressively more and more factors, until there are many more factors in his latest analyses than there were tests in the battery upon which Thurstone based his primary mental abilities. Moreover, as Guilford uncovered more and more factors, he has tended to find a more and more important role for encounters with circumstances in their origin. Similarly, Philip Vernon's (1961) hierarchy of abilities corresponds nicely with the hierarchy which Humphreys (1962b) has described, although Vernon has been essentially silent about the role of transfer training in determining the hierarchy he finds.

The Order in Behavioral Development

Perhaps the chief empirical support for the once dominant view of the development of behavior as genetically predetermined came from the observable order of this development. Coghill's (1929) work on the development of behavior in frogs and salamanders is reported in every textbook of either child psychology or developmental psychology. Coghill saw the basis for behavioral development in anatomical maturation. Thus he explains the shift from nonmotility to motility to be associated with microscopic changes in nerve terminals (Coghill, 1929, pp. 84-85). Coghill went on to assert that "the normal experience of the animal with reference to the outside world appears to have nothing to do with the determination of the form into which the behavior of the animal is cast" (Coghill, 1929, p. 87).

Coghill's laws of cephalocaudal progression and proximodistal progression got generalized to human infants through the observations of such investigators as Arnold Gesell (1954) and Mary Shirley (1931, 1933). Gesell (1954) asserted that "the growth of tissues, of organs, and of behavior is obedient to identical laws of developmental morphology" (p. 337). Coghill's cephalocaudal principle is Gesell's first "principle of developmental direction." The second of Gesell's principles is that of reciprocal interweaving, the third is that of functional asymmetry, the fourth is that of individuating maturation, and the fifth is that of self-regulatory fluctuation. Only one of these developmental principles, that of individuating maturation, makes a role for environmental encounters in the process of development. While Gesell occasionally made statements giving at least lip service to the interaction between the organism and the environment, he was also explicit in saying that "the so-called environment, whether internal or external, does not generate the progressions of development. Environmental factors support, inflect, and specify; but they do not engender the basic forms and sequences of ontogenesis."

Mary Shirley (1931, 1933) also noted that the developmental principles of Coghill were applicable to the locomotor development of human infants. She wrote, for instance, that "motor control begins headward and travels toward the feet. Beginning with the eye muscle, and progressing through stages in which the head and neck muscles are mastered, arms, and the upper trunk come under control . . . the baby at last achieves mastery of his entire body . . ." (pp. 204-205). Moreover, when she found that all the correlations between the orders in which locomotor responses appeared in her 20 infant subjects and the order of the modal series were above +.93, and that 60 per cent of them were above +.97, she concluded: "Motor development sweeps in an orderly course, and apparently is little influenced by the exigencies of time, place, and cultural fashion in child dress and child training." This work of Mary Shirley got described in nearly all of the textbooks of child psychology and developmental psychology.

Such evidence coupled with the norms for various kinds of

mental growth deriving from the work of Gesell *et al.* (1940) lends support to the notion of development as a maturational process predetermined by heredity. The notion of development as a predetermined process, in turn, lends support to the notion of fixed intelligence.

Although learning was a major topic in psychology during this period when the notion of predetermined development was most prominent, the conceptual separation of maturation from learning had the effect of minimizing the role of the young infant's encounters with circumstances in his development. When, in the 1930's, I proposed to investigate the effects of early infantile experiences on later development in both human children being reared in orphanages and in rats being reared in laboratories, even such outstanding investigators of the learning process as Walter Hunter and Clark Hull were anything but encouraging. Only after seeing the apparently dramatic effects on pellet-hoarding in the first of my experiments on the effects of infantile feeding-frustration did they become interested. Then they became very interested. I myself presumed that intellectual development was essentially fixed. The idea for the feeding-frustration studies came from Freud's (1905) theory of psychosexual development, and more specifically from Roger Money-Kyrle's (1939) summary of the effects of the fate of the hunger drive during infancy on the typical personal characteristics of people in various primitive tribes. Undoubtedly Freud's emphasis on the role of early experience in development had an important role in undermining the acceptance of the notion of predeterminism. Yet, by 1940, the influence of Freud and the psychoanalytic movement had not become strong enough to permit the evidence dissonant with the predeterministic view of intelligence to be acceptable in even a suggestive sense. For instance, the now classical suggestive finding of Skeels & Dye (1939), wherein marked increases in IQ came from shifting infants from an orphanage to a ward in an institution for the retarded where the older and brighter girls became very much attached to the children, were treated with the utmost derision. After the war the findings of Rene Spitz (1945, 1946a, 1946b) wherein retardation, as measured by the Hetzer-Wolf (1928) baby test, was related to "mothering," had tremendous influence on the views of social workers and psychiatrists, but very little influence on the views of psychologists and especially on the views of developmental psychologists. To be sure, Spitz's studies had major defects, as Pinneau (1955) so ably pointed out.

It is exceedingly difficult to obtain logic-tight evidence of the effects of environmental encounters on the development of human subjects. During the first half of this century, those with a strong belief in predetermined development (and they were the preponderant majority) could easily pick flaws in any of the studies using human subjects that yielded evidence dissonant with their view. The tide began to turn with the appearance of dissonant evidence from experiments with animal subjects. Many of these studies were prompted by the theorizing of Donald Hebb (1949). In these studies, perceptual experience in rats and dogs during the period immediately after weaning was found to have a substantial influence on ability to solve problems in adulthood (see Hunt, 1961, pp. 100-106). Hebb (1949) also noted in his concept of the A/S ratio that that portion of the cerebrum not directly connected with either sensory inputs or motor outlets increases up the evolutionary scale. A comparison of the findings of Hebb (1947) on rats and the findings in other studies suggests that the influence of early perceptual experience on problem-solving ability may increase up this evolutionary scale with increases in the A/S ratio.

Such findings from the animal studies lent new weight to the older evidence dissonant with the conception of predetermined development. In my own case, and also in the case of a good many of the people with whom I talked about the matter during the 1950's, these findings from the animal studies inspired by Hebb's theorizing encouraged an attitude which prompted one to take very seriously not only the older findings from studies with human subjects that were dissonant with the dominant view, but also the work of Jean Piaget.

Translation of Piaget's (1924, 1926, 1927, 1932) early studies had stirred up a flurry of interest in America during the early 1930's. The interest faded rapidly, however, when American investigators were unable to find the evidences of the "egocentricity" that Piaget had described. With his studies of the *Origins of Intelligence in Children* (Piaget, 1936) and the *Construction of Reality in the Child* (Piaget, 1937) and with *Play Dreams and Imitation* (Piaget, 1945), Piaget relinquished his purely verbal approach and changed to one of confronting his infant subjects with situations designed to elicit intelligent behavior and/or constructions of reality. Again, as was the case with the observations of Gesell and of Shirley, an order appeared in the course of development. In a sense, Piaget did no experiments to test the influence of encounters with environmental circumstances on development. Yet, Piaget's theorizing served to reverse the conceptual relationship between order in development and the role of heredity and environment. Where all except one of Gesell's principles of development emphasized predeterminism, Piaget saw the order in development deriving from this conceptual invariance in the organism-environment interaction. I refer to his notions of *accommodation* and *assimilation*. The term *accommodation* refers to the process of change and changes in the structure of behavior and of the central processes mediating behavior that come with encounters with circumstances. The term *assimilation* refers to the process of consolidation that comes with repeating the changed structure of behavior in situations that do not call for adaptive change. Piaget has also described a series of stages in the course of sensorimotor development during the first two years, another series of stages during the preoperational phase between age two and six or seven, a series of stages during the operational phase, and a series of stages in the final formal phase of psychological development. In the course of these stages, both intelligence and the conception of reality are conceived to go through something essentially similar to the epigenesis of somatic structures that occurs in embryonic development. This epigenesis and the notion of structural change in behavioral development helped reinforce a hierarchical conception of both intelligence and the construction of reality.

Piaget & Inhelder (1947) have been explicit about a basic sequential ordinality in the development of concrete operations of later childhood. In this ordinality, conservation of quantity comes first, conservation of weight comes second, and conservation of volume comes third. Piaget and Inhelder were quite explicit on the point that any child that conserved volume will also conserve both weight and quantity, that any child that conserves weight will also conserve quantity; a similar relationship could well hold for many of the successive transitions in the course of development during the sensory motor phase.

It is on the assumption that these early transitions of development would show ordinal relationships, that Dr. Uzgiris and I have attempted to construct a series of ordinal scales of development for the first two years (Uzgiris & Hunt, 1970). In constructing these scales, however, we have chosen schemata, or behavioral elements, which are clearly subject to modification by experience. In many instances, however, the ordinality is built into the system logically. For instance, the infant who can follow an object visually through 180° can obviously follow it through a lesser arc. Similarly, any infant who has central processes or images which permit objects perceived to be permanent in the absence of perceptual contact while he takes three covers off the object also has images of such firmness that they will survive through taking a single cover off the goal object.

In other instances, the ordinality is not logically built into the system. Any given system appears to develop with use. It is thus that White & Held (1966) have found that experiential enrichments involving several kinds of enrichment including a stabile over the crib can decrease the median age at which mature reaching appears from 145 days to something like 88 days. Experiences that foster eye-hand coordination, however, need have little or no influence on ear-vocal coordinations. In fact, moreover, the infants in the experiments of White and Held who are so advanced in eye-hand coordination are actually quite retarded in ear-vocal coordination. Conversely, the children of graduate students and younger staff whom Dr. Uzgiris and I have studied in their homes are quite advanced in ear-vocal coordination, but they fall considerably behind those subjects of White and Held who have experienced their enrichments. On the basis of such observations, I suspect that some of Piaget's stages are artifacts of encountering a variety of different kinds of circumstances at approximately the same rate. Thus, while Piaget's theorizing has helped to reverse the relationship between order in development and heredity and environment at the conceptual level, the reversal poses a number of issues for empirical investigation. In some instances, this ordinality appears to be built into the system logically even though it is greatly modifiable in rate by encounters with circumstances. In other instances, this is not the case. It is not always easy to see what is logically built in and what is not. For instance, Dennis (1960) found a marked exception to Shirley's generalization that creeping precedes standing and cruising and walking. The preponderant majority of young children in the Tehran orphanage that Dennis observed scooted rather than crept before they stood, cruised, and walked. We have here a problem calling for investigation and the investigation is likely to be highly informative about the nature of intellectual development and about the role of the circumstances encountered in it.

Changes in the Nature of Psychological Practice

These changes in our conceptions of intelligence and of the development of intelligence and its relation to heredity and environment bring with them some implications for practice which, I believe, are actually beginning to be manifest in practice. The conceptual distinction between genotypic potential and phenotypic ability is being much more generally recognized. Hebb (1949) recognized this distinction in his *Intelligence I* for genotypic potential and his *Intelligence II* for phenotypic abilities that emerge from the interaction of genotypic potential with the environmental circumstances encountered.

So long as intelligence tests were presumed to have the impossible ability to assess genotypic potential, the task of psychologists was limited largely to personnel selection. This has been the function of not only tests of intelligence but other tests as well in industry, in the military services, and even in the schools. So long as development was conceived to be predetermined, such matters as "school readiness" were conceived to be a function of maturation. In this context, although various clinicians and various teachers did more, the task of practice was limited largely to determining whether a child had achieved a mental age that would permit him to profit from the experience in school. The task of practice associated with getting an IQ was limited largely to decisions on how far one can expect a child to develop.

The notion of using test findings to guide the design of remedial procedures, although it is as old as the work of Itard and Seguin and Montessori, is relatively new for us American psychologists and child specialists. To be sure, a few clinicians have used scatter on the Binet-derived tests as a diagnostic guide to the design of materials and procedures that would evoke corrections in intellectual development, but this approach was left largely to the personality sphere in clinical practice. Within the domain of intellectual development, the first test designed specifically to provide a guide for the development of corrective experiences, so far as I know, is the Illinois Test of Psycholinguistic Abilities developed by Kirk & McCarthy (1961). The wide appeal of this test, which has admitted limitations, suggests the readiness of special educators and school psychologists for the new approach to psychological practice in which the findings of testing procedures are employed as a guide to the preparation of environmental materials and circumstances for corrective educational procedures.

Similarly, the findings of such investigators of deficit in culturally deprived children as Cynthia Deutsch (1964), Vera John (1963), John & Goldstein (1964), and the Kendlers (1956) have led Martin Deutsch to the idea of a "therapeutic curriculum." In the same vein, the evidence from this same series of studies has lead Bereiter & Engelmann (1966) to design an academically oriented preschool curriculum for culturally deprived preschool children specifically to overcome their faulty pronunciation of language, their lack of terms for propositional relationships, and their failure to master English syntax. Bereiter and Engelmann have designed this curriculum with the notion that the failure to have learned these various linguistic skills in the homes of the poor may account for the failure of children of poverty in standard school situations.

This shift in the tasks of psychological practice produce some twists in the standard psychometric orientation. One twist calls for distinguishing what one may term contemporary prediction from longitudinal prediction. In contemporary prediction, the problem-solving performance of individuals in one situation, typically the test situation, is used to predict their performance in other situations. In this case of contemporary prediction, however, the time between encountering the test situation and encountering the criterion situation is very short. In the case of longitudinal prediction, the performance of subjects in the test situation is employed to predict their later, often much later, performances in other test situations. These two kinds of prediction provide the bases for two quite different kinds of validities. Tests may be highly valid for contemporary prediction without having much validity for longitudinal prediction. Moreover, it is the contemporary prediction which provides the basis for that diagnosis which permits the planning of corrective educational procedures. Moreover, ironically, the more effective are these corrective educational procedures, the more damage they do to longitudinal validity of tests.

Another twist needs to be made in connection with longitudinal prediction and the concept of validity. If the hierarchical conception of the organization of abilities is correct, and I believe it is, longitudinal prediction involves a part-whole relationship. This makes the improvement in longitudinal abilities that has long been observed to occur with increasing age an artifact of the predictor, becoming a larger portion of the criterion. The older a child gets, the larger becomes the part one uses to predict the whole performance later in life. It is, I believe, intrinsically impossible to predict from the performances of infants or very young children on any test what their performances on other tests will be at a much later age unless one specifies the circumstances that child will encounter and cope with in the interim.

The new task of practice in which tests are employed to diagnose the structure of abilities so that children can be confronted with circumstances appropriately prepared to foster their development and educational growth differs quite radically from the traditional task of psychometric practice. Much remains to to be learned about it. Important in pointing the way is the work of Piaget, the theorizing of Robert Gagné & Paradise (1961), and the factor analytic studies of intellect (Ferguson, 1954, 1956, 1959; Guilford, 1959; and Humphreys, 1962b). I dare to hope that the work "Toward Ordinal Scales of Psychological Development in Infancy" which Dr. Uzgiris and I have done may also be useful in this process, uncovering more of the nature of psychological development and of changing the task of psychological practice.

Differential Fertility and Intelligence

It was pointed out as early as the seventeenth century that those of the lower socioeconomic classes have larger families than those of the upper classes and thereby contribute more than their share of the next generation (United Nations, 1953, 1955). Because the IQ's of unskilled laborers have typically averaged about 20 points below the IQ's of people in the professions (see Anastasi, 1958, p. 515), it has been common to view this fact of differential fertility as evidence that human potential is drifting downhill. Moreover, in as much as investigators have repeatedly found negative correlation between the numbers of children in families and the tested intelligence of the children in these families of the order of approximately —.3 (see Anastasi, 1956), this evidence has been considered to be quite direct. In 1937, Cattell multiplied the number of people at each IQ level by the reproduction rate at that level and computed the new mean as an estimate of the IQ of the next generation. From this procedure, which assumes a perfect correlation between the IQ's of parents and children, he got an estimated drop of little over three points a generation, or about one point a decade. This he characterized as a "galloping plunge toward intellectual bankruptcy."

This dire prediction has been disconfirmed by a rising IQ in those populations where the children have been tested and re-tested after intervals of a decade or more. Thirteen years after his own dire prediction, Cattell (1950a) himself published a study comparing ten-year-old children living in the city of Leicester in 1949 with the ten-year-old children living in that same city in 1936. In place of the predicted drop by something slightly more than one point in mean IQ, Cattell actually found an increase of 1.28 points. This increase, although small, was highly significant from a statistical standpoint. Moreover, this upward shift occurred with a nonverbal and supposedly culture-free test which was given to both samples by the same examiner. In perhaps the largest study of this kind, the Scottish survey by Godfrey Thompson and his collaborators (1933, 1949, 1953), a gain of 2.28 points in IQ appeared over this 15-year period in the place of the predicted drop of 1.5 points. In other studies, the predicted drop in IQ has been disconfirmed by gains which are substantially larger than these. That reported by Smith (1942) between the scores of children at the various schools of Honolulu in 1924 and the scores of children in those same schools of Honolulu in 1938 was of the order of 20 points. That reported by Wheeler (1942) was ten points and it occurred between the averages for samples of children taken before and a decade after the social changes instituted by the Tennessee Valley Authority. Both samples of children came from the same families. When Finch (1946) compared the tested intelligence of all students in a sample of high schools in the 1920's with the tested intelligence of the students of those same high schools in the 1940's, he found the average increases for the various schools ranging between 10 and 15 points of IQ. These gains occurred despite the fact that a substantially larger portion of the total population was attending these high schools in 1940 than in 1920.

In considering causation, it is worth separating the matter of the negative correlations between the family size and the intelligence scores of children from the matter of these population improvements. The latter appeared to have occurred despite the validity of the former. So far as the causation of the former is concerned, it is worth noting that the negative correlation between number of siblings and intelligence does not hold for families at the top of the socioeconomic scale where outside help for the care of young children can be afforded (see Hunt,

1961, pp. 341-342). Second, it has been repeatedly observed that twins have lower average intelligence than singletons and also that doubletons differing less than a year and a half in age average in IQ about the same as twins while doubletons differing by more than a year and a half in age average in IQ nearly as high as single children. Such findings (see Hunt, 1961, pp. 337-343) indicate that the negative correlation between number of children in a family and measures of intelligence may well be a matter of inferior parental care during the preschool period. At any rate, in the light of such evidence, it is just as reasonable now to attribute the low average intelligence of the children in large families to deficiencies in early experience as it is to attribute it to heredity.

Changes in the Conceptions of School Readiness

Starting young children in school at six or seven years of age is a time-honored custom that goes back to the days of Rome and Greece. During most of the past century we have explained this custom in terms of the concept of *readiness*. As a corollary of the belief in predetermined development, readiness has been conceived to be a stage in development at which the child arrives more or less automatically through the predetermined process of maturation. When individual children failed to respond in the expected way to school tasks, their parents were urged to hold them out for a time to let their readiness mature, or the children were held over to repeat the grade. In the terms of intelligence testing, readiness has typically been a matter of mental age—a mental age of six.

The concept of intelligence as a hierarchial organization of abilities acquired in the course of the young child's ongoing interaction with circumstances has implications for school readiness which are not fully appreciated. Some public recognition of differential opportunities for learning in the various socioeconomic classes of our society has been recognized in the appropriation of federal funds for such preschool programs as Head Start. On the other hand, teachers and we psychologists still show evidence of confusion about the matter. Age still determines the admission of the child to such a program of compensatory education as Head Start. In the various Head Start programs, the curricula typically consist of mere transfer of what teachers have been doing in the nursery schools, kindergartens, or first grades where they have been accustomed to teach, to their Head Start classes.

We psychologists have not been very helpful. We have continued to talk of school readiness in terms of mental age, and we have continued to predict future developments by extrapolations of the DQ or IQ for individuals without knowing their circumstances. Such talk and such usage implies considerably less plasticity in development than the evidence warrants. In our own laboratory, merely providing infants with the opportunity to use their eyes by looking at a stabile pattern placed over their cribs at five weeks of age decreased the age at which the blink-response appears from an average of 10.4 weeks to an average of seven weeks (Greenberg, Uzgiris, & Hunt, 1968). In the familiar terms of the DQ, this constitutes an increase of the order of 48 points for this particular behavioral item, and this took place in the home-reared infants of parents of the middle class. Similarly, the decrease in the age at which mature, visually-directed reaching appeared in the infant subjects of White & Held (1966) from 145 days before any enrichment, to 87 days following their second enrichment program, constitutes an increase of about 68 points in the familiar terms of the DQ. This increase is undoubtedly limited largely to the behavioral item assessed. Although such changes in the DQ for specific items clearly demonstrate a level of plasticity which belies our customary predictions from the DQ, it is not to be expected that these increases are of general import. On the other hand, if visual accommodation is ready for use at seven weeks rather than at 10.4 weeks, the possibility of incorporating this visual accommodation into a new ability permits that ability to make its appearance earlier than would otherwise be possible. Thus, one might expect accumulative effect of deprived and/or enriched circumstances that would justify the variation of 70 points in mean IQ on tests such as Dennis (1966) found among typical samples of children aged seven and eight from some 50 cultures over the world. Such evidence would suggest that school readiness may be just as much a matter of the circumstances encountered in a child's ongoing interaction as it is of his hypothetical genotypic limitations.

Unfortunately our ignorance is still tremendous. We lack adequate studies of the social psychological conditions in child rearing in various cultures and in various socioeconomic classes within cultures which will account for the class differences in readiness. To be sure, we have a number of pioneering studies in this domain (Davis, 1948; Davis & Havighurst, 1946; Cynthia Deutsch, 1964; Deutsch & Brown, 1964; Hess & Shipman, 1965; John, 1963, 1964; and John & Goldstein, 1964). These pioneering studies lend suggestive illumination, but they hardly produce that detailed and hard information required to guide corrective measures. Similarly, in the domain of experimentation we have not yet conducted investigations which demonstrate the kind of cumulative effect of enrichments and deprivations that I have inferred from our existing information. Neither have we obtained the information required to describe clearly the hierarchy of abilities with sufficient precision to permit us to deduce a curriculum of enrichments. The best we can do is to suggest enrichment programs for children at various levels of development, and to try out their effectiveness empirically. Even so, we have enough information to justify a major change in the conception of school readiness from that of a stage of maturation to that of a series of achieved abilities. Moreover, we have enough information to indicate that the curricula for compensatory education should be adapted to the already achieved abilities of individual children.

Conclusion

These past twenty years we have lived through and witnessed a major transformation in our conception of intelligence, of its development, and of its relation to heredity and environment. This transformation is still an unfinished process. At the cutting edge of our knowledge many issues remain unresolved. Even now, however, the implications of the transformation for educational practice are only beginning to be realized.

3

Traditional Personality Theory in the Light of Recent Evidence

Knowledge of persons has been disturbingly static over the centuries. Those changes which have occurred have all too often come like the swings in the pendulum of opinion. Knowledge within this domain of persons and of conduct has been too little touched by that cumulative dynamic process of science which followed the Renaissance and which transformed forever the shape of knowledge and understanding within other domains.

Yet, a science of persons and of conduct has been one of the serious hopes of this century. Critics of this hope have been quick to point out, nevertheless, how those propositions about persons, their development, and their conduct that have been passing for a science of persons have derived from such arts of practice as psychotherapy and from the naturalistic observation of administrative behavior rather than from controlled in-

Originally prepared for presentation at the International Congress of Psychology (Washington, D.C., August 30, 1963). Later versions were presented at the Academic Exercises Celebrating the Dedication of the Allan Memorial Institute of Psychiatry at McGill University in Montreal (November 10, 1963), as an invited address for a meeting of the Arizona State Psychological Association in Tucson (February 5, 1964), as a public address at the Educational Testing Service in Princeton, N.J. (March 12, 1964), and as the invited dinner-address for a meeting of the Illinois Psychological Association in Chicago (October 30, 1964). Copyrighted 1965 by The Society of the Sigma Xi and reprinted by permission of the copyright owner.

vestigation. They have noted how schools of conviction about such matters have contended and debated with one another without controlled evidence ever entering the discourse. They have also noted how hard it is actually to apply the experimental method, which has become the chief source of controlled evidence elsewhere, in the domain of persons and their life histories. They have wondered, therefore, if this hope for a science of persons may not be in vain.

Although science does ultimately yield a body of relatively definitive knowledge about a domain, it is in essence less this definitive knowledge that is science than the dynamic, self-corrective process of ongoing inquiry. This process of science, to quote Conant (1947, p. 37), consists in the "development of [I would prefer the phrase *creating of*] conceptual schemes" where the relative validity of competing concepts is tested against concept-directed observations so that "new concepts arise from . . . these observations [and experiments]." It has been common for many critics to contend that the failure of this dynamic yeast of science to get underway within our knowledge of persons results from the vagueness of the conceptual schemes which pass for personality theory. I wish to counter that any beliefs definite enough to make observed phenomena surprising or incredible constitute a suitable starting point. Moreover, a majority of personologists have been sharing a number of beliefs which are sufficiently definite to render a good many of the observations made since World War II, and some made earlier, very surprising and so incredible that they call for revision of these beliefs. My purpose in this paper is to state five of these beliefs and to synopsize some of the observations which they make surprising.

Are Personality Traits the Major Source of Behavioral Variance?

According to the first of these beliefs, the source of most of the variations in behavior resides within persons. Psychoanalysts, clinicians generally, personologists, and students of individual differences have shared this belief. Moreover, they have shared it in opposition to those social psychologists—their thought rooted in the work of C. H. Cooley (1902), George Herbert Mead (1934), and W. I. Thomas (see Volkart, 1951)— who have contended that the major source of variation in behavior resides in the "situation."

In this context, individual differences have been conceived typically after the fashion of static dimensions and have been called traits. Those who have attempted to measure personality traits, however, have all too often found even the reliability and validity coefficients of their measures falling within a range of 0.2 and 0.5. If one takes the square of the coefficient of correlation as a rough, "rule-of-thumb" index of the proportion of the variance attributable to persons, it would appear to be limited to somewhere between 4 and 25 per cent of the total. This is incredibly small for any source which is considered to be *the* basis of behavioral variation, but we personologists have blamed our instruments rather than our belief in the importance of static dimensional traits. Such results, when coupled with the opposition of the social psychologists, suggest the desirability of a direct attempt to determine the relative amounts of common-trait variance attributable to persons, to the modes-of-response which serve as indicators of the traits, and to situations.

Norman Endler and Alvin Rosenstein, two of my former students, and I have attempted this for the trait of *anxiousness* (Endler, Hunt, & Rosenstein, 1962). We asked our subjects to report the degree (on a five-step scale) to which they had manifested a sample of 14 modes-of-response which are commonly considered indicative of anxiety. These included, for instance, "Heart beats faster," "Get an 'uneasy feeling,'" "Emotions disrupt action," "Feel exhilarated and thrilled," "Need to urinate frequently," "Mouth gets dry," "Seek experiences like this," "Experience nausea," and "Have loose bowels." We asked our subjects to report the degree to which they had manifested each of these modes-of-response in each of a sample of 11 specified situations. This sample of situations included, for instance "Going to meet a [blind] date," "Crawling along a ledge high on a mountain side," "Getting up to give a speech before a large group," "Sailing a boat on a rough sea," "Being alone in the woods at night," "Going into an interview for a very important job," and "Entering a final examination in an important course."

When we made a three-way analysis of variance of these quantified reports of response, the largest main source came from the modes-of-response. This finding in itself is trivial, for one might expect an individual to "get an 'uneasy feeling'" to an extreme degree in many situations without ever having "loose bowels" in any. Far from trivial, however, is the fact that the second largest main source came from the situations. In one sample of Illinois sophomores, with the middle 70 per cent on a measure of anxiousness removed, the mean square for situations (152) was 3.8 times that for persons (40); and in another sample of unselected Penn State freshmen, the mean square for situations (244) was somewhat more than 11 times that for persons (21).

When we have recited these facts to our colleagues, some of them have criticized our comparing of mean squares. Nevertheless, they have typically paid us the compliment of staring in disbelief. Such a reaction implies that personality theory has contained at least one proposition sufficiently definite to be the basis for incredibility of observational evidence. The compliment derives from the implication that we have apparently found evidence, the inappropriateness of comparing mean squares notwithstanding, which is sufficiently relevant to the belief in static trait-dimensions to be surprising. We admitted that the generality of our findings could not be inferred from comparing mean squares. Rather, the generality of our findings would have to derive from their reproducibility with other samples of modes-of-response, with other samples of situations, with other samples of subjects, and with other personality traits. If these results should prove to be reproducible in general, as I have defined general, they imply that our brethren from social psychology have had a conceptual slant which is more nearly congruent with reality than has been the slant of us personologists.

On the other hand, like many disputes in the history of science, this one is based on what is, in a sense, a pseudo-question.

Behavioral variance is due primarily to neither persons nor situations. Although a comparison of mean squares for situations and for subjects may have surprise or shock value, actually the mean square for the situational source is a composite of the variances from situations *per se,* from the interaction of situations-by-subjects, from the interaction of situations-by-modes-of-response, from the triple interaction, and from the residual. Also, the mean square for subjects is a similar composite. If one employs the equations of Gleser, Cronbach, & Rajaratnam (1961) to partition these various sources properly, one finds that the modes-of-response do contribute about one-fourth of the variance, again a trivial point. But one also finds that neither situations nor subjects contribute substantially. Typically, neither contributes 5 per cent of the total, and for subjects this is what would be expected from the reliability and validity coefficients for tests of personality traits. The simple interactions contribute nearly a third of the total variance (about 10 per cent each), and the triple interaction with residual contributes about the final third. Thus, main sources, simple interactions, and triple interaction with residual each contribute about a third of the total variance (Endler & Hunt, 1966). Three-way analyses of variance for some 15 samples of subjects with three forms of the S-R Inventory have served to indicate that the percentages of total variance from these various main sources and interactive sources are quite stable. While increasing the variability of situations increases the percentage of variance from situations, the increase is only one from something of the order of 2 or 5 per cent to something of the order of 7 or 8 per cent. Thus, it is neither the individual differences among subjects, *per se,* nor the variations among situations, *per se,* that produce the variations in behavior. It is, rather, the interactions among these which are important.

In the words of a Vermont farmer once quoted by Henry A. Murray, "people is mostly alike, but what difference they is can be powerful important." I am now guessing to be "powerful important" the variations in the meanings of situations to people and the variations in the modes-of-response they manifest. These results imply that, for either understanding variations of behavior or making clinical predictions, we should be looking toward instruments that will classify people in terms of the kinds of responses they make in various categories of situations. Osgood has provided us with the Semantic Differential, an important method of assessing the interaction between people and situations (Osgood, Suci, & Tannenbaum, 1957). Perhaps our own approach may also be helpful.

Is All Behavior Motivated?

The second belief which I wish to confront with evidence from recent investigation concerns personality dynamics or, particularly, motivation. It has most commonly taken the form of the assertion that "all behavior is motivated." In this form, which either originated with or was popularized by Freud, the assertion is indeed too vague to provide a basis for observational surprise, but Freud (1900, 1915), such physiologists as Cannon (1915), and such modern behavior theorists as Hull (1943), Miller & Dollard (1941), and Mowrer (1960), have all shared in filling out the statement so that it has come to say, "all behavior is motivated by painful stimulation, homeostatic need, sexual appetite, or by acquired drives, i.e., originally neutral stimuli which have been associated with painful stimuli, homeostatic need, or sex in the organism's past experience."

This is the well-known drive-reduction theory. According to this theory, the aim or function of every instinct, defense, action, habit, or phantasy is to reduce or to eliminate either stimulation or excitation within the nervous system. Once the assertion gets this form, it can readily provide the basis for observational surprise, for it implies that, in the absence of such motivation, organisms will become quiescent.

They do not become quiescent. I have reviewed these surprising observations elsewhere (1960, 1963a). It has been contended that I have reviewed them *ad nauseam*, so let me be brief here. These observations derive from the studies of play in children by Bühler (1928) and in animals by Beach (1945) and others, the studies of monkeys and chimpanzees manipulating puzzles by Harlow (1950) and by Harlow, Harlow, & Meyer (1950), the studies of spatial exploration in rats by Berlyne (1960) and by Nissen (1930), the studies of spontaneous alternation of rats in a T-maze by Montgomery (1953, 1955), the finding that monkeys will learn various things merely to get a peek at a new scene by Butler (1953), the studies of human beings under conditions of homogeneous input by Bexton, Heron, & Scott (1954), and the now classic studies by Hebb (1946b) which found that fear in chimpanzees will occur with encountering something familiar in an unfamiliar guise.

Such evidence, however, has recently been given theoretical recognition in several unfortunate fashions. One of these is drive-naming. The literature is now full of drives (manipulative, exploratory, curiosity, etc.) and of needs (stimulus, change, etc.). This naming of new motives which merely describes the activities they are designed to explain, helps little. Moreover, in motive-naming, we are revisiting the instinct-naming which McDougall (1908) popularized early in this century but which was discredited just after World War I. We should know better.

A second unfortunate fashion of theoretical recognition is naming motives in terms of their telic significance. I refer to the "urge to mastery" promulgated by Ives Hendrick (1943) and to the concept of "competence motivation" proposed by Robert White (1959) in his excellent review of the evidence concerned. Unfortunately, concepts of telic significance seem to me to provide no means of developing hypotheses about antecedent-consequent relationships that can be tested against observations.

A third unfortunate fashion of theoretical recognition has consisted of postulating spontaneous activity. Some activity can be said to be spontaneous, from a descriptive standpoint, as Hebb has pointed out to me. But this does not make spontaneity a useful explanation, and I am indebted to my colleague, L. I. O'Kelly, for noting that postulating spontaneous activity as an explanation may be just as useless as postulating a list of instincts and drives, and for precisely the same reasons.

As I see it, these various lines of evidence combine to indicate that a system and a mechanism of motivation inheres within the organism's informational interaction with its environmental circumstances. I have described this mechanism elsewhere (Hunt, 1963a). The news of its existence was, I believe, one of the implicit messages of that now classic book entitled *The Organization of Behavior* (Hebb, 1949). This message has since been made explicit, and it has been confirmed by various lines of evidence.

It is no easy matter to characterize properly what it is in the informational interaction with circumstances that is essential. I have termed it "incongruity" (Hunt, 1963a). By this term, I have intended to designate the discrepancy between the incoming information of the moment and that information already coded and stored within the brain in the course of previous encounters with the category of circumstances concerned. Berlyne (1960) uses the term "collative variables" and sees these underlying "arousal potential"; Festinger (1957) speaks of "cognitive dissonance"; Hebb (1949) has referred the matter to a stage of development in cortical organization; Munsinger & Kesson (1964) and Eckblad (1963), a Norwegian psychologist, are calling it "uncertainty." The role of arousal in this informational organism-environment interaction is also a moot point (see Hunt, 1963a). Whether there is one factor or several in it is another moot point. Nathan Isaacs, in Britain, likes to distinguish between novelty, for discrepancies between input and that already stored in mere information processing, and incongruity, where inputs are discrepant from established commitments and plans (personal communication). He may well be correct.

Whatever the essential character of this informational organism-environment interaction and its relationship to arousal turns out to be, there appears to be an optimum amount of it for each organism at any given time. I suspect that this optimum is to a considerable degree a function of experience, and that it may obey Helson's (1959) notion of the adaptation level. When a situation offers too much, i.e., when the inputs from a situation are too incongruous with the information already coded and stored, the organism withdraws as illustrated by Hebb's (1946b) fearful chimpanzees, and by some of the human beings whom Festinger (1957) has found to be avoiding or discrediting information dissonant with their commitments and plans. On the other hand, when a situation offers too little incongruity, i.e., when the inputs from a situation are too similar to the information already in storage, boredom results, and the organism withdraws from that situation to seek another one offering more incongruity, stimulus-change, novelty, dissonance, uncertainty, or what-have-you. It is this seeking of incongruity which is apparently illustrated by the college students in the McGill experiments of Bexton, Heron, & Scott (1954) who refused to remain under conditions of homogeneous input even though they were paid $20 a day. It is this seeking of incongruity which is also illustrated by the fact that Butler's (1953) monkeys will learn merely in order to get a peek at the world outside their monotonous cage-situations, and by that early study of Nissen's (1930) in which rats left their familiar nests and crossed an electrified grid (one of Warden's obstructions) to get to a Dashiell maze filled with objects fresh and novel to them. This work of Nissen's never got into the textbooks, probably because it was too dissonant with the traditional propositions about motivation presented therein.

This line of conceptualizing has still largely unacknowledged implications for our traditional notions of both psychodynamics and psychological development. Both Sigmund Freud (1926) and Anna Freud (1936) conceived the mechanisms of defense as serving to protect a person from anxiety. Sigmund Freud, at least in his later days when he came to see repression as a consequence of anxiety rather than as its source, saw anxiety originating from castration threats, Oedipal anxieties, and other overwhelmingly intense experiences of painful stimulation. The fact that Hebb (1946b) has found chimpanzees withdrawing from sources of input which could never have been associated with painful stimulation (by virtue of the fact that the infants had been reared under observation in the Yerkes Laboratory), coupled with the fact that Festinger (1957) and his students have found human subjects utilizing various strategies to avoid dissonant information, and coupled again with the fact that evidence dissonant with prevailing theories—like that of Nissen's early study—seldom gets into the textbooks, suggest that the mechanism of defense may sometimes, or may even typically, function chiefly to protect individuals from information too incongruous with that which they already have coded in the storage or with that already involved in their commitments and plans. Probably the most important category of stored information in this theoretical context is that concerning the self, as the theorizing of Hilgard (1949) and as the clinical observations and theorizing of Rogers (1951) and George Kelly (1955) would indicate. I dare not take the time to elaborate; here it must be enough to point a direction.

Within the domain of psychological development, it is generally believed that the existence of fears implies that the feared sources of input, when they are not themselves painful, have been associated in the past with painful stimulation. But separation anxiety (or perhaps *separation grief* is a better term) typically appears in infants who are least likely to have had the disappearance of a familiar adult associated with painful stimulation or intense homeostatic need. Moreover, this separation anxiety or grief does not develop while infants are still very young and at a stage of life when the painful stimulation from colic and homeostatic need would be most likely to be prominent. Instead, as the observations of Anna Freud & Burlingham (1944) have indicated, separation grief becomes prominent and prolonged only during the latter part of the first year and during the second year. It is significant to note that this is the time, according to the observations of Piaget (1936), that objects are beginning to have permanence. This emerging permanence of objects implies that some kind of coded template must have been gradually established within the brain-storage in the course of repeated encounters with these objects. Again, I dare not take time to elaborate. My main point is to bring to your attention these indications that there is a highly important system of motivation which is inherent in the organism's informational interaction with the environment and that it has a developmental basis in experience quite different from that of the now traditional acquired drives. I tend to think of this kind of motivation as "intrinsic motivation," a term which distinguishes it from the motivation deriving from painful stimulation, homeostatic need, and sexual appetite, all of which are extrinsic to the organism's informational interaction with the environment.

Are Emotional Factors So Much More Important Than Cognitive Factors in Psychological Development?

The third belief which I wish to discuss in the light of recently uncovered evidence is also motivational and dynamic, but it is developmental as well. Freud probably did more to emphasize the importance of infantile experience in psychological development than anyone else in the history of thought. Freud's (1905) theory of psychosexual development put the emphasis on the fate of the instinctive modes of infantile pleasure-striving, i.e., sucking, elimination, and genitality. Freud's influence has led to the very widespread belief among personologists that these extrinsic motivational or emotional factors are much more important in development than are cognitive factors. This minimization of the importance of cognitive and perceptual factors in early infantile, or preverbal, development has been abetted, moreover, by the beliefs in fixed intelligence and predetermined development so widely held among the earlier students of individual differences in intelligence.

Recent evidence indicates, perhaps, that just about the opposite should hold. Reviews of those relatively objective studies of the effects of the emotional factors pointed up in the theory of psychosexual development have generally tended to depreciate the importance of those factors (see Child, 1954; Hunt, 1946, 1956; Orlansky, 1949). Every study finding significant effects can be matched with another which does not. Moreover, the better controlled the study, the less likely is it to have found significant effects. Similarly, while infantile feeding-frustration in rats appeared to increase eating speed and hoarding in adulthood (Hunt, 1941; Hunt et al., 1947), thereby lending support to the importance of extrinsic motivational factors, these studies have not always been reproducible so far as the effect on hoarding is concerned (Marx, 1952; McKelvey & Marx, 1951). Moreover, having done the first of these studies, perhaps I should admit that I probably misinterpreted the facts anyway. Of course, it is still true that painful stimulation can inhibit eating and drinking and that prolonged failure to eat and drink can kill an organism. On the other hand, the studies of the effects of variations in the richness of early perceptual experience in animals have regularly shown (Forgays & Forgays, 1952; Forgus, 1954, 1955a, 1955b; Hymovitch, 1952) substantial effects on adult problem-solving. These studies have stemmed from Hebb's theorizing, and the first of the kind (Hebb, 1947) compared the performances of pet-reared rats with those of cage-reared rats in the Hebb-Williams (1946) test of animal intelligence. The pet-reared animals proved much superior to their cage-reared littermates. Thompson & Heron (1954) have made a similar experiment with dogs, and the evidence of the superiority of the pet-reared dogs over their cage-reared littermates is even more striking than that for rats. The fact that the evidence from dogs is stronger than that from rats suggests that the importance of early experience, and particularly the importance of early cognitive or perceptual experience, probably increases up the phylogenetic scale as that portion of the brain without direct connection to sensory input or motor outlet increases relative to the portion which does have direct sensory and/or motor connections (i.e., with the size of what Hebb (1949) has termed the A/S ratio). Moreover, there is direct evidence that such effects can be generalized from animal subjects to human beings in studies by Goldfarb (see 1955 for summary) which indicate that being reared in an orphanage, where the variety of circumstances encountered is highly restricted, results at adolescence in lower intelligence, less ability to sustain a task, less attentiveness, and more problems in interpersonal relations than being reared in a foster home. Moreover, those findings of Dennis (1960) that 60 per cent of the two-year-olds in a Tehran orphanage, where changes in ongoing stimulation were minimal, were not yet sitting up alone and that 85 per cent of the four-year-olds were not yet walking alone, serve to dramatize how very much the factor of variety of circumstances encountered in infancy can affect the rate of development—even the rate of development of posture and locomotion.

As I see it, these various lines of evidence combine to indicate that cognitive experience—or, more precisely, the organism's informational interaction with the environment—can be as important for psychological development as emotions based on the fate of instincts, and perhaps it is typically more important. In corollary fashion, these same bits of evidence would also appear to indicate that we have been wrong in our widespread belief that it is the intellectual characteristics of a person which are most nearly fixed by the genotype and that the emotional characteristics of a person are highly subject to substantial environmental influence. Although the life history is of considerable importance in the development of both types of characteristics, it appears that it may be the intellectual variety which is the more subject to substantial effects of environmental encounters, particularly those coming in early infancy.

Must Emotional Attachments Derive from Gratification of Libidinal or Homeostatic Needs?

According to a fourth belief commonly held by personologists, the emotional attachments to objects, persons, and places—called cathexes in psychoanalytic terminology—derive from their association with the gratification of libidinal or homeostatic needs. In his *Three Contributions to the Theory of Sex,* Freud (1905) not only assumed a separation of libidinal from nutritional needs, but he also attributed all object-cathexes to libidinal energy (see p. 553, p. 611, and p. 743 footnote 2). These points, coupled with Freud's (1915) conception of instinct, appear to indicate that he attributed all emotional attachments to libidinal gratification, as he defined it. As I (Hunt, 1946) pointed out nearly 20 years ago, any such generalization is contradicted by the wide variety of studies in which preference for objects, persons, and places has been changed by association with food reward (see, e.g., Mowrer, 1960; Razran, 1938a, 1938b; Williams, 1929; Williams & Williams, 1943) or by association with success in goal-achievement (see Mierke, 1933; Nowlis, 1941; Rosenzweig, 1933).

More recently, it has been generally believed that such emotional attachment derives from the association of objects, persons, and places with homeostatic gratification. And so it is sometimes, but Harlow's (1958) work indicates that association with homeostatic gratification is far from the whole story. In his studies, you will recall, monkey babies, when frightened, went for solace to the soft surrogate-mothers covered with padded terry cloth rather than to the wire surrogate-mothers on which they had sucked to gratify their need for food. Nor can softness of contact be the whole story, for behavioral criteria defining emotional attachment appear to have another basis. Infants of various species appear to approach, to seek, and to take delight in objects which are becoming recognizably familiar in the course of repeated encounters (see Hunt, 1963b), and they show varying degrees of distress as these objects escape their perceptual ken. Piaget (1936) has described how his children came to make what is clearly an "intentional effort" to keep interesting spectacles within perceptual range. Anyone who has ever jounced an infant on his knee and stopped his motion only to find the infant starting a similar motion of his own, is familiar with this intentional effort of the infant to hold on to an interesting spectacle. One gathers from Piaget's (1936) observations that these interesting spectacles very commonly consist of objects or persons that are becoming familiar through repeated encounters. In an exploratory study of this phenomenon, Dr. Ina Uzgiris and I have got evidence consonant with this idea that the young human infant prefers a mobile which has been hanging over his crib to another mobile which he has never encountered before (Hunt & Uzgiris, 1964). Here, the term *prefers* is based on looking time. When the familiar mobile has been withdrawn for a time and is then returned with another unfamiliar one beside it, the infant looks more at the familiar than at the unfamiliar one. Similar phenomena of emotional attachment are to be found in animals. Since it is following an object and distress at its escape from perceptual ken that characterizes the one major component of what the ethologists (Heinroth, 1910; Lorenz, 1935; Thorpe, 1944) call "imprinting," it intrigues me to consider that this effort to follow and to keep interesting spectacles within view and the distress of losing them in lower mammals and birds may be a special case of this more general principle of emotional attachment deriving from recognitive familiarity. If this be sensible, and I believe it is, one can then relate the marked variation in the number of encounters required to establish such recognitive emotional attachments to

Hebb's A/S ratio. There appears to be a progression in the number of encounters or in the amount of exposure time required, from two or three hours in the greylag goose, through two or three days in the sheep or deer, some two weeks in the monkey infant, and some six or so weeks in the chimpanzee infant, to some six or so months in the human infant. Maternal attachment appears to be another special case of this same principle, but it is well contaminated also with contacts and with the gratification of homeostatic need. In all probability, fear of strangers is a direct derivative comparable to the fear of the familiar in an unfamiliar guise found in adult chimpanzees by Hebb (1946b) and already mentioned.

But following is alone no indication of emotional delight. Evidence of the delight comes from the infant's smile and laugh of recognition. Spitz (1946c) and others have considered smiling to be a social response, one based, presumably, on the fact that the human face is repeatedly associated with homeostatic gratification, but Piaget's (1936) observations and those of my colleague, Dr. Uzgiris, indicate that the infant will smile and show laughing delight at the appearance of various objects which are merely becoming familiar with repeated encounters (Hunt, 1963b).

Such observations and considerations strongly suggest that recognitive familiarity is in itself a source of emotional attachment, and this attachment is attested further by the fact that separation grief always concerns familiar objects and persons and by the fact that such grief is but transient in infants too young to have established object permanence. In a sense, this is a further elaboration of the importance of that intrinsic system of motivation which inheres in the organism's informational interaction with the environment.

Do Encounters with Painful Stimulation in Infancy Result in Sensitivity and Proneness to Anxiety?

According to a fifth belief, which we may call the "trauma theory of anxiety," encounters with painful stimulation or strong homeostatic need inevitably leave a young child or a young animal prone to be sensitive and anxious in most situations. This trauma theory assumes the conditioning conception of fear. Thus, it is presumed that the various sources of inputs present immediately before and during encounters with painful stimulation will acquire the capacity to evoke the autonomic and central emotional features incorporated within the total response to painful stimulation.

In spite of Hebb's (1946b) strong evidence to the contrary, most clinicians of all professions act as if *the only source* of anxious emotional disturbance were this association of originally neutral sources of input with pain. Recently, however, another source of evidence dissonant with this widely held belief has been the investigations of the effects of shocking infant animals before they are weaned. Although there may well be both species and strain differences in some of these effects, as indicated by reports—based on studies using mice as subjects—which deviate from those which I am about to mention (see Hall, 1934; Lindzey *et al.*, 1960), rats shocked in infancy have been repeatedly found as adults to be less fearful than rats which have been left unmolested in the maternal nest. This is to say that they urinated less and defecated less in, were less hesitant to enter, and were more active in unfamiliar territory than were rats which had been left unmolested in the maternal nest (see Denenberg, 1962; Levine, 1959, 1961).

In two other investigations, moreover, rats shocked before weaning, with sufficient intensity to keep them squealing continually for three minutes each day, have been found as adults to require stronger shocks to instigate escape-activity than do rats left unmolested (Goldman, 1964; Griffiths, 1960). Finally, in a very recent study by Salama, one of my own students, rats shocked daily from their 11th through their 20th day were found to show much less "fixative effect" of shock after the choice-point in a T-maze than did rats left unmolested in the maternal nest or than did rats either gentled or handled for this same period (Salama & Hunt, 1964).

Let me explain this last experiment briefly. Some 16 years ago, Farber (1948) reported a study of "fixation" which showed that rats intermittently shocked just after the choice-point on their way to one of the goal-boxes in a T-maze, where they were fed, required substantially more unrewarded trials to give up going to that goal-box than did rats merely given food-reward in it. Salama (1962) has replicated this finding and found the mean number of unrewarded trials to be 20.7 for the shocked animals but only 2.8 for those merely given food-reward. He has gone further; he has compared the number of unrewarded trials required for rats shocked in infancy to give up the goal-box with the numbers required by rats gentled and handled. The means for those gentled (21.4) and for those handled (17.6) differed little for the mean for those left unmolested in the maternal nest (20.7), but the mean for those shocked (9) approximates only half the means for these other groups, and it differs significantly ($p < 0.001$) from these and from the unmolested group not shocked after the choice-point.

It is very interesting in connection with these studies that Holmes (1935) has found the children of lower-class backgrounds from a day-care center to be less fearful than children of an upper-middle-class background from a nursery school. Holmes's study was conducted in 1935, right in the midst of the Great Depression, when children of lower-class parents could be expected to have encountered more painful stimulation and homeostatic need than children of the upper middle class. This result suggests that the findings from these animal studies may well generalize to human beings.

It is clear from the evidence that all of these studies tend to disconfirm the present formulation of the trauma theory of anxiety based on the conditioning principle as the only experiential basis for anxiousness. They also suggest that encounters with painful stimulation may serve instead to raise what Helson (1959) calls the adaptation level for painful stimulation and thereby to reduce its aversiveness. The force of such evidence is hardly yet sufficient to warrant—and certainly not sufficient to call for—a change in child-rearing practices, for trauma is also a fact. There are varieties of early experience that leave infants prone to be sensitive and anxious, but we cannot yet clearly specify their nature. Perhaps it should be remembered in connection with this evidence, however, that the Spartan culture survived for several centuries while holding to a belief that infants should be exposed to cold and to painful stimulation to prepare them to bear the dire exigencies of later life.

Summary

I have been calling your attention to the fact that, vague as the propositions in traditional personality may have been, some have been sufficiently definite to provide those who have believed them with an experience of surprise or incredulity when they have encountered some of the observations deriving from investigation, largely from that investigation done since World War II.

I have cited five beliefs which have served as a basis for such surprise: (1) that personality traits are the major sources of behavioral variance; (2) that all behavior is motivated; (3) that emotional factors are much more important than cognitive factors in psychological development; (4) that emotional attachments derive from gratification of libidinal or homeostatic needs; and (5) the trauma theory of anxiousness, that encounters with painful stimulation in infancy always result in sensitivity and proneness to anxiety.

I have synopsized some of the evidence which these beliefs make surprising, and I have indicated some new interpretations which have implications for further investigation. In the light of these developments, perhaps the hope for a science of persons is not in vain. Perhaps the yeastful and self-corrective dynamic of science has at last found its way into knowledge of persons and of personality development.

4

The Epigenesis of Intrinsic Motivation and the Fostering of Early Cognitive Development

Even as late as 15 years ago, a symposium on the stimulation of early cognitive learning would have been taken as a sign that both participants and members of the audience were too soft-headed to be considered seriously. During the last 20 years, however, various lines of evidence have produced changes in our conceptions of intelligence and motivation (discussion of such changes is omitted here because they have been described in Chapters 1, 2, and 3). The geneticist's conception of genotype-environment interaction and the psychobiological conception of ongoing organism-environment interaction now make it quite sensible to consider deliberately fostering early cognitive development or learning. The new evidence and changes of conception, however, do not indicate clearly how to go about it. A fruitful source of suggestions concerning how to proceed derived from an examination of the relationship between what I call intrinsic motivation (see also Hunt, 1963a, 1963b, 1965a) and early cognitive development.

This paper was originally prepared for a symposium on the Stimulation of Early Cognitive Learning, chaired by J. R. Braun, and presented at the Annual Meeting of the American Psychological Association, Philadelphia, 30 August 1963. It is reprinted from *Current Research in Motivation*, R. N. Haber, ed. (New York: Holt, Rinehart, & Winston, 1966). Reprinted by permission of the publisher.

The Concept of "Intrinsic Motivation"

The term "intrinsic motivation" involves a substantial change in our conception of motivation. Intrinsic motivation derives from recognition that there is a motivating system inherent in the organism's informational interaction with its circumstances. Although it is quite clear that the traditional motivating systems of painful stimulation, homeostatic needs, and sex exist and operate as genuine motivating systems, nevertheless, a very large share of an organism's interaction with its circumstances is informational in character. This interaction occurs through the distance receptors, the eyes and the ears, and, to a much lesser degree, through touch.

Elsewhere I have documented the basis for this idea that a major motivational system inheres within the organism's informational interaction with its circumstances (Hunt, 1963a). Here let me be brief. The Russian investigators have found both an emotional aspect and an attentional aspect to even an infant mammal's response to change in ongoing visual or auditory input. Pavlov (1927) called this the "what is it?" response, but it has come to be known as the "orienting response" (see Berlyne, 1960; Razran, 1961; and Sokolov, 1963). The emotional aspect of this "orienting response" can be registered by such impressive indicators as vascular changes (plethysmograph), changes in blood pressure (sphygmomanometer), changes in heart rate (cardiotachometer), changes in palmar sweating (electrical conductance of the skin), changes in muscular tension (electromyograph), and changes in brain potentials (electroencephalograph). The attentional aspect can be seen in efforts to turn to the source of an input that has stopped abruptly. William James recognized the phenomena in his well-known statement that we do not hear the clock until it stops, and recognized the principle that the factor in the situation which draws attention and arouses the individual is a change in some characteristic of the ongoing input.

The fact that the response to such changes of input has both emotional and attentional aspects indicates, at least to me, that these changes of input through the distance receptors were motivational in character. Moreover, the fact that these emotional and attentional aspects occur to changes of ongoing inputs through the eyes and the ears indicates that its motivational power is intrinsic within the organism's informational interaction with the environment. This is the meaning of the term "intrinsic motivation."

Stage One in the Epigenesis of Intrinsic Motivation: The "Orienting Response"

The fact that this "orienting response" is present at birth or as soon as the ears are cleared and the eyes are open, implies that it is a fundamental motivational mechanism which is ready-made at birth.

Indications of the motivational importance of this "orienting response" and of encounters with variations in informational inputs derive from the marked retardation observed in children whose auditory and visual inputs have been severely restricted. Although such retardation has been observed by many during the past century, it was usually explained by assuming that the alert infants escaped orphanages through adoption and only those phlegmatic and unmotivated remained. The well-known studies of Rene Spitz (1945, 1946a) helped greatly to rule out this attribution of retardation to a process of selection. More recently, Wayne Dennis (1960) has found two orphanages in Tehran where even more severe retardation was evident. Of those infants in their second year, 60 per cent were still unable to sit up alone; of those in their fourth year, 85 per cent were still unable to walk alone. By way of explanation, Spitz emphasized the emotional factors associated with lack of mothering as the basis for the greater retardation that he observed at "foundling home" than at "nursery." Dennis, on the other hand, has attributed the extreme retardation of sitting and walking to lack of learning opportunities, or more specifically, to the "paucity of handling, including failure of attendants to place children in a sitting position and the prone position" (1960, p. 1958). These may well be factors of importance, but it should be noted that the conditions of these infants provided a paucity of variation in auditory and visual inputs, or, perhaps I should say, a paucity of meaningful variation in these inputs. On the visual side, those infants in the orphanages in which 90 per cent had been admitted at an age of less than one month had plenty of light, but they continually faced homogeneous off-whiteness interrupted only by passing attendants who seldom stopped to be perceived. On the auditory side, while the noise level of the surrounding city was high and cries of other children were numerous, seldom did clear variations in sound come with such redundancy as to become recognizable, and very seldom did such sound variation herald any specific changes in visual input. Thus, opportunities for the development of specific variations in either type of input and opportunities for auditory-visual coordinations were lacking. Moreover, since no toys were provided, the children had little opportunity to develop that intentional behavior calculated to make interesting spectacles endure. Since the "orienting response" rapidly becomes extinguished to any unchanging input or to any unchanging iterative pattern of input (see Hunt, 1963a, pp. 61-63), one would expect this lack of variation in input, especially during the earliest months, to result in a kind of learned phlegmatic state that would prevent early cognitive development.

In the light of our traditional behavioristic belief that the observable motor response is all-important in psychological development, it is worth noting that the marked retardation that I am attributing to the homogeneity of input does not occur with mere inhibition of motor function during the first year. This latter observation is another by Dennis, or by Dennis & Dennis (1940). You will recall that the distribution of ages for the onset of walking in Hopi children cradled for their first year did not differ from the distribution of ages for onset of walking in Hopi children reared in an unrestrained fashion. While the motions of the legs and arms of the cradled infants were restrained during most of their waking hours, the fact that these cradled infants were often carried about, once they were 40 days old, means that they probably encountered an enriched variety of redundant changes in auditory and visual input. Such a comparison suggests that it may be changes in perceptual input rather than opportunity for motor response that is most important in the motivation of psychological development during the earliest months (see also Fiske & Maddi, 1961).

FIRST SUGGESTION FOR STIMULATING EARLY COGNITIVE LEARNING

This brings me to my first concrete suggestion for stimulating cognitive development during the earliest months, and the process can begin at the child's birth. I suggest that the circumstances be so arranged that the infant will encounter a high variety of redundant changes of auditory, visual, and tactual inputs.

But this suggestion needs elaboration. While changes in ongoing stimulation are probably of basic motivational importance, it may not be mere change in itself that is sufficient to foster cognitive development; redundance of the input changes and of intermodal sequences of input changes are probably necessary. Piaget's (1936) observations of his own infants suggest that, during approximately the first half-year, one of the major accomplishments of interaction with the environment consists in the coordination of what are at birth largely independent sensorimotor systems. According to Piaget, these systems include sucking, listening, looking, grasping, vocalizing, and wriggling. Without use, any one of these systems will wane. As is well known to any farm boy who has pail fed a calf, the sucking wanes after ten days or two weeks of pail feeding and the calf can be trusted completely among fresh cows with full udders. Moreover, the work of Alexander Wolf (1943) and of Gauron & Becker (1959) on the effects of depriving infant rats of audition and vision on the readiness of these systems to respond in adulthood, coupled with the work of Brattgård (1952) and of Riesen (1947, 1958, 1961) showing that the visual system fails to develop properly when rabbits and chimpanzees are reared in darkness, indicate that this principle holds for listening and looking as well as sucking. Parenthetically, I should add that the role of organism-environment interaction in early development appears to be tied biochemically with later capacity to synthesize RNA, as the work of Brattgård (1952), Hydén (1959), and others (see Riesen, 1961) appears to indicate. Perhaps the earliest of such interactions serve chiefly to sustain and to strengthen and develop the individual ready-made sensori-motor organizations or, as Piaget terms them, the "reflexive schemata." Very shortly, under typical circumstances, however, the sounds that evoke listening come to evoke looking, and the things seen come to evoke grasping and reaching, and the things grasped come to evoke sucking, etc. Such changes indicate progress in the coordination of the originally separate systems. During this phase, which is the second stage in Piaget's (1936) system, the progressive organization of schemata consists chiefly in such coordination, and it appears to consist in sequential organization, of which Pavlov's *conditioning* and Guthrie's *contiguity learning* are special cases.

If one tries to imagine how one can introduce redundant changes in visual and auditory inputs in order to provide for the sequential coordination of listening with looking, of looking with reaching, etc., one finds it no easy matter without actually having on hand human beings whose approaches and withdrawals supply the auditory-input changes that are regularly followed by visual-input changes. I have found myself wondering if the emphasis on mothering may not have a somewhat justified explanation in that it is the human infant's informational interaction with this coming and going of the mother that provides the perceptual basis for this coordination of relatively independent schemata.

Stage Two in the Epigenesis of Intrinsic Motivation

But the nature of this intrinsic motivational process changes with experience. Any attempt to stimulate early cognitive learning must, I believe, take this change in form, or epigenesis, into account if it is to be at all successful. Moreover, if this epigenesis is taken into account, the circumstances encountered by the infant should not only motivate a rapid rate of cognitive development but should contribute substantially to the satisfaction the infant gets from life. As observers of infant development have long noted, the human infant appears to learn spontaneously, that is, in the absence of the traditional extrinsic motivators, and to get superb enjoyment from the process (see Baldwin, 1895; Bühler, 1918, 1928; Hendrick, 1943; Mittlemann, 1954). This is a new notion to most of us, but it is also old. For instance, it was implicit in the "self-activity" of Froebel (1826) and in the "intrinsic interest" of Dewey (1900). Moreover, Maria Montessori (1909), to whose work I shall return shortly, built her system of education for young children on the notion that children have a spontaneous interest in learning.

In what appears to be the first major transition in the structure of intrinsic motivation, the infant, while continuing to respond to changes in ongoing stimulation, comes to react toward the cessation of inputs which have been encountered repeatedly in a fashion designed to continue them or to bring them back into perceptual ken. Piaget (1936) called this a "reversal transformation." He considered it to be the beginnings of intention. Each of you who has ever dandled an infant on your knee is familiar with at least one example: when you stop your motion, the infant starts a motion of his own that resembles yours, and when you start again, the infant stops. The prevalence of infants' actions that are instigated by an absence of repeatedly encountered changes in input suggests, at least to me, that the repeated encounters with a given pattern of change in receptor input lead to recognition that provides one basis, and I believe it an important one, for cathexis, emotional attachment, and positive reinforcement (see Hunt, 1963b). My colleague Morton Weir prefers to refer to what attracts the infant as "predictability." Perhaps this is the better term. I have, however, preferred "recognition" because I suspect that what is happening is that the repeated encounters with a pattern of change in ongoing input serve to build into the storage of the posterior intrinsic system of the cerebrum a coded schema that can be matched to an input from the repeatedly encountered pattern of change. As the pattern is becoming recognizable, or when it is newly recognized, I suspect it provides a joyful basis of cathexis and positive reinforcement.[1] I believe, at least tenta-

[1] Since this was written, data consonant with this hypothesis have come from several studies (Greenberg, Uzgiris, & Hunt, 1968; Hunt & Uzgiris, 1964; Uzgiris & Hunt, 1969; Weizmann, Cohen, & Pratt, 1968).

tively, that it is this recognition that is one of the most consistent evokers of the infant's smile. Such an interpretation gains some support from the fact that maternal separation and encounters with unfamiliar persons bring little emotional disturbance, anxiety, or grief until the second half of the first year of life (Freud & Burlingham, 1944). In fact, these observations of emotional disturbance are important indicators that the cathexis or maternal attachment has been formed. It is this emotional disturbance that supports the observation that an infant acts to retain or to obtain a pattern of familiar input that attests his cathexis of that pattern. Moreover, it should be noted that emotional distress accompanies maternal deprivation only after the age at which objects have begun to acquire permanence for the child. Presumably this permanence of objects is based on the development, in the course of repeated encounters with a pattern of change in input, of a set of semiautonomous central processes that can represent the pattern deriving from an encounter with an object.

Parenthetically, may I suggest also that the following-response within what is called "imprinting" may well be a special case of this more general principle that emotional attachment grows out of the recognition coming from repeatedly encountering an object, place, or person; the fact that the following-response occurs after a shorter period of perceptual contact with an object in a species such as the greylag goose, or in the sheep or deer, than is required in species such as the chimpanzee or man suggests that the number of encounters, or duration of perceptual contact, required may well be a matter of the portion of the brain without direct connections with receptors or motor units, or what Hebb (1949) has termed the A/S ratio.

Out of such observations comes the empirical principle, which I have imbibed from Piaget (1936), that "the more an infant has seen and heard, the more he wants to see and hear." The avidity of an infant's interest in the world may be seen to be in large part a function of the variety of situations he has encountered repeatedly. Moreover, it would appear to be precisely the absence of such avid interest that constitutes the regularly observed apathy of orphanage-reared children who have encountered only a very limited variety of situations. It may well be that this seeking of inputs that have been made familiar by repeated encounters is what motivates the behavior Dennis & Dennis (1941) have termed "autogenous." Outstanding examples of such behavior are the hand-watching and the repetitive vocalizations called "babbling." It is, apparently, seeking to see the hands that motivates the motions to keep them within view, thereby providing the beginnings of eye-hand coordination. It is, apparently, seeking to hear voice sounds that motivates spontaneous vocalizing and keeps it going, thereby providing the infant with a beginning of ear-vocal coordination.

SECOND SUGGESTION FOR THE STIMULATION OF EARLY COGNITIVE LEARNING

This brings me to my second suggestion for fostering early cognitive learning. It comes in connection with the development of intrinsically motivated intentions or plans, as the terms *intention* and *plan* are utilized by Miller, Galanter, & Pribram (1960). In fact, it is in connection with this development of intrinsically motivated intentions or plans that one basis for this change in the conception of motivation may be seen. Psychologists and psychoanalysts have conceived of actions, habits, defenses, and even of every thought system, as an attempt to reduce or eliminate stimulation or excitation within the nervous system arising out of painful stimulation, homeostatic need, or sex. To anyone who has observed and pondered the struggle of a young infant to reach and grasp for some object he sees, it is extremely difficult to find such an extrinsic motivational basis for his reaching and grasping. What is suggested by Piaget's observations is that in the course of repeated encounters with an object, there comes a point at which seeing that object becomes an occasion for grasping it. In this coordination between looking and grasping, it would appear that grasping the object becomes a goal even though it is quite unrelated to pain, to homeostatic need, or to sex. Once an infant has the grasping goal of an object he has seen repeatedly, his various other motor schemata of striking, pushing, and even locomotion become also means to achieve this goal. Anyone who ponders this phenomenon in the light of the traditional theory of extrinsic motives will ask, "but why grasp the object?" And, "why grasp one object rather than another?" My tentative answer to these questions is that the object has become attractive with the new-found recognition that comes with repeated visual or auditory encounters. While reading Piaget's (1936, 1937) observations, one gets the impression that a smile very frequently precedes the effort to grasp, as if the infant were saying, "I know what you are, I'll take hold of you." Of course, nothing is so explicit; he has no language; he is merely manifesting a kind of primordial plan or intention. It is my hypothesis that this primordial intention is instigated by recognitive perception. If this hypothesis is true, then once an infant is ready to grasp things and to manipulate them, it is important that he have perceptual access to things he can grasp. It is important that there be a variety of such things that he has encountered earlier. The more varied the objects that are available, the more interest the infant will have in his world and the more sources of attractive novelty he will have later on.

As already indicated, it is probably also important that the infant have an opportunity to interact with human beings as well as with inanimate objects. Perhaps one of the chief functions of early interaction with human beings is to make the vocalized phones of the parental language and the gestures of communication familiar, for one of the most common forms of action designed to hold onto newly recognized inputs is imitation.[2] Such imitation is important for socialization and for intellectual development because the roots of human culture reside in the sounds of language and the various gestures of communication. An infant imitates first those phones and gestures that are highly familiar to him. In fact, one of the most feasible ways to start an interactive relationship with a young infant is to make one of the sounds that he is making regularly or to perform one of his characteristic gestures. The very fact that the sounds or gestures are the infant's helps to insure his

[2] This conception of imitation differs radically from that given by Miller & Dollard (1941), but it does not deny that their conception may be true under certain circumstances.

recognition of them. Seeing them in another person commonly brings delighted interest and, not infrequently, imitative effort to recover them when the adult has stopped. The infant's jouncing in the dandling relationship is a special case of such imitative effort. Again we have a kind of encounter hard to arrange without involving human beings. This paucity of encounters that can be arranged without human beings supports the idea that the stories of feral men, including Romulus and Remus, are probably myths.

Stage Three in the Epigenesis of Intrinsic Motivation

The second major transformation in intrinsic motivation appears to occur when repeatedly encountered objects, places, and events become "old stuff." The infant then becomes interested in *novelty*. The breakdown of the meaning of a given input with repeated perceptual encounters and the monotony that comes with repeated participation in given events are phenomena that psychologists have long observed (see Titchener, 1926, p. 425). Hebb (1949, p. 224), moreover, has observed that a major source of pleasure resides in encountering something new within the framework of the familiar. The sequence—of "orienting response" to stimulus change, recognition with repeated encounters, and interest in the variations within the familiar—may well be one in the interaction of an organism with each completely new class of environmental phenomena. What look like stages in the development of the first year may possibly be derived from the fact that an infant tends to be repeatedly encountering a fairly extended variety of situations at a fairly consistent rate. In any event, in his observations of his own children, Piaget (1936) noticed that this interest in novelty appears toward the end of the first year.

There are those who dislike the very notion of such an epigenesis in the structure of motivation. There are those who seek single explanatory principles. Some have tried to explain this series of transformations in terms either of a process in which the new is continually becoming familiar or of a process whereby the earlier interest in the familiar exists because recognizability itself is novel at this phase. We may someday get a biochemical understanding of this phenomenon, but such attempts to find a unitary psychological principle of explanation are probably doomed to failure. Numerous studies indicate very clearly that organisms first respond to change in ongoing inputs. It is less certain that they next prefer the familiar, but the evidence is abundant that they later prefer objects and situations that are relatively less familiar than others available (see Dember, Earl, & Paradise, 1957; Hebb & Mahut, 1955; Montgomery, 1952, 1953). There is one instance in which a study shows that the lowly rat will endure even the pain of electric shock to get from his familiar nest-cage to an unfamiliar situation where there are novel objects to manipulate (Nissen, 1930). Studies also exist, moreover, in which organisms withdrew in fear from "familiar objects in an unfamiliar guise." These were objects that could never have been associated with painful stimulation in their previous experience because the animals had been reared under known conditions at the Yerkes Primate Laboratory. Festinger (1957) has also found people withdrawing from information dissonant with their strongly held beliefs, plans, or commitments.

It is no easy matter to characterize properly what is essential in that glibly called "novelty." I believe, however, that we can say that novelty resides within the organism's informational interaction with its environment. I have termed this essence "incongruity" (Hunt, 1963a); Berlyne (1960) has written of the "collative variables" underlying "arousal potential"; Festinger (1957) has talked of "dissonance"; Hebb (1949) has written of the stage of development in cortical organization; and Munsinger & Kessen (1964) are using the term "uncertainty." Whatever this essence is called, too much of it gives rise to withdrawal and gestures commonly connoting fear. Too little appears to be associated with boredom. That novelty that is attractive appears to be an optimum of discrepancy in this relationship between the informational input of the moment and the information already stored in the cerebrum from previous encounters with similar situations.

Once interest in novelty appears, it is an important source of motivation. Perhaps it is the chief source of motivation for cognitive learning. Interest in novelty appears to motivate the improvement of locomotor skills, for the novel objects "needing" examination or manipulation are typically out of reach. It appears to motivate imitation of unfamiliar verbal phones and unfamiliar gestures and even of fairly complex actions. Imitated vocalizing of unfamiliar phones and vocal patterns appears to be exceedingly important in the acquisition of language. The notion that all infants vocalize all the phones of all languages (Allport, 1924) has long been hard to believe. The social side of language acquisition appears to be more than the mere reinforcing with approval or notice of those vocal patterns characteristic of the parents' language. If the interest in novelty provides an intrinsic motivational basis for (imitatively) vocalizing phones that have never been a part of the infant's vocal repertoire, then we have a believable explanation for the fact that most of the first pseudo-words are approximations of adult vocalizations that have occurred repeatedly in connection with novel and exciting events. Repetition of encounters with a given class of events may be presumed gradually to establish central processes representative of that class of event, that is, *images*, if you will. Imitation of the novel phones verbalized by adults in association with the class of events may provide the infant with a vocalization that can serve him as a sign of his image. Later, reinforcement, partially based on approval-disapproval and partially based on growing cognitive differentiation, may lead gradually to images and phonemic combinations that are sufficiently like those of the people taking care of an infant to permit communication.

Once language is acquired, the human child comes into basically the same existential situation in which all of us find ourselves. He then has two major sources of informational input: first, the original one of perceiving objects and events and, second, the new one of learning about them through the language of others. One of his major intellectual tasks is to make what he learns about the "real world" through the communications of others jibe with what he learns about it directly through his own receptors. This is a creative task of no mean proportion, and it is not unlike the task with which mature men of science are continuously concerned. This is one of George Kelly's (1955) major points.

The considerations already outlined in connection with my suggestions concerning repeated encounters with a given class of stimulus change and "recognition" show again the basis for the principle that "the more a child has seen or heard, the more he wants to see and hear" and do. If an infant has encountered a wide variety of changes in circumstances during his earliest days, and if he has encountered them repeatedly enough to become attached to them through recognition, and if he has had ample opportunity to act upon them and to manipulate them, he will become, I believe, ready to be intrigued by novel variations in an ample range of objects, situations, and personal models.

The fact that too much novelty or incongruity can be frightening and too little can be boring, however, creates a problem for those who would stimulate cognitive development. They must provide for encounters with materials, objects, and models that have the proper degree of that incongruity (Hunt, 1963a). This is one aspect of what I have termed the "problem of the match" (Hunt, 1961, pp. 267ff).

THIRD SUGGESTION FOR THE STIMULATION OF EARLY COGNITIVE LEARNING

Consideration of the problem of the match brings me to my third concrete suggestion for stimulating cognitive learning in the very young. I must confess that I have borrowed this suggestion from Montessori (1909; see also Fisher, 1912). The first portion of this suggestion is that careful observation be made of what it is in the way of objects, situations, and models for imitation that interests the infant. Once it is clear what objects and models are of interest, then I suggest providing each infant with an ample variety of them and with an opportunity to choose spontaneously the ones that intrigue him at a given time. This latter suggestion assumes, of course, that the infant is already comfortable, that he feels safe, and that he is satisfied so far as homeostatic needs are concerned. I really feel that we do not have to worry too much about gratifying the sex appetite of a child under three years of age.

When I wrote *Intelligence and Experience* (1961), this problem of providing a proper match between the materials with which a child is confronted by teachers and what he already has in his storage loomed large because of our tremendous ignorance of the intricacies involved. This ignorance is a major challenge for investigation; in the meantime, however, as Jan Smedslund pointed out to me in a conversation in Boulder last summer, Montessori long ago provided a practical solution. She based her system of education on intrinsic motivation, but she called it "spontaneous learning." She provided young children with a wide variety of materials, graded in difficulty and roughly calculated to be the range of materials that would provide a proper match for children of ages three to six if they were given opportunity of choice. She also gave each of the children in her school an opportunity to occupy himself or herself with those materials of his or her own individual choice. To do this, she broke the lockstep in the educational process. A Montessori school was socially so structured that the children were obviously expected to occupy themselves with the materials provided. Moreover, by having together within a single room children ranging in age from three to six years, she provided a graded series of models for the younger children and an opportunity for some of the older children to learn by teaching the younger ones how to do various things. You will be interested to know that a substantial proportion of the slum children in Montessori's school began reading and writing before they were five years old. In the Casa di Bambini, which Montessori founded in 1907 in the basement of a slum apartment-house in Rome, the teacher was the apartment house superintendent's 16-year-old daughter who had been trained by Montessori. You will also be interested to know that the old nursery school bugaboo that children have very brief spans of attention did not hold. Dorothy Canfield Fisher (1912)—the novelist who spent the winter of 1910-1911 at the original Casa di Bambini— has written that it was common to see a three-year-old continuously occupied with such a mundane task as buttoning and unbuttoning for two or more hours at a stretch.

Montessori's contributions to the education of the very young were discussed with excitement in America until the time of World War I. Thereafter the discussion ended almost completely. I suspect that this occurred because Montessori's theoretical views were so dissonant with what became about then the dominant views of American psychologists and American educators. Her theory that cognitive capacity could be modified by proper education was dissonant with the dominant and widely prevailing notions of "fixed intelligence" and "predetermined development." These notions were implicit in the doctrine of a constant IQ. Her notion of spontaneous learning was sharply dissonant with the doctrine that all behavior is extrinsically motivated by painful stimulation, or homeostatic need, or sex. Moreover, the importance she attributed to sensory training was dissonant with what became the prevailing presumption that it is the observable motor response that counts. We need to re-examine her contributions in the light of the theoretical picture that has been emerging since World War II. I am grateful to Jan Smedslund for calling her contributions to my attention.

My discourse has skipped roughly half of the second year and all of the third year of life, because interest in novelty typically makes its earliest appearance toward the end of the first year or early in the second. (Montessori's schools took children only at three years of age or older.) I suspect that the basic principle involved in stimulating cognitive learning is fairly constant once the interest in novelty appears. On the other hand, I would not be surprised if it were precisely during this period between 18 months and three years of age that lower-class families typically most hamper the kind of cognitive learning that is later required for successful performance in school and in our increasingly technological culture. Let me explain briefly.

During the first year, the life of an infant in a family crowded together in one room—as Oscar Lewis (1961) has described such living in his *Children of Sanchez* and as I have observed it in the slums of New York—probably provides a fairly rich variety of input. On the other hand, once an infant begins to use his new-found locomotor and linguistic skills, his circumstances in a lower-class setting probably become anything but conducive to appropriate cognitive learning. Using his new loco-motor skills gets him in the way of problem-beset adults and, all too likely, may bring punishment which can be avoided only by staying out of their way. This in turn deprives the infant of the opportunity to hear and imitate the verbal phones that pro-vide the basis for spoken language. If a slum child should be lucky enough to acquire the "learning set" that things have names and to begin his repetitive questioning about "what's that?" he is not only unlikely to get answers but also likely to get his ears cuffed for asking such silly questions. Moreover, in the slum setting of lower-class family life, the models that an infant has to imitate are all too often likely to result in the acquisition of sensorimotor organizations and attitudes that inter-fere with rather than facilitate the kinds of cognitive learning that enable a child to succeed in school and in a technological culture such as ours. How long such interference with develop-ment can last without resulting in a permanent reduction in cognitive potential remains an unsolved problem. It is likely, however, that day-care centers and nursery schools prepared to face such children with situations, materials, and models that are not too incongruous with the schemata and attitudes that they have already acquired, can counteract much of the detri-mental effect of lower-class life. Such preschool experience dur-ing the second and third, and possibly even during the fourth, years of life can perhaps serve well as an antidote to this kind of cultural deprivation (see Hunt, 1964).

Summary

I have limited my discussion to the implications, for the stimu-lation of early cognitive learning, of the epigenesis of intrinsic motivation that I believe I can see taking place during preverbal development. I have identified three stages of intrinsic motiva-tion that are separated by two major "reversal transformations." In the first of these, repeated encounters with patterns of change in perceptual input lead to recognition that I believe, as of now, to be a source of pleasure and a basis for cathexis or for affectional attachment. The second consists in a transition from an interest in the familiar to an interest in the novel. During the first few months, when the child is responsive chiefly to changes in the character and intensity of ongoing stimulation, I suspect it is most important to provide for repeated encounters with as wide a variety as possible of changes in receptor input. It may also be important to provide for sequential arrangements of these inputs that will provide a basis for a coordination of all combinations of the ready-made reflexive sensorimotor systems. As the infant becomes attached to objects, people, and situations by way of the hypothetical joys of new-found recognition, it is probably most important to provide opportunities for him to utilize his own repertoire of intentional activities to retain or elicit or manipulate the objects, people, and situations, again in as wide a variety as is feasible. Once interest in novelty appears, I suspect it is most important to give the child access to a variety of graded materials for manipulation and coping and to a variety of graded models for imitation. With what little we now know of what I call the "problem of the match," I suspect it is important to follow Montessori's principle of trusting to a considerable degree in the spontaneous interest of the individual infant instead of attempting to regiment his learning process in any lockstep method of preschool education.

5

Political and Social Implications of the Role of Experience in the Development of Competence

Various changes have been taking place since World War II in our conceptions of intelligence and of all those factors determining the development of the abilities and motives which underlie competence and social responsibility. These changes in our conceptions have social implications, and our attempts to utilize these changes in conception for social change have political implications about which we should be witting. Since I have been analyzing and trying to foster these changes since 1956, I feel that most of them should now be obvious. Yet, wherever I go among educators, teachers, and even among my psychological colleagues, I hear language clearly implying the continued existence of notions which were dominant through a period beginning a decade before World War I and lasting through World War II. These are notions that I now consider to be clearly untenable. These are notions which unfortunately hampered research and development in early childhood education. The changing conceptions appear to be reaching lay leaders even before they reach many of us trained in the psychological sciences. These lay leaders, however, may be hoping for too much from the changes in conception without the development of the necessary educational technology. The political

Invited address for Psi Chi, Honorary Psychological Fraternity, at the Meeting of the Midwestern Psychological Association, Chicago, Illinois, 6 May 1967.

consequences of excessive hope may be an "oversell" to be followed by an "overkill" of support for the efforts required to develop an effective technology.

Let me summarize for you now.

With respect to intelligence, I believe, first, that it is no longer tenable to conceive of intelligence tests as indicators of fixed capacity or innate potential. I believe, second, that it is untenable to consider tests of intelligence as fundamentally different from, or even very different from, tests of achievement. I believe, third, that it is semantically unfortunate to speak of intelligence as a dimension of persons and to speak of the tests as scales.

With respect to psychological development, I believe, first, that it is no longer tenable to conceive of such development as predetermined in rate, as the notion of the constant IQ implied. I believe, second, that it is, therefore, quite wrong to think of predicting from the IQ of a child from a test administered at an early age what his level of intelligence will later become so long as one cannot specify the circumstances that the child will encounter in the interim. Third, I feel it is wrong to consider the behavioral order existing in behavioral development as evidence of a preprogrammed maturation. Moreover, I believe there are several bases for order in behavioral development and that the matter is one important for empirical investigation. Finally, I believe these conceptions, particularly these I have labeled as untenable, have been and continue to be harmful because, insofar as they make it seem hopeless to alter what is presumably fixed and predetermined, they have interfered with and continue to interfere with their investigation and with efforts to improve the circumstances in which children develop and to improve the techniques of education.

On the other hand, I also find myself perturbed by the haste now evident in efforts to improve the competence of children of the poor. Note that my perturbation concerns only the *haste*, not the efforts. It would appear that our political and social leaders outside the profession and science of psychology have read clearly the message of the changing nature of our professional views about the role of experience in the development of the abilities and motives underlying competence. Once the circumstances controlling experience in the course of development are conceived to have an important role in the development of competence, it takes only a very little imagination to infer that the children of parents of low socioeconomic status, once very widely considered to be naturally inept and lazy, may instead be viewed as children cheated of that equality of opportunity which our forefathers considered to be a birthright of all.

It has probably been the contemporary social challenges of technological advance and racial discrimination which have prompted our political and social leaders to catch the message of our changing conceptions of the role of experience in the development of competence. What perturbs me is their tendency to confuse a scientifically justifiable hope that the competence of children of the poor can be improved with the existence of the science-based educational technology required to plan broad-scale educational programs, and to set up these programs immediately.

The new challenges, to be sure, have become obvious and urgent. The industrial revolution has come to farming. No longer can a family obtain a livelihood from a few acres of land with a mule, a sulky plow, and a hoe. As a consequence, we have been witnessing a tremendous increase in the rate of migration from our farms to the cities. It has been said that the magnitude of this migration since World War II is equivalent in number of persons to all such migrations in the states and colonies from the landing of the Pilgrims to World War II. This migration is, in a very large measure, responsible for the current plight of our cities. Within our cities, moreover, self-monitoring machines under the label of automation are coming to both factories and offices. As they come, they have the effect of contracting sharply the economic opportunities for people with limited skills in the use of symbols, in the solving of problems, and with limited motivational bases for achievement and responsibility. At the same time, the economic opportunities for people with strong symbolic skills and strong motivation for achievement and responsibility are expanding perhaps even more sharply. Thus, while the grade school dropout can hardly expect to participate meaningfully in the mainstream of our increasingly technological society, the demand for Ph.D.'s in almost all fields continually outstrips the supply by an increasing margin. All this is a major part of the challenge that has motivated the appropriation of federal funds to help equalize the educational opportunities of children from our slums in Project Head Start. Even as recently as 25 years ago, the appropriation of federal funds for such a purpose would have been as utterly unthinkable as the appropriation of federal funds to put someone on the moon.

Achieving racial desegregation, another major part of the challenge which has motivated such projects as Head Start, is not unrelated to the challenge posed by our technological advances. Those who hold that the races differ in inherited potential for competence are far from extinct. Although one cannot with utter certainty rule out such a possibility, this possibility is one of little import so long as the great majority of black children grow up in poverty with grossly limited opportunities to acquire the abilities to use language and numbers and the motivation for achievement and social responsibility.

The matter of how we conceive of intelligence and competence; the matter of how we conceive of psychological development, both intellectual and motivational; and the matter of what circumstances will best foster the development of competence are no longer merely academic. These matters have clearly acquired urgent social and political significance.

Intelligence

TEST SCORES NOT INDICATORS OF CAPACITY OR POTENTIAL

It should have been obvious from the beginning that scores on tests of intelligence could not possibly serve as indicators of hereditary potential or ultimate capacity. It is a truism to say that the genotype sets limits on intellectual potential and also that it greatly influences the nature of the consequences of encountering any given series of environmental circumstances. As a scientific statement, however, this is basically meaningless, as Binet (1909) recognized from the start. He deplored the fact that:

. . . some recent philosophers appear to have given their moral support to this deplorable verdict that the intelligence of an individual is a fixed quantity . . . we must protest and act against this brutal pessimism . . . [for] a child's mind is like a field for which an expert farmer has advised a change in the methods of cultivation, with the result that in the place of a desert land, we now have a harvest. It is in this particular sense, the one which is significant, that we say that the intelligence of children may be increased. One increases that which constitutes the intelligence of a school child, namely the capacity to learn, to improve with instruction (pp. 54-55).

Although it was the complex tests of Binet & Simon (1905) which survived in the intelligence-testing movement, it was the conceptualizing of Francis Galton and G. Stanley Hall, rather than that of Binet, which emphasized from the beginning the role of heredity as a fixer of intelligence and a predeterminer of development in the interpretation of test scores. It was Galton's student, J. McKeen Cattell, who, for instance, first brought the tests to America. It was such students of G. Stanley Hall as H. H. Goddard, Frederick Kuhlmann, and Louis M. Terman who set in motion the intelligence-testing movement, and it was Arnold Gesell, another of his students who developed the normative approach to the study of behavioral development.

Moreover, authors of the textbooks on genetics in America tended throughout more than the first four decades of this century to emphasize the work of Mendel on the transmission of traits and to neglect the work of Johannsen on interactionism. It was Johannsen (1903, 1909) who authored the concepts of *genotype* and *phenotype*. By the genotype, Johannsen meant any constellation of genes that an organism receives from its progenitors. By the phenotype, he meant any combination of characteristics of an organism that can be observed and measured at any point in its development. It was Johannsen who also pointed out that the genotype can only be inferred from its effects on the observable phenotype. It was Johannsen who did the early work of showing that phenotypic characteristics of chrysanthemum plants are a function of the interaction between the genotype and the circumstances under which the plants develop. Had American students of intelligence and development known this work and conceptualizing of Johannsen from the outset, perhaps they would never have conceived of intelligence test scores as indicators, even as indirect indicators, of fixed capacity or of hereditary potential.

To be sure, some of the early evidence was quite consonant with the notion of intelligence tests as indicators of capacity. For instance, the IQ's of groups of children showed great constancy (an artifact of the way the tests were constructed) and also considerable individual constancy once children got into school. Moreover, efforts at training children directly on the functions tested turned out to have but short-lived effects. Furthermore, the IQ's of persons closely related proved to be more similar than the IQ's of persons less closely related or unrelated.

Yet, other bits of even the early evidence were highly dissonant with the belief in the tests as measures of fixed capacity (see Hunt, 1961, p. 19ff). Unfortunately, the faith in this belief was so strong that it prompted attempts to reduce the resulting dissonance by arguments aimed at reducing the credibility evidence.

Since World War II evidence highly dissonant with the belief that the tests indicate fixed innate capacity or potential has been accumulated to a degree that leaves the belief no longer tenable. Perhaps the most incontrovertible of this evidence is that of rising intelligence in the face of predicted deterioration. The prediction of deterioration came from combining two observations. First, it has been obvious since the seventeenth century that families of the low socioeconomic status have more children on the average than families of the middle and upper classes. Second, people from low socioeconomic background typically average about 20 points of IQ below people in the upper-middle class (see Anastasi, 1958, p. 515). In 1937, for instance, R. B. Cattell multiplied the number of people at each IQ level by the reproduction rate at that level and computed the new mean to estimate the IQ of the next generation. From this procedure, he estimated a drop of a little over three points a generation, or about one point a decade. This dire prediction has been repeatedly disconfirmed by rising IQ's in those populations where the children of a given age have been tested and retested after intervals of a decade or more. Thirteen years after his own dire prediction, Cattell (1950) himself published a study comparing ten-year-old children living in the city of Leicester in 1949 with the ten-year-old children living in that same city in 1936. In the place of the predicted drop of something slightly more than one point in IQ, Cattell actually found an increase of 1.28 points. Although small, this increase was highly significant from the statistical standpoint. Findings of a similar order have come from the Scottish survey of Godfrey Thompson and his collaborators (1933, 1949, 1953). In other studies, the predicted drop in IQ has been disconfirmed by gains which are substantially larger than these. That reported by Smith (1942) between the scores of children in the various schools in Honolulu in 1924 and the scores of children in those same schools of Honolulu in 1938 was of the order of 20 points. That reported by Wheeler (1942) between the mean IQ for samples of children from a single group of families, taken before and a decade after the social changes instituted by the Tennessee Valley Authority, was ten points. When Finch (1946) compared the tested intelligence of all students in a sample of high schools in the 1920's and again in those same high schools in the 1940's, he found the average gains for the various high schools ranging between 10 and 15 points of IQ. These gains occurred despite the fact that a substantially larger portion of the total population was attending these high schools in 1940 than in 1920. Perhaps the most dramatic evidence of an upward shift comes from comparing performances of the soldiers in World War II with the soldiers of World War I on military intelligence tests (see Anastasi, 1958). Clearly, if the tests measure fixed intellectual capacity or innate potential, and if the majority of each new generation comes from parents in the lowest third in tested intelligence, something very, very strange is happening.

It was obvious to Binet even in 1909, however, that intelligence as measured by tests was far from fixed, and that the very nature of the tests depended on learning or the effects of experience.

SIMILARITY OF TESTS OF INTELLIGENCE AND TESTS OF ACHIEVEMENT

It has long been customary to differentiate intelligence tests from achievement tests. Some differences do exist. At the level of item selection or item content, Humphreys (1962a) has recognized three. All are differences in degree, however, rather than in kind. First, intelligence tests include items of a wider variety of kinds than do achievement tests. Intelligence tests are more heterogeneous with respect to content than achievement tests. Thus, when the total scores on a broad series of achievement tests are correlated with scores on an intelligence test, the resulting coefficient is about as high as the coefficients obtained by correlating the scores for a group from one form of a test with the scores of the group on another form.

Second, as a corollary of the first difference, intelligence tests tend to tap a wider variety of experience both in and out of school than do achievement tests. Most achievement tests are closely tied to specific courses of study. Intelligence tests are not. School experience is still contributive, however, to performance on more broadly based tests of intelligence. Moreover, experiences in the home and in social groups contribute to performance on achievement tests.

Third, intelligence tests differ from achievement tests in the amount of time between original learning and the administration of the test. The achievement tests are aimed at relatively new learning. Intelligence tests depend typically on older learning. I agree with Humphreys that whatever other differences exist with respect to the functional relationship involving these two kinds of tests, they appear in every case to follow logically from these three differences in item selection. Thus, both intelligence tests and achievement tests are measures of current performance depending directly upon previously acquired skills and information and motivation. Binet saw this at the turn of the century, but he had escaped the "advantages" of the tutelage from men with strong theoretical beliefs in intelligence fixed by heredity.

SEMANTICAL CONSEQUENCES OF TERMS: DIMENSION AND SCALE

Semantics can often have unfortunate theoretical consequences. One may view these unfortunate semantical consequences either as unwarranted response-produced generalization, in the language of Miller & Dollard (1941), or as the unwarranted extension of conceptual learning-sets. I find myself thinking of the object-constancy, quantity-conservation, and number-conservation of Piaget as special cases of the learning-sets described by Harlow (1949). Such learning-sets appear to me to be ubiquitous in human psychological development.

In this context, intelligence has commonly been termed a *dimension,* and seen as a dimension of persons. Similarly, the tests of intelligence have been termed *scales,* and seen as measures of a fixed dimension of persons. Such terminology has its source in the physical sciences where objects *are* constant with respect to such dimensions as height, circumference, weight, volume, and shape, and where the systems of relationships among their dimensions *are* closed. The constancy of each of these various dimensions of objects appears to develop in each of us, with experience, as a kind of learning-set. Thus, object-permanence, conservation of quantity and number, size-constancy, and color-constancy emerge gradually in the course of psychological development (see Piaget, 1947).

As I have said elsewhere (Hunt, 1961, p. 309),

The application of such terms as dimension and scale may at once tend to carry their meaning in the physical world over to the world of organismic behavior and to imply that the concept of constancy of dimensions is being generalized from static objects to non-static persons and their behavior. On the conceptual side, since persons change relatively slowly, especially in adulthood, it is easy to see how such Piaget-type conceptual sets as object-constancy, quantity-conservation, and number-conservation would readily be generalized from the world of static things to the world of changing organisms and persons. Once change has come to be conceived to be a matter of mere appearances behind which exists a constant essense, it is no easy matter to distinguish essences which are not static from essences which are in fact changing. It is probably that unwarranted generalization of conceptual constancy-sets is one factor behind the persistence of the belief in fixed intelligence. Fixed intelligence is a conception like the preformationistic notion that the bodily structure of a species is to be found within the egg or the sperm. . . . Once one has acquired such a conceptual constancy-set, the idea that something like intelligence can change tends to produce "cognitive dissonance." And one tends to build defenses against such emotional dissonance. In the light of such considerations, calling intelligence a *dimension* and speaking of tests as *scales* may be unfortunate in providing semantic capsules which resist the dissonance of observation and obscure reality.

Such semantic capsules are highly unfortunate when they sap in teachers the motivation to change their approaches and curricula in order better to promote development in children who do not respond to the standard approaches and curricula.

Development

Let me turn next to those propositions concerning development which I believe are no longer tenable and which I believe are highly unfortunate in their influence upon those working in programs of early childhood education.

DEVELOPMENT NOT PREDETERMINED IN RATE

First, I am confident that the belief that development is predetermined in rate is no longer tenable. In the history of our thought about psychological development, the constant IQ was the epitome of this notion. Elsewhere I have traced the origin of this notion back to G. Stanley Hall's interpretation of Darwin's theory of natural selection (see Chapter 2, and Hunt, 1961, p. 42ff). This notion got support from the influential work of Coghill (1929) relating the development of behavior patterns to histological and microscopical studies of neuromuscular maturation. The notion also got support from the widely cited studies of Carmichael (1926, 1927, 1928) on the embryonic development of swimming in salamanders and frogs. You will recall that those immobilized with chloretone for some five days showed the same general patterns of body development and motion as did those free to exercise in tap water—once the chloretoned embryos were put into tap water. This notion also got apparent support from various other observations that I cannot take time to review here (see Hunt, 1961, Ch. 3). Suffice it to say that maturation and learning were seen as two distinctly separate processes with maturation predetermined by heredity and learning controlled by the circumstances encountered.

Evidence dissonant with the notion of a predetermined rate of development also appeared. It appeared in Kuo's (1932a, 1932b, 1932c, 1932d) splendid studies of the embryonic development of behavior in chicks. Although Cruze (1935) found that the amount of practice required by newly hatched chicks to acquire a given level of accuracy in pecking decreased with age from one to five days, he also found that when chicks are allowed only some 15 minutes of pecking a day, the accuracy of their pecking failed to improve. And Padilla (1935) reported that chicks prevented from pecking for ten days after hatching would starve beside a pile of grain. Moreover, the early longitudinal studies of intellectual development in human children (see Jones, 1954, p. 639ff) uncovered individual growth curves with changes in IQ as large as 60 points. Moreover, increases in the IQ's of young children were found associated with nursery-school experience (Ripin, 1933; Skeels, Updegraf, et al., 1938; Wooley, 1925). At the time, the credibility of these observations of change in the rate of development and the belief in a predetermined rate of development were reduced by argument. The observations were, so to speak, explained away by assuming differing inherited patterns of growth (Goodenough & Maurer, 1942), by calling the predictive validity of the infant tests into question (Anderson, 1939, 1940), or by finding methodological weaknesses in the studies (McNemar, 1940). Differences of more than 20 points of IQ were found between identical twins reared apart under differing kinds of circumstances, but, because such instances were rare, they were considered to be merely examples of errors of measurement.

One of the most impressive of the early studies yielding evidence highly dissonant with the notion that the rate of development is predetermined is that of Skeels & Dye (1939). You may recall that this study was prompted by a "clinical surprise." Two residents of a state orphanage, one aged 13 months with a Kuhlmann IQ of 46 and the other aged 16 months with an IQ of 35, were committed to an institution for the retarded. After six months there, where the mentally retarded women doted on them, these two children showed a remarkably rapid rate of development. Coupled with a change in motivation from apathy to liveliness was an improvement of 31 points of IQ in one and 52 points in the other. Following this "clinical surprise," a group of 13 infants—ranging in age from 7 months to 30 months and in IQ's from 36 to 89, with a mean of 64—were transferred from the orphanage (but not committed) to these wards for moron women in the institution for the retarded. After being on these wards for periods ranging from 6 months for the one 7 months old to 52 months for the one 30 months old, every one of these infants showed a gain in IQ. The minimum gain was 7 points; the maximum was 58 points, and all but four showed gains of over 20 points. On the other hand, 12 other infants—ranging in age from 12 to 22 months and in IQ from 50 to 103, with a mean IQ of 87—were left in the orphanage. When these infants were retested after periods varying from 20 to 43 months, all but one of them showed decreases in IQ which ranged from 8 to 45 points, and five of the decreases exceeded 35 points. These findings suggested strongly that the effects of these two institutional environments differed greatly, but the idea of finding improvements in test performance as a consequence of moving children from an orphanage to a school for the feebleminded was merely ridiculed, and the ridicule deprived the findings of their highly suggestive import.

In the light of the evidence which has accumulated since World War II, this study of Skeels & Dye (1939) has acquired the status of a classic, and the notion of a predetermined rate of development has become almost incredible.

The studies of the effects of early experience in animal subjects have been especially important in altering this belief in a fixed rate of development predetermined by heredity. The earliest of such studies derived from Freud's (1905) theory of psychosexual development (Hunt, 1941; Hunt et al., 1947), but it was those instigated by the theorizing of Donald Hebb (1949) that were most important for the change in the belief in predetermined development. Hebb (1949) distinguished intellectual potential (intelligence I) from actual test performance (intelligence II). Moreover, his hypothesis that form-vision derives from the integration of the traces of sensory inputs (S-S relationships) based on the contiguity principle prompted two major lines of investigation.

First, it prompted Riesen and his colleagues to rear chimpanzees in the dark for the purpose of determining the effects of visual experience on the development of perception. Infant chimpanzees reared for a period of 16 or 18 months in total darkness showed drastic defects. On the functional side, these included absence of the blink to a threatening blow to the face, failure to develop visual accommodation upon which the blink depends, absence of visual fixation and pursuit of objects, absence of recognition of even the highly familiar feeding bottle until it was touched, failure to develop fear of strange objects and persons, and partial loss of pupillary reflexes. These changes for the most part proved to be essentially irreversible in chimpanzees submitted to total darkness for 16 months or longer. On the structural side, the defect was manifest as a pallor of the optic disc. Later, in histological examination following autopsy after some six years in full daylight, the basis for this pallor was found in changes in the ganglion-cell layer cell of the retina and in the optic nerve (see Riesen, 1958; Rasch, Swift, Riesen, & Chow, 1961).

Another variety of this first line of investigation stemmed from Hydén's (see 1960) biochemical hypothesis that the metabolism of riboneucleic acid (RNA) in the interactive relationship between neural and glial cells of the retina and brain is highly important in learning. This hypothesis prompted Brattgård (1952), one of Hydén's students, to rear rabbits in the dark. Histochemical analysis of the retina of these dark-reared rabbits revealed a deficiency of both Mueller fibers and of RNA production of the retinal ganglion cells. Such histological and histochemical effects of dark-rearing have now been found not only in rabbits (Brattgård, 1952) and in chimpanzees (Rasch, Swift, Riesen, & Chow, 1961) but also in kittens (Weiskrantz, 1958) and even in the lowly and coneless-eyed, color-blind rat (Liberman, 1962).

Conversely, in this first line of investigation, evidence of increased growth of central structures following the enrichments of experience involved in encounters with complex environments have been repeatedly reported in the work of Bennett, Diamond, Krech, & Rosenzweig (see 1964) and in the work of Altman & Das (1964). Such findings from these various sources appear to indicate that Piaget's (1936) aphorism that "use is the aliment of a schema" is more than a metaphor. Even maturation itself appears to be affected by informational interaction with circumstances.

Second, Hebb's (1949) theorizing prompted a number of investigators to rear animals under circumstances varying in complexity, especially in perceptual complexity. In the first of this kind of study, Hebb (1947) himself compared the adult problem-solving ability, as measured in the Hebb-Williams (1946) test of animal intelligence, of rats reared as pets with their littermates reared in laboratory cages. The former were much the better learners in the test. Other investigators in the McGill laboratory found that rats reared, after the opening of their eyes and weaning, in free and perceptually complex environments, were better as adults at learning mazes than those reared with homogeneous perceptual environments (Forgays & Forgays, 1952; Forgus, 1954; Hymovitch, 1952). Moreover, Thompson & Heron (1954) found pet-reared Scottish terriers to be superior performers in the Hebb-Williams test than cage-reared littermates. Indeed, they found this superiority even though the differences in rearing conditions lasted only from weaning till the animals were eight months old, and both the pet-reared and the cage-reared dogs were allowed ten months of unrestricted life in the dog pasture before they were tested at 18 months of age.

I believe these investigations employing mammals below man for subjects have been especially important in altering the belief in predetermined development partly because it was easier, with animal subjects, to avoid the methodological defects of the early human studies and partly because they stemmed from a theory that made the new evidence more plausible. Not unimportant is the conception of Hebb (1949) that the portion of the brain without direct connections to either receptors or effectors increases up the evolutionary scale. I refer to his notion of the A/S ratio. But new evidence from the development of human subjects has not been wanting since World War II.

In the domain of locomotor development, Dennis (1960) found an orphanage in Tehran where 60 per cent of those infants in their second year were still not sitting up alone, and where 84 per cent of those infants in their fourth year were still not walking. When one considers that nearly all family-reared infants are sitting alone by eight months of age and nearly all such infants are walking by 20 months of age, it becomes clear that locomotor development does not come at a constant rate under all kinds of conditions. What specific conditions are responsible for such retardation is still a matter of debate and investigation, but such evidence greatly weakens belief in a predetermined rate of locomotor development independent of circumstances.

Especially relevant and impressive for us is the evidence from a series of studies of visuo-motor development in human infants by White & Held (see 1966). These began with a normative study of the visuo-motor function in infants being reared at the Tewksbury State Hospital (White, Castle, & Held, 1964). The components of this functioning assessed at successive ages in infants under the customary regimen of the hospital included (1) visual accommodation, (2) defensive blinking at an approaching visible object, (3) visual attention, and (4) visually directed reaching. Let me focus on visually directed reaching for the point I wish to make. In the normative study, this reaching developed through a series of phases beginning with "fisted swiping" and terminating with "top-level reaching." The fisted swiping, which consisted of "swiping at objects introduced within their visual range with fists closed" appeared at a median age of 65 days. The "top-level reaching and grasping," wherein the hand is opened and is shaped in anticipation of reaching the seen object, made its appearance at a median age of 145 days, some 80 days after the infants first began to respond to seen objects with "fisted swiping."

White and his colleagues asked specifically whether this period of 80 days between the "fisted swiping" and "top-level reaching" was inevitable. It was not. In their first attempt at "massive enrichment," they (1) attempted to increase tactile-vestibular input by handling each infant for 20 minutes each day from day 6 through 63; (2) attempted to increase motility by placing each infant in a prone posture for 15 minutes after each of three feedings from day 37 through day 124; and (3) attempted to enrich the visual surroundings by suspending above each infant's eyes a stabile with highly contrasting colors and numerous forms against a dull white background from day 37 to day 124. Apparently this "massive enrichment" was too rich at first. It served to decrease visual attention during the first six weeks (to day 72), and it delayed the onset of "fisted swiping" by nearly a week (to 71 days). Moreover, the infants submitted to this massive enrichment program appeared to cry more than those "control" infants in the normative study. Even so, they achieved "top-level reaching" some 40 days earlier than did those in the normative study, namely, at a median age of 105 days.

In a second attempt at enrichment, White attempted to avoid the overstimulation that decreased visual attention and delayed "fisted swiping." He continued the extra handling and the prone positions, but from day 37 to day 68, he substituted for the too complex stabile round surfaces of solid white some 6 inches in diameter with a red pacifier in the center. One of these was mounted on each crib-rail. From day 68 to day 124, the complex stabile of the first enrichment study was employed. The result of this second approach to enrichment served to increase visual attention substantially during the first 60 days. It reduced the median age for the onset of "fisted swiping" from day 71 to day 58. It reduced the median age for the onset of "top-level reaching" to 89 days. Clearly, the rate at which eye-hand coordination develops cannot be wholly predetermined. In fact, a remarkable degree of plasticity exists in its development and also in the other aspects of visuo-motor development.

LONGITUDINAL PREDICTION IMPOSSIBLE

Despite such an accumulation of evidence as I have indicated, the belief in a constant IQ has given us the habit of thinking of the validity of tests in longitudinal terms. We have used and still use the scores based on the performances of children on tests administered at one age to predict what their performances will be at later ages. Such longitudinal validity needs to be differentiated from cross-sectional validity where the performances which children show in the test-situation are used to predict

their performances in other contemporary situations or to predict their readiness to profit from given kinds of tutelage. Clearly
the tests do have a considerable degree of cross-sectional validity.

On the other hand, if the rate of organic maturation can be
influenced by the circumstances encountered, and if psychological development is as plastic as these bits of evidence imply,
longitudinal prediction is impossible from test scores alone. The
plasticity which appears to exist in the rate at which human
organisms develop renders longitudinal prediction basically impossible unless one does specify the circumstances under which
this development is to take place. In fact, trying to predict what
a person's IQ at 20 will be merely from his IQ at ages one, two,
or three is like trying to predict how heavy a calf will become
at age two years from his weight at two weeks without knowing
whether the calf will be reared in a dry pasture, in an irrigated
pasture, or in a feed lot.

To be sure, longitudinal prediction improves with age. This
results from the fact that test-retest validities involve part-whole
relationships. Thus, if one is predicting IQ at 20, the older the
child is at the time of the initial test, the larger becomes the
predictor part of the criterion *whole.* Moreover, in actual situations, individuals tend to remain within sets of social, economic,
and educational circumstances which are relatively stable. Thus,
a very large share of whatever constancy individual IQ's have
had can be attributed to a combination of a part-whole relationship and to the constancy of these circumstances.

Believing that the rate of development is a predetermined
constant and that longitudinal prediction is possible has had
very unfortunate consequences for educational practice. When
children fail to learn and are found to have low scores on intelligence tests, teachers are prompt to feel and say that "these
children are doing as well as can be expected." Such an attitude dampens any inclination teachers may have to alter their
approach to such children. Consequence? A self-fulfilling prophecy: the tutelage that the child encounters remains essentially
stable, and the child continues in his rut of failure.

An important corollary of the finding that the rate of development depends upon the circumstances encountered is a

needed change in the conception of "readiness." The notion that children are ready for certain kinds of experiences and not for others has validity. On the other hand, the notion that this "readiness" is a matter of predetermined maturation, as distinct from learning or past encounters with circumstances, is basically wrong and highly unfortunate. What is involved is what I have called "the problem of the match" (Hunt, 1961, pp. 267-288; 1965b, pp. 230-231; 1966, pp. 131-132). If encountering a given set of circumstances is to induce psychological development in the child, these circumstances must have an appropriate relationship to the information already accumulated in the child's mental storage from his previous encounters with circumstances. The problem of presenting particular children with circumstances which will foster their particular development is no easy matter. On the cognitive side, the circumstances presented must be relevant to the information accrued among the child's central brain processes from circumstances encountered in the past. Ordinarily, the best indicators of an appropriate match are to be found, as I now believe, in emotional behavior. These indicators are evidences of interest and mild surprise. If the circumstances are too simple and too familiar, the child will fail to develop and he is likely to withdraw in boredom. If the circumstances presented demand too much of a child, he will withdraw in fear or explode in anger.

Those holding the traditional theory of child development worry about dire effects from pushing children. These worries have a basis in fact, but so long as the child can withdraw from the circumstances encountered without facing punishment, loss of love, fear of disapproval, or what-not, I believe it is impossible to overstimulate him. The complex stabile of White & Held (1966) was apparently distressing to children under 70 days of age because it filled 60° of the visual angle, and, being directly over the child, was almost inescapable. On the other hand the white discs with red nipples in the center that White placed on opposite sides of the cribs in his second enrichment study were both less complex and much more easily escaped. The challenge in such a conception of "readiness" as that involved in the "problem of the match" is basically that of preparing the environment to provide the child with an optimal challenge. We are still a long way from solid knowledge of how to do this, but I believe we do have some sensible suggestions about how to proceed.

DEVELOPMENTAL ORDER AND PREDETERMINISM

One more point about development, and its implications. Order has always been obvious in behavioral development. In locomotor development, for instance, it is obvious that an infant is at first rooted to a given spot, that he learns to wheel and twist even before he sits up, that he sits up alone before he can creep, that he creeps or scoots before he stands, that he stands before he cruises, that he cruises while holding on to things before he toddles, that he toddles before he walks, and that he walks before he runs. Arnold Gesell and his collaborators (Gesell *et al.,* 1940) devoted their entire normative enterprise to describing the order in the various domains of behavioral development which takes place with advancing age. Piaget and his collaborators (see Hunt, 1961, Ch. 5 & 6) have also been concerned in describing the order in the development of intelligence and in the construction of such aspects of reality as object permanence, as constancy of quantity, of shape, and of color, and as causality, space, and time. Ina Uzgiris and I have been utilizing these orderly landmarks in development as a basis for what, in terms of the evidence we have, appear to be ordinal scales of psychological development in infancy (Uzgiris & Hunt, 1970). In short, order in development is an obvious fact.

Throughout most of the past half-century, according to the dominant view, this order has been interpreted as evidence of genetic preprogramming. In a certain sense and degree, this order is predetermined. Species are genetically predetermined. One does not get rats by breeding elephants. Moreover, such order as that which served as evidence for Coghill's (1929) cephalocaudal and proximodistal principles does, indeed, appear to be preprogrammed. Coghill, however, went on to assert that "the normal experience of the animal with reference to the outside world appears to have nothing to do with the determination of the form into which the behavior of the animal is cast" (1929, p. 87). He based this statement upon his observations of the development of behavior in such lowly, cold-blooded amphibia as salamanders and frogs. After observing the development of behavior in chick embryos, Kuo (1932a), who also saw the evidences of cephalocaudel progression, objected that the additional interpretation went well beyond Coghill's data and that it is not true for chicks. Kuo found definite evidences of experience in the behavioral development of chicks. Even so, such investigators as Gesell (1954) and Mary Shirley (1931; 1933) repeatedly pointed out that the developmental principles of Coghill could be observed to operate in human infants, and they drew the inference that order in behavioral development follows the preprogramming of maturation. Responses were presumed to appear as the myelin sheath matured around the nerve fibers mediating those responses.

Although Gesell (1954) gave occasional lip service to organism-environment interaction in behavioral development, all but one of his various principles of ontogenesis (that of "individuating maturation") described predetermined processes. Moreover, Gesell said explicitly that "the so-called environment, whether internal or external, does not generate the progressions of development. Environmental factors support, inflect, and specify; but they do not engender the basic forms and sequences of ontogenesis" (1954, p. 354).

Similarly, Mary Shirley wrote that "motor control begins headward and travels toward the feet beginning with the eye muscle and progressing through stages in which the head and neck muscles are mastered, arms and upper trunk come under control . . . the baby at last achieves mastery of his whole body . . ." (1933, p. 204). Moreover, when she found that the order in which responses appeared in each of her 20 individual children exhibited correlations of +.93 or higher with the order of the modal series, she interpreted the findings to mean that the order is indeed predetermined.

Yet such an interpretation is not a necessary implication of the observed fact of orderliness in development. Piaget, like Gesell, has found order in psychological development. Unlike Gesell, however, Piaget has emphasized the role of organism-environment interaction in his interpretative theorizing. According to Piaget (1936, 1947), development occurs in the course of adaptive interaction between the organism and the environment. This interaction involves two complementary and invariant processes: *assimilation* and *accommodation*. Piaget conceives these processes as basically common to both the physiological and the psychological domain. *Assimilation* occurs whenever an organism utilizes something from the environment and incorporates it into its own structures. Biochemically, this is exemplified by the ingestion of food which is incorporated in somatic structures. Psychologically, it operates whenever the organism receives and responds to something new in terms of something familiar, whenever the organism acts in a new situation as it has acted in other situations in the past. Thus, assimilation includes such familiar phenomena of American theorizing as that of conditioning, that of stimulus generalization, and that of response generalization. It is thus that Piaget (1947) speaks of assimilation as "the action of the organism on surrounding objects, insofar as this action depends on previous behavior involving the same or similar objects" (p. 7). *Accommodation,* the complement of assimilation, operates whenever encounters with environmental circumstances evoke a change in the existing organization of the organism by modifying the central processes that mediate the interpretation of events and control action. Thus, accommodation is a term for adaptive learning in the broad sense.

Although I wish to make no defense of these constructs of Piaget, they have definitely influenced my own thinking about learning. Attempting to understand them has opened my own eyes to the fact that circumstances influence development in ways quite other than those under the traditional rubrics under which we have studied learning. These traditional rubrics include the rote learning of Ebbinghaus (1885), the skill learning of Bryan & Harter (1897), the classical conditioning of Pavlov (see 1927), and the trial-and-error learning of Morgan (1894) and Thorndike (1898) or the "instrumental learning" of Hull (1943) or the "operant conditioning" of Skinner (1938,

1953). They do not, however, cover the whole gamut of ways in which circumstances influence development. Elsewhere, I have identified 11 other forms of influence from organism-environment (Hunt, 1966, pp. 103-118). If we are ever to have an appropriate theory with which to guide the development of our young, I am convinced we will have to broaden our conception of learning to include such phenomena as input habituation, the effect of the use and disuse of systems on their maturation, image formation through perception, perceptual learning-sets, the role of interest in the novel and the more complex, the role of disconfirmation of constructions of reality, and perhaps others. It is through these still relatively strange ways in which encounters with circumstances affect development that the humorous aphorisms of Marshall McLuhan (1964) acquire a certain degree of serious significance. In a sense, "the medium is the message," and "the medium is the massage."

Order in behavioral development, however, is quite as consonant with interactionism as with predeterminism. The order in visual following and object permanence will illustrate part of this point. If an infant's eyes will follow an object through 180°, they must necessarily be able to follow an object through lesser arcs. If an infant holds his eyes where an object has disappeared until it returns, he must necessarily be able to follow the object with his eyes. If an infant will maintain his interest in an object that has disappeared long enough to pull a screen off it and obtain it, he will obviously obtain it when it is only half covered. If the infant will maintain his interest in the object long enough to pull three screens off, he can obviously sustain his interest in the object long enough to pull one off. And so it goes. And yet, such evidence of the developing central processes that give objects permanence can hardly develop except in the course of visuo-motor interaction with objects.

The work of White & Held (1966) already described illustrates the manner in which an opportunity to encounter visually circumstances properly geared to their development and past experience will hasten eye-hand coordination in visually directed reaching. The children at the Tewksbury State Hospital achieved "top-level reaching" at a median age of 89 days whereas we have seldom observed such behavior in the home-reared infants of our graduate students and younger staff before something like 120 days of age. On the other hand, these home-reared babies of graduate students, who served as subjects in the development of our ordinal scales, commonly developed the ear-vocal coordination implied in pseudo-imitative behavior before they were four months old whereas I was unable to get such behavior in the babies who were experiencing one of White's enrichment programs at age six months without resorting to the noises involved in play with saliva. Note in this connection that any behavior involving the coordination of eye-hand coordination with ear-vocal coordination must inevitably follow the achievement of both the subordinant coordinations. This illustrates the principle of hierarchical organization that appears to be emerging from several sources of evidence. One of these sources is the observations of Piaget (1936, 1937, 1947) and the various confirmations of these observations by others. A second source is the factor-analytic studies of abilities (Guilford, 1959; Humphreys, 1962b; Vernon, 1961). A third source is the studies of human problem-solving (Gagné, 1966b; Gagné & Paradise, 1961). Order is just as inherent in the hierarchical structures emerging in the course of the young organism's informational interaction with his circumstances as it is in preprogrammed maturation.

This model of hierarchical structures has other implications. It implies an epigenesis in the development of intellectual structures and of the conceptualization of reality which is analogous to that epigenesis of organ structures in embryonic development. The existence of such an epigenesis of intellectual structures in turn implies that the various experiences underlying the development of a given kind of ability may resemble very little the use of that particular ability. This helps to explain why those early studies of practice in such skills as stair-climbing, tower-building and the like were evanescent. These skills have a limit reached quickly, and only as they are early incorporated in more complex organizations of behavior can they have prolonged effects.

Social Implications for Class Differences

As I have already noted, the factors which control the development of competence and the factors which control early childhood development are no longer purely academic topics. They have acquired both social and political significance from the fact that our advancing technology is rapidly decreasing the economic opportunities for those without linguistic and mathematical abilities and the motivation to solve problems and to carry social responsibility, and from the fact that a large majority of black people, who come from a background of poverty, lack these skills and motives. In the light of these challenges, what are the implications of the foregoing?

Two of the implications are already explicit in what I have said. First, the intellectual capacity that underlies competence is not fixed; it may be modified substantially by the circumstances encountered, particularly in the earliest years. Second, the rate and course of psychological development are far from predetermined. If the circumstances that children have an opportunity to interact with control in a substantial degree the rate and the course of their development and the ultimate level of their competence, it becomes untenable to consider poverty and lower-class status to be the consequences of an inevitable incompetence. Although it is true that incompetence tends to result in poverty, that incompetence may also be a consequence of being reared in poverty.

Various lines of evidence suggest that being reared in poverty deprives a child of opportunities to develop the linguistic and mathematical skills and the motivation to solve problems and to take social responsibility which constitute the basis for socioeconomic competence. The children in poor families have typically encountered many fewer kinds of objects than children of middle-class background. Often as infants the children of poverty in crowded circumstances are submitted to a continuing vocal racket to which they become habituated. This habituation may account for the inadequacies of auditory discrimination found by Cynthia Deutsch (1964) and by Deutsch & Brown (1964). Too often, the verbal interaction of children of the poor with their elders is limited to commands to cease whatever the child is doing; seldom two- and three-year-olds are asked questions which demand that they formulate matters verbally in response (John, 1964; John & Goldstein, 1964). They are especially unlikely to learn prepositional relationships and the syntactical rules of the standard language (Bernstein, 1960, 1961). Seldom are the reasons for actions explained; seldom is ingenuity rewarded, except for that ingenuity in avoiding the punishment that comes for getting caught at something prohibited (see Chilman, 1965). In such circumstances, the low test scores repeatedly observed in those of low socioeconomic status (Anastasi, 1958) and in children of the poor (John, 1963, 1964) would be expected.

On the motivational side, moreover, children have little opportunity to take initiative, to give up present satisfactions for future goals, or to take pride in problem-solving achievement. For that matter, parents in poverty have seldom learned such kinds of motivation themselves (Lewis, 1961, 1966a). Their responses to their children are typically dictated by their own immediate impulses and needs, not the child's (see Bronfenbrenner, 1958; Chilman, 1965; Davis, 1948; Davis & Havighurst, 1946). To them, a good child is typically a quiet child who does not bother them (Klaus & Gray, 1968). Also, the standards of conduct to which these children of the poor are exposed are hardly those described by the middle class. What these children have an opportunity to imitate in the behavior of their parents and their peers often serves to make them unfit for adaptation in schools and in economic competition.

From such bits of still tenuous evidence, it appears that the accident of being born to parents in poverty serves to deprive children of that equality of opportunity which has been considered a birthright of all Americans.

Corrective Measures and the Danger of Hopes Too High

From the academic standpoint, these relatively new findings concerning the role of circumstances in psychological development, in intelligence, and in motivation are exceedingly intriguing. Various lines of evidence show that it becomes increasingly difficult to alter the effects of early experience the longer the young organism has encountered a given kind of circumstances (Hunt, 1961, p. 321ff). It follows that corrective efforts should be focused upon the young, and preferably upon the very young. The evidence we have suggests that early childhood education can have a tremendous social significance if we learn how to do it effectively. It is a long step from justifiable hopes that a particular kind of corrective measures will work, however, to having developed those measures in workable form. The question is, can we extend these findings concerning the importance of the interaction between children and their circumstances in psychological development of competence into programs of early childhood education fast enough to forestall a loss of hope in the public and in our political leaders that will take away the support required for the opportunity to continue trying?

Project Head Start is a tremendous step in the right direction. The danger is that it may have been taken before an adequately effective technology of early childhood education had been developed. All too often the Head Start programs have consisted in supplying children of the poor with an opportunity to play in traditional nursery-school settings. Such an opportunity may help to get these children accustomed to the school regimen. It may even help motivationally to change some of what they expect from adults. Such opportunities are unlikely to be very helpful, however, in motivating the children of the poor to forego gratification of the present in order to gain long-term gratifications, or to develop those linguistic and numerical skills essential for success in elementary school.

Nursery schools appear to have been invented originally for the purpose of compensatory education. During the first decade of this century, Montessori developed a program for the culturally deprived children of the San Lorenzo district of Rome which, according to the reports of those who visited, was highly successful (see Hunt, 1964b). Montessori's effort was supported by the Roman Association of Good Building, and the owners of the buildings in the San Lorenzo district were motivated in large part by the hope that keeping the unruly children, usually left alone during the day by their working parents, in something like a school would prevent vandalism and save damage to their property. According to reports, these children, aged three to seven years, became avid pupils and even learned the basic skills of counting, reading, writing, often before they were five years old. Somewhat later, Margaret McMillan (1919) established her nursery schools in the slums of England to give these children whom she considered to be environmentally handicapped an opportunity to learn what middle-class children learn spontaneously. She, too, achieved considerable success. As developed in the United States, however, the nursery school was adapted to the needs of young children of the middle and upper middle class. Two of the goals were to provide for these children an opportunity for spontaneous exercise, and an opportunity to learn through play. Since such children came even to nursery school with established linguistic and number skills, special tutelage in language and number skills was considered quite unnecessary. Even the Montessori schools were modified in America for the culturally privileged children. The practice of including children ranging in age from three to six years was dropped in most of these schools, thereby depriving younger children of a graded series of models for imitation and older children of the opportunity to help teach the younger ones. Thus, this approach, once observed to be effective, is probably inadequate to overcome the deficit in linguistic and numerical skills of the disadvantaged children from American slums.

In consequence of this historical state of affairs, we have no ready-made practices of early childhood education designed to develop in children of the poor those skills they have failed to develop as a consequence of the circumstances of their rearing. As the inadequacy of the traditional nursery school for compensatory education has been recognized, we have had a tremendous explosion in new curricula for young children. Unfortunately, none of these has been adequately tested for effectiveness. Impressionistic observations suggest that these schools achieve little in the way of compensatory development in the children of the poor unless they focus on language and number concepts and on the motivation to extend the time interval in which these children of the poor operate psychologically. I see no substitute for painstaking investigation of what works and what does not work coupled with theoretical synthesis calculated to give us an accurate picture of the various kinds of deficits to be found in slum children and effective ways either to prevent or overcome these deficits.

I am inclined to believe that we shall have to extend our programs to include children of ages less than four. I believe we shall have to involve the help of parents in these programs. Unfortunately, attempts to influence the child-rearing behavior of parents from the lowest socioeconomic status by means of psychotherapy-like counseling have regularly failed. On the other hand, involving parents as aides in nursery schools where they have an opportunity to observe the effects of modes of dealing with children which are new to them coupled with home demonstrations appear to be promising. Here the work of Rupert Klaus & Susan Gray (1967) and their colleagues at the George Peabody College for Teachers in Nashville, Tennessee, may be showing a way. In a summer nursery school for culturally deprived children, they developed a curriculum which aimed to teach children the language skills, attitudes, and motives required to cope with elementary school. During the summers, moreover, a home visitor brought each mother to the nursery school. There the mother could see for herself not only what the teachers were doing with her child, but also the results of the teacher's approach with her child and with other neighborhood children. This home visitor interpreted for these mothers what the teachers were doing and why. Moreover, during the period between the summer sessions of the nursery school, the home visitor saw each of the mothers every other week. During these bi-weekly visits, she undertook to demonstrate for the mothers such things as how to read a story with enthusiasm, how to reinforce children for acquiring new skills and finding new ways to cope with such children's problems as getting dressed, how to talk with the children about such home-making operations as peeling potatoes while in the process of doing so, etc.

This effort has been evaluated by means of standard tests of intelligence given at regular intervals. The tests given before and after the summer nursery school have shown spurts which do not appear in the children who did not go to the nursery school. The results of this program also show two other highly promising phenomena. First, the younger siblings of the children in the nursery school groups whose mothers regularly saw the home visitors turned out to be significantly superior in test performance to the younger siblings of four-year-old children in the two contrast groups who got neither nursery school nor the home visits. This suggests that the mothers must have been learning something about child rearing which was affecting their management of their younger children as well as of those in the nursery school. Klaus and Gray call this "vertical diffusion." Second, the younger children of the mothers in the contrast groups who lived in the same neighborhood as those attending the nursery school and receiving the home visits got higher test scores than did the children of mothers in a contrast group living some 60 miles away. This Klaus and Gray termed "horizontal diffusion." It suggests that the mothers who learned new child-rearing practices from their observations at the nursery school and from the home visitor were somehow communicating them to their neighbors, a communication which could not occur with those some 60 miles away.

Conclusion

The new evidence and these new curricular efforts form a basis for justified hope that our society can cope with the challenge of that incompetence and poverty which constitute a major factor in the problems of our cities. What perturbs me about our present state of affairs is that our failure to investigate these matters during those decades before they acquired social and political urgency—a failure deriving largely from our pessimistically presuming intellectual competence to be fixed and psychological development to be predetermined—leaves us puny now when we need to be strong in terms of theory and scientific evidence and in terms of the technology of early childhood education. I fear that the very limited success of the effort in Project Head Start may lead to an unjustified discouragement on the part of our political leaders and of the public who must provide the voting support for the leaders to continue these efforts. I fear that our ignorance of how to proceed effectively may soon deprive us, for an indefinite period, of that opportunity to do what I am confident ultimately can be done to meet these challenges. What we need is the opportunity to innovate and investigate, to fail, to correct our misinterpretations from our failures, and gradually to create programs of encounters with circumstances that *are* effective in fostering the development of those skills and motives required for success in elementary school and in economic competition. In the language of education, the development-fostering programs of encounters with circumstances which we need are analogues of what have been termed "curricula." At this stage of history, it is extremely important that our political leaders and our voters understand the limited status of our knowledge, understand the basis for our justified hopes, and understand the need for support of fundamental research on child development and for the development of an adequate technology of early childhood education.

6

Toward the Prevention
of Incompetence

The United States Public Health Service has built
a tradition of utilizing knowledge of natural resources to prevent
diseases and to improve the health of the populace. Classic examples are the purification of water to prevent typhoid and
other diseases, universal vaccination to prevent smallpox, and
the spraying of ponds to kill mosquitoes to prevent yellow fever
and malaria. Today, we are witnessing something of a struggle
over fluoridation of water supplies to prevent tooth decay. This
tradition of the Public Health Service has utilized the results
of biological and ecological research to guide its interventions
into the circumstances of human beings to prevent disease.

The notion of mental health has, by a largely verbal analogy,
called for a public mental-health service. This analogy is the basis
for a hope that investigators of human development and of the influences of social interaction in the family and in neighborhoods
will lead to knowledge permitting a Community Mental-Health
Service to provide innovations in the social processes of communities to prevent mental disorders and to improve the general
level of human well-being. Although the mental disorders, or
what are commonly called mental diseases, may have in common

Written for a symposium entitled "Research Contributions from Psychology
to Conceptions of Community Mental Health," organized by Dr. Jerry W.
Carter, Jr., and presented at the Meeting of the American Psychological
Association, 2 September 1967, Washington, D.C. Partially revised for
this volume.

the element of discomfort or suffering with other diseases, their etiology typically appears to be fundamentally different. The etiology of traditional diseases consists of infections or of breakdowns in organic functioning. Although it is true that infections and breakdowns in organic functioning can disorganize an individual's behavior and social functioning, mental health traditionally has become concerned with those defects in functioning which arise out of the history of defects in the individual's informational interaction with his circumstances. These result in distress-producing conflicts among the individual's motives, in frustrations of goal-directed behavior, and in failures of social communication with such foregoing consequences as their result. What is now being called community mental health is an extension of the Public Health Service to prevent these distressful disorders of behavior and social functioning. From the analogy of mental health to organic health, the limiting goals of community mental health have extended not merely to a hopeful emptying of the psychiatric hospitals by preventing psychoses and neuroses, but also to the prevention of instances of mass violence and to the general improvement in the quality of human life. These are the broad goals and hopes.

Those concerned with mental health have most commonly focused their attention on the emotional aspects of behavior disorders. Although it is true that emotional distress is the most evident aspect of many disorders of behavior and functioning, focusing upon the emotion is much like a physician focusing upon the fever which is a highly evident aspect of a plethora of infections and of many breakdowns in organic functioning. The emotional distress in behavior disorders is an inherent aspect of frustration (see Brown & Farber, 1951; Amsel, 1958; Amsel & Roussel, 1952) and of conflict between intentions and purposes (see Hunt, 1963a, p. 58ff). But emotional distress can also be an aspect of encountering information that is incongruous, strange, and unexpected (see Hebb, 1946a, 1946b; Hebb & Riesen, 1943). It can be an aspect of interference among attitudes and beliefs in what Festinger (1957) has called "cognitive dissonance." In fact, the emotions are an integral aspect of all functioning, though they need not be distressful, and sometimes I wish

Aristotle had not fastened upon us the triune conception of mind in which emotion (affection) was separated from motivation (or conation) and from thought (or cognition). In our day, one of the major bases for frustration and for the emotional distress that goes with it, in that large share of our population which we are coming to call the culturally deprived, is inadequate competence to cope with the circumstances encountered and to obtain the gratification that our affluent society makes highly evident by the advertising in our mass media.

Incompetence as a Verbal Analogue of Disease

We live in a day when the opportunities for those with high competence—consisting in symbolic skills, in ability to solve problems, in future-oriented motivation to achieve and to be concerned with the welfare of all men—greatly outrun the supply. At the same time, automated machines do the tasks of heavy labor, many of the routines of manufacturing and of clerical work, and even many of the tasks in farming. As a consequence, the demand-opportunities for those with low competence have been dwindling rapidly. Without the abilities and skills required, they lose their stake in the mainstream of American culture with its high hopes and high productivity.

One basis for the plight of our American cities resides in the fact that the industrial revolution has come to agriculture. It is said that more people have moved from the farms to the cities since the end of World War II than moved from the farms to the cities from the time of the landing of the Pilgrims to the end of World War II. At the turn of this century, nearly 90 per cent of our population lived on farms or in very small towns. Now that percentage is of the order of 10 per cent, and 90 per cent live in urban centers—a majority of them in our expanding, impersonal megalopoli.

Most of those who have moved from the farms to the cities in recent years have been poor and marginal farmers with highly limited skills. A very large share of them were Negro sharecroppers from our rural South. Nowhere has the industrial revolution in agriculture proceeded more rapidly than in our southern states. As a consequence, the ghettos of black people in our large cities have been expanding very rapidly. At the same time, the Supreme Court decision of 1954 has provided the promise of desegregation and a hope for increased economic and social opportunities for black people. Unfortunately, because of their history in slavery coupled with the historical limits of their economic opportunities to sharecropping or menial work, a large share of these black people have never had an opportunity to move out of poverty and lower-class status in our society. They, like lower-class white people, provide their children with very limited opportunities for learning during their preschool years. Because of these factors and because of the inadequacy of schools in the South and in the slums, entirely too few young Negroes have been equipped to grasp the new opportunities provided for them at levels above the unskilled. Because opportunities for the unskilled have been shrinking rapidly, the proportion of Negroes who are unemployed is especially high. Add to this the fearful impersonality of the newly formed neighborhoods in black ghettos. When asked, for instance, why northern Negroes appear to be more violent than southern Negroes, the NAACP's Roy Wilkins replied that "In the North the Negro finds himself in new surroundings, usually without his family, without his old neighbors, without his church. In Harlem, he's just John Smith." Combine these factors and one has the setting for the urban problems of our day with their attending violence.

These factors, in brief outline, are also the main sociological factors underlying the increased, and continually increasing, importance of incompetence in our highly technological society. Incompetence is far from the only factor to be overcome in our coping with the violence in our cities which has become so prominent. But, even after we have invented economic devices to provide jobs for the unemployed, even after we have coped with inadequate housing, and even after we have coped with racial prejudice, the burden of the incompetence of the poor will remain as it does in the case of poor whites. Moreover, the impoverished impersonality of our urban neighborhoods will remain to encourage incompetence. From the standpoint of community mental health, even though the analogy may be weak, incompetence is like a disease. As such, it is one of the major etiological sources of the frustration and the emotional distress associated with the inability of the poor to participate in the mainstream of our increasingly technological and increasingly affluent society.

Education Versus Mental Health

If one accepts for the purposes of exposition this conceptual twist which makes incompetence an analogue of disease, then it follows that our educational institutions have been and are one of the major resources of community mental health. Unfortunately, educators have tended to focus their attention on the cognitive—on skills and knowledge and their acquisition. Also, they have traditionally neglected the affective and conative aspects of acquiring skills and knowledge. To be sure, educators have moved a long way from the traditions set by Luther and Calvin who founded the reading schools in the days of the Reformation to give young Protestants a direct avenue to God's word in the Bible. Then, insofar as the affective was considered at all, it was a matter of inducing fear for conative or motivational purposes. The goal of inducing this fear was to eradicate the original and natural sin of laziness, and to make learning to read less undesirable and painful than other activities or remaining idle. Student adjustment and student satisfaction in the process of acquiring skills and knowledge are still all too often considered by members of school boards, by educators, and by teachers to be side issues when they are actually essential aspects of the processes of development and skill-acquisition—or learning, if you will.

On the other hand, it is equally unfortunate that those whose central focus has been on mental health and mental hygiene have so emphasized the emotional factors of social adjustment that they have commonly lost sight of the skills, knowledge, motives, and values which underlie competence. These are essential goals of education. Despite the 2,600 years that separate the days of Aristotle from our own, we still chop up the individual student in terms of the logical constructs with which Aristotle divided mind in general (affection, conation, cognition). We even carry this division of mind into our governmental institutions. The National Institute of Mental Health must compete with the Office of Education for Congressional appropriation. Thus, those in the bureaus concerned with mental health and the emotional side of man become the competitors of those in the bureaus concerned with education and the skills and cognitive side of man. Moreover, this conceptual division is also reflected down at the level of the community where those in mental health clinics are all too often competitors and critics of the teachers in the school instead of their collaborators who join with them to foster fully the development of each child's potential competence.

This schism, which I see deriving historically from the Aristotelian conception of triune man, is but one conceptual relic from the history of thought that has hampered our dealing with incompetence through community mental health. Another is the conception of incompetence as something fixed, as something basically inborn, as something predetermined that will inevitably become manifest in the course of the individual's development. Such a conception was dominant in Western thought from the days of the debates over Darwin's theory of evolution and the interpretation of its implications for improving the lot of man by Francis Galton until very recently (see Chapter 3 above). Investigations in the domain of genetics, in the domain of psychological development in animals and human beings, and in the domain of the social conditions of development in various social classes, largely since World War II, have greatly weakened the faith in these traditional beliefs about the basis for incompetence (Hunt, 1961). In doing so, the evidence from these investigations has also provided us with justification for a hope that we may ultimately be able to prevent a substantial share of incompetence.

Recent Evidence and Our Traditional Conceptions of the Basis for Incompetence

Evidence dissonant with these beliefs began to appear even before World War II, but it was largely discredited. For instance, Skeels & Dye (1939) reported increases in the IQ of every one of a group of 13 retarded infants from an orphanage who were transferred to a women's ward at an Iowa state school for the mentally retarded. There, the mentally retarded women doted on the infants, then aged from seven months to 30 months. The infants thrived on the doting. The resulting increases in IQ ranged from 7 to 58 points, and all but four of these infants gained by more than 20 points. These gains came with periods on the ward ranging from six months to 52 months. Another group of 12 somewhat less retarded infants, who ranged in age from 12 to 22 months, were allowed to remain in the orphanage. After periods varying from 20 to 43 months, all but one showed decreases in IQ ranging from 8 to 45 points. When these findings were reported, they met with scathing derision (Goodenough, 1939) and with the most searching statistical criticism (McNemar, 1940). To be sure, this investigation was not an ideal experiment, but the findings were highly suggestive. The criticism and the derision, probably motivated by the dissonance between the findings and strongly held beliefs, deprived the findings and others like them of the suggestive, corrective value that they might have had.

But it was only for the time being. Since World War II evidence clearly dissonant with beliefs in predetermined development and fixed levels of competence has been accumulating. Let me synopsize at least the nature of these various kinds of evidence.

Within the domain of genetics, the fatherhood of that science has now come to be credited to Johannsen (1909, 1911) as well as Mendel. The observable, measurable characteristics of organisms, which Johannsen called *phenotypes*, have come to be seen as products of the interaction between the hereditary constitution, which Johannsen termed the *genotype*, and the circumstances encountered in the course of development. At the

University of Illinois, for instance, William Horsfall and his colleagues (Horsfall & Anderson, 1961) have got what appear to be phenotypic female mosquitoes from genotypic male larvae by exposing the eggs and the larvae continually to a temperature of 29° C. In consequence of such evidence, no longer is it seriously argued that the genotype guarantees either any given rate of development or any given outcome unless the organism encounters circumstances appropriate to bring out the genotypic potential, unknowable in advance, at each phase of development. Obviously the genotype is both an essential and a tremendous factor in the product. Species are predetermined. Limits are set. Rats, for instance, may learn something in psychological laboratories, but they do not learn to talk or to do calculus. The genotype even determines the nature of the developmental consequences of encountering any given kind of environment. Horsfall's findings, for instance, apply only to snowpool mosquitoes. In human beings also the limits imposed by any genotype are unknown and basically unknowable. As in the case of the so-called Mongolian idiocy, these genotypic limits may be very low, but they depend in very considerable part upon circumstances encountered and upon our educational ingenuity. Nowadays, for instance, a good many of these Mongolians escape idiocy by achieving "trainable" or even "educable" status among the mentally handicapped. One implication of Johannsen's interactionism, moreover, is that children of different genotypes may need different kinds of circumstances to foster their development and to enable them to achieve their potential level of competence. As Hirsch (1963, 1967) has been pointing out, the principle of interactionism calls for individualization of educational efforts.

In the domain of psychological development, recent evidence has brought recognition of the importance of early experience in the development of competence. In this domain, studies of the role of early experience in the problem-solving ability of animal subjects have been important. Because both the genotype and the circumstances of the life history are easier to control in animal subjects, the results of such investigation have tended to be more convincing to many people than the evidence from such studies as that of orphanage infants by Skeels and Dye. It was the theorizing of Donald Hebb (1947) of McGill that instigated many of these animal studies. He himself also did the first of these experiments. It was one in which pet-reared rats proved to be better problem-solvers than rats reared in laboratory cages. Evidence of a similar sort has come repeatedly from the work, which started from a different theoretical orientation, of a group at the University of California (Bennett, Diamond, Krech, & Rosenzweig, 1964). Rats provided with a variety of auditory and visual experience, following the opening of their ears and eyes, proved to be better problem-solvers than rats reared in opaque laboratory cages as Hebb's theorizing suggested (Forgays & Forgays, 1952; Forgus, 1955a, 1955b; Hymovitch, 1952). When the problem-solving of pet-reared dogs was compared with that of their cage-reared littermates (Thompson & Heron, 1954), the differences were, if anything, more pronounced than the differences in the problem-solving performances between pet-reared and cage-reared rats. This and other evidence suggest that the importance of early experience on later problem-solving competence probably increases up the evolutionary scale.[1]

Within this same domain of psychological development, a variety of investigations have indicated that the longer a young organism lives under any given kind of circumstances, the harder it is to alter their influence. When Carmichael (1926, 1927) kept the eggs of frogs and salamanders in chloretone solutions that immobilized their swimming movements for eight days, they recovered the ability to swim within half an hour after getting into tap water, but when Matthews & Detwiler (1926) left the tadpoles of salamanders immersed in a chloretone solu-

[1] This suggestion may be untrue, for Margaret Harlow told me after my presentation that monkeys reared in solitude were no less able, presumably to acquire learning-sets, than monkeys reared by their mothers even though those reared in isolation did lack the normal repertory of social responses. Whether the learning-sets utilized in the Wisconsin experiments demand the past acquisition of earlier learning-sets and are thereby appropriate to bring out an intellectual deficit in the monkeys reared in isolation is unclear. I simply wish to warn the reader that the Wisconsin findings do call this suggestion into question, and that further analysis and investigation are needed.

tion for 13 days or more, their ability to swim was permanently impaired when they were returned to tap water. When Cruze (1935, 1938) kept chicks in darkness for five days or less, they developed accuracy in pecking very readily, but when he limited practice in pecking to the testing situation and kept them in the dark the remainder of the time for 20 days, the sensori-motor organization of pecking and swallowing failed to develop. When Padilla (1935) kept chicks in darkness for a period of eight days or longer, moreover, they would starve with a pile of grain immediately available. Bloom (1964) has organized the evidence from longitudinal studies of human development based on measures of intelligence, of academic achievement, and of attitudes, interests, and values and found evidence of this same import. In the case of measurements for each of these kinds of characteristics, stability increases with age. With IQ at age 17 as the criterion for intelligence, about 50 per cent of the variance among individuals is accounted for by age four, and about 80 per cent by age eight. With vocabulary at age 18 as the measure of academic achievement, about 50 per cent of the variance among individuals is accounted for by age nine. With measures of aggression, dependency, and intellectual interest at adolescence as the criterion, about 30 per cent of the variance is accounted for by age two and about 50 per cent by age five. Because these correlations between successive measures of every such characteristic involve part-whole relationships with the predictor-part becoming a larger and larger portion of the criterion-whole with time, it becomes clear that the inertia increases with age because more and more of the individual's abilities, attitudes, motives, and values must be changed. It appears that the longer a developing organism lives under any given kind of circumstances, the harder it is to alter their influence on both developing behavior and body.

I have added "body" here on purpose. Austin Riesen (1958), stimulated by Hebb's theorizing, reared chimpanzees in the dark for 16 months with not only a behavioral result such as failure to develop the blink response, recognition of highly familiar objects, and fear of the strange but also defects in anatomical maturation. These showed first as a pallor of the optic disc which turned out in a histological study of the retinae following autopsy as a paucity of both the nerve cells and Mueller fibers in the retinal ganglia (Rasch, Swift, Riesen, & Chow, 1961). Other evidence that the circumstances encountered will influence even the anatomical maturation of the nervous system has stemmed from the biochemical theorizing of Hydén, a Swedish biochemist. When Brattgård (1952) reared rabbits in the dark, he found in histochemical analysis of the retinae of the dark-reared rabbits a deficiency in RNA production of the ganglion cells as compared with that of their light-reared littermates. Similar findings have been obtained also in kittens (Weiskrantz, 1958) and in rats (Liberman, 1962) reared in the dark. Evidence of both greater weight and thickness of cortical tissue and of higher total acetylcholinesterase activity of the cortex has been reported for rats reared in complex environments than for littermates reared in simpler environments of laboratory cages has been reported repeatedly by the California group (see Bennett, Diamond, Krech, & Rosenzweig, 1964). Something of the way in which these anatomical modifications of cerebral tissue occurs has appeared in the studies of Hubel & Wiesel (1959, 1960, 1961). Thus, it would appear than even anatomical maturation which is associated with problem-solving competence is influenced by the circumstances the young organism encounters.

Within the domain of behavioral development in human infants evidence of the effects of circumstances has also been accumulating. The rate of development during the first year following birth is especially plastic in human infants. At the Tewksbury State Hospital, for instance, Burton White (see White & Held, 1966) has reduced the median ages of appearance of two landmarks in the development of eye-hand coordination very substantially. The earlier of these landmarks, fisted swiping at objects presented to view, has appeared at the median ages of 72 days, 65 days, and 55 days, depending upon the circumstances of the infant's rearing. The later landmark, mature reaching for objects presented to view with the hand shaped in anticipation for grasping, has appeared at median ages of 145 days (in a normative study without any enrichment),

105 days, and 87 days. In the familiar terms of the IQ ratio, the change from 145 days to 87 days is an increase of the order of 67 points. It was achieved by turning the infants onto their stomachs for 15 minutes after each feeding, 20 minutes of handling a day, and arranging things appropriately for the infants to look at objects and feel them with their hands. Inasmuch as the difference between 105 days and 87 days involved only the opportunity for looking, the looking is probably the most important of the three elements in the enrichment program.

In my own laboratory, David Greenberg, Ina Uzgiris, and I (1968) have found that the infant children of middle-class parents in Champaign-Urbana who have had our mobiles hung over their cribs at five weeks of age show blinking to an object approaching their eyes at an average age of seven weeks, while other infants, whose mothers have agreed not to put anything over their cribs, failed to show this blink-response until an average age of 10.4 weeks. In the familiar terms of the IQ ratio, this is an increase of the order of 48 points.

From the domains of investigation in the development of intelligence, in the factor-analytic studies of intelligence, and of success and failure in problem-solving, comes evidence of a hierarchical conception of the intelligence aspect of competence which is replacing the conception of intelligence as a dimension of individual persons (see Chapter 3). In the light of this hierarchical conception of intelligence, it is not that eye-hand coordination or the blink-response have any special or permanent significance in themselves even though these findings illustrate the plasticity of that early development of human infants once considered to be predetermined in rate. Rather, these findings suggest that such increases in the rate of development may be cumulative. In the hierarchy, such simple sensorimotor organizations as the accommodative mechanism, which permits both the blink-response and seeing clearly patterns at various distances from the eyes, and eye-hand coordination become incorporated into more complex organizations. When such simple sensorimotor organizations are hastened in their development, they become available for coordination with others at this earlier age, and this allows these more complex organizations to become available for incorporation into still more complex organizations at a progressively earlier age. This suggests that such increases in the rate of development may possibly be cumulative. We must investigate this possibility.

No one can now say how large these decreases and increases in human competence deriving from encounters with hampering and fostering circumstances might be. Yet, Wayne Dennis (1966) published some interesting findings of relevance to the matter. They are based on the results of the Draw-a-Man Test given to groups of typical children of six and seven years in age from some 50 cultures over the world. This Draw-a-Man Test was devised by Florence Goodenough (1926), as you will recall, to be culture free. Its freedom from cultural influence was called into question, however, when typical Hopi Indian children aged between six and ten years turned up with an average IQ of 124 on the test (Dennis, 1942). This IQ of 124 approximates the average IQ's for samples of suburban American children and for suburban English children and for samples of children in Japanese fishing villages (Dennis, 1966). At the other end of the distribution, Dennis (1966) finds samples of typical Bedouin Arab children with an average IQ of 52. Here, then, we find a range of about 70 points in mean IQ for groups of typical children from these various cultures. The most obvious correlate of this variation in mean IQ is the amount of contact with the pictorial arts. Among Hopi Indian children, the children of suburbia in America and England, and the children of Japanese fishing villages, contact with the pictorial arts begins early and is continuous. Among Moslem Arab children, where religion prohibits representative art as graven images, IQ's are low, and the IQ's of those Bedouin children with a minimum of contact with pictorial arts are lowest. Even among Moslem Arab children, the range in average Draw-a-Man IQ's is from 52, for the nomadic Bedouins, to 96, for Lebanese children, who, among Arab children, have the most contact with the pictorial arts of Western culture. Although the Draw-a-Man Test is one that requires but a limited set of abilities, such variation in average IQ is highly suggestive, nevertheless, of the degree to which circumstances may alter the intelligence underlying competence, as that intelligence is now tested.

Clearly, the level of competence is not fixed; the rate, course, and ultimate level of development are far from fully predetermined.

Evidence Concerning the Nature of the Circumstances Fostering Incompetence in the Children of the Poor

So long as it was tenable to believe in fixed intelligence and predetermined development, parsimony encouraged the attributing of class differences and even of race differences in competence, as indicated by the IQ, to unmodifiable hereditary constitutions. Although it is still impossible to rule out an appreciable role for heredity in class differences and even in race differences, the evidence just synopsized above indicates that the circumstances encountered in the child-rearing of people in poverty could readily enough have sufficient effect on a major share of children to make the difference between incompetence and competence quite sufficient for full participation in our technological culture.

Recent investigations demonstrate that the child-rearing practices of parents in poverty do indeed make for incompetence. These investigations include those of unskilled laborers in Britain by Bernstein (1960, 1961), of immigrants from various impoverished cultures to Israel by Smilanski (1961, 1964), of inhabitants of the Negro slums of Chicago by Davis (1948), Davis & Havighurst (1946), and by Hess & Shipman (1965), and of poor Puerto Ricans in both the United States and Puerto Rico by Oscar Lewis (1966a). These investigations indicate that children of parents in poverty all over the world lack opportunities to acquire the language and number skills, the motivational habits, and the values and standards which underlie competence.

On the matter of language skills and number skills, parents in poverty typically talk less often to their children than do parents of the middle class (Bernstein, 1960, 1961; Bronfenbrenner, 1958; Chilman, 1965). These parents themselves have often failed to utilize prepositional relationships with precision and to talk of topics demanding abstract concepts. Moreover, their syntax differs substantially from that of the standard language of the mainstream of society. Thus, they serve as poor linguistic models for their young children. Furthermore, these parents seldom ask questions that prompt their young children to note the various perceptual characteristics of objects, to attend to the various relationships among them, and to respond with language describing these characteristics and relationships. On quite the contrary, when these children ask questions, their parents all too often tell them to "shut up," without giving a reason. Supplying reasons is important for developing a conceptual basis for limits on behavior.[2]

On the matter of motivation, the competence required for participation in the mainstream of our technological society calls for some willingness to forego the gratifications of the moment in favor of future goals, and it calls for ambition to achieve and willingness to take initiative. Parents living in poverty have seldom learned such motivational habits themselves (Bronfenbrenner, 1958; Chilman, 1965; Davis, 1948; Lewis, 1961, 1966a). Since these parents have never known enough consumable goods to go around, they, like rats frustrated in infancy (Hunt, 1941), are prone to take urgently what goods are available at the moment. In turn, they react to their children's needs largely in terms of their own, and their children have little reason to do

[2] Since this was written, Maxine Schoggen of the Demonstration and Research Center for Early Education at the George Peabody College for Teachers in Nashville, Tennessee, has started a study that promises to be especially illuminating on this matter. She has selected three samples of eight families, one of professional people, one of rural poor, and one of the urban poor. Each family contains a three-year-old who is the target child of the study. After becoming very well acquainted with each of these families, the investigator-visitors record instances of verbal interaction initiated by both older children and the parents with the target three-year-old in such functionally equivalent situations as meal time. These units of interaction she terms "environmental force units." In the evidence thus far available, not only are there more than twice as many such units in the families of professional status as in the families of either the rural or urban poor, but the quality of such interaction differs radically. Although restraining commands of "don't do that" in one from or another are common in all families, they constitute nearly a total of the environmental force units to be found in the families of the poor, whereas a substantial portion of these units in the families of professional status do call upon the child to discern various characteristics of things and various kinds of relations among things and people and to formulate his impressions in his own language (Schoggen & Schoggen, 1968).

otherwise. Seldom do their children learn anything about time. They do not even learn how to tell time because clocks are seldom available. In such a setting, even fantasies of the future tend to be meaningless. Moreover, to such parents, a good child is a quiet child who does not disturb their own preoccupations (Gray & Klaus, 1963; Klaus & Gray, 1967). Though these mothers in poverty love their children, take pride in them, and may even overdress them for school, they typically send them off with the counsel to "be good, and do like the teacher says." Defining "being good" as being quiet and compliant hardly encourages initiative and hardly builds a high valuation of achievement. As a consequence, these children of poverty have little or no opportunity to acquire the orientation toward the future, the concern for achievement, and the initiative which constitute some of the important motivational aspects of competence.

On the matter of standards of conduct, the competence for life in the mainstream of society calls for certain values and inner controls. These are more fundamental than middle-class norms or matters of taste. They are values and controls upon which a peaceful, organized, technological society depends. Although one must acknowledge that certain laws are either unjust or out of touch with the current realities, these values include a respect for law that demands compliance except in those exceedingly rare instances where breaking the law while accepting the personal consequences appears to be required to force the changes toward a higher level of justice. They include concern for the needs of others, basic honesty, that dependability which makes a man's word as good as his bond, and a degree of tenderness coupled with recognition that violence is almost always a matter of destruction without solving the problem. The children of our slums have little opportunity to develop such values and standards. Because the mothers have a multitude of unmet needs, they cannot cope with their children's requests for satisfactions that do not exist for them. Thus, despite their love for the children and concern for their future, these mothers typically respond to children's verbalized requests with "shut up," or with "leave me be," and they call their inquiring questions "silly" (Bloch & Flynn, 1956; Chilman, 1965).

It is hardly surprising that children in this context look to children of their own age for human companionship and contact. These unsupervised children, of which there are hundreds of thousands in our slums, get such satisfactions as they can from their peer associations; sex play and stealing commonly become routine in the lives of even the very young (Childers, 1936). These children form peer gangs which tend to set the norms for all the children in a neighborhood, and it is from these peer gangs that children of the slums typically acquire their values and standards of conduct (Short & Strodtbeck, 1965, Ch. 3). In these slum neighborhoods, the very young children copy children a few years older, and, especially among boys, the preadolescents have as models the adolescents who are members of the local delinquent gangs (Cloward & Ohlin, 1960; Cohen, 1955; Cohen & Short, 1958; Shaw, 1931; Thrasher, 1936; Whyte, 1943). The standards and the patterns of delinquent behavior may vary considerably from neighborhood to neighborhood (Shaw, 1929). Even the structures of the groups vary (Short & Strodtbeck, 1965; Whyte, 1943). Traditionally, the motivation for the delinquent behavior noted has been seen as part of a search for fun and excitement. In the slums where poverty deprives adolescents of desired materials, fun becomes burglary and stealing (Cohen, 1955; Shaw, 1931; Warner & Lunt, 1941). The motives for delinquent behavior, however, appear to be changing. Various bits of evidence suggest that in recent years delinquent behavior has come to be motivated less by a search for fun and excitement than by frustration and protest against social conditions. Although violence was always part of the picture in the gang wars, this new motivation increases the proneness to violence (Cohen, 1955; Miller, 1958; Short & Strodtbeck, 1965). Violence is also increased by the fact that leaders have little with which to maintain their positions and to hold their members together. They turn, therefore, to fomenting hostility from other groups to motivate cohesion among their own membership and to retain their own positions of status where hostility and violence have become the valued norm (Short & Strodtbeck, 1965). In such a social context, the children of the slums have little opportunity to develop respect for law, concern for the needs of others, basic

honesty, and tenderness. Instead, they acquire chiefly the anti-
theses of these values and standards required for an organized
society that operates its technology peacefully.

In short, what these children of poverty and lower-class background learn in the way of language, motivation, and standards
of conduct before they are old enough to enter our traditional
schools makes them incompetent and typically unfits them to
profit from the circumstances provided by the curricula of our
traditional schools. This occurs despite the abundant love these
poor parents have for their children. Lacking the competence to
cope with the school situation, it is hardly surprising that these
slum-reared (rural or urban) children soon lose hope of succeeding there, become fed up with the school, and drop out as
soon as they can.

Evidence Pointing Toward a Prescription for the Community

Project Head Start was devised to provide compensatory education for the children of the poor that would ameliorate their
incompetence and enable them better to cope with the circumstances in our traditional schools. The goal is right; the direction is right. In the light of the institutionalization of the logical
constructs from Aristotole to separate mind-in-general into components, it is interesting and significant that our political leaders
found it expedient to house Project Head Start in neither the
National Institute of Mental Health, where affection and conation are the central concern, nor the Office of Education, where
cognition and intellect are the central concern. Rather, they
house Project Head Start in the new Office of Economic Opportunity. The consequences are only partially successful. Although
some of the historical leaders of nursery-school education were
explicitly concerned with compensating children of poverty for
the inadequacies of their early experience (see especially Margaret McMillan (1919) of England and Maria Montessori (1909)
of Italy), what become the traditional curricula of our day have
consisted largely of group activities and free play to promote
the spontaneity, the muscular growth, and the social adjustment
of the highly controlled children of middle-class mothers. Be-

cause educators, psychologists, and public health workers considered it too soft-headed during the past half-century to be worthwhile even to try experimentally to improve the competence of the children of the poor, no compensatory educational technology was ever developed. Animals, people, and institutions regularly meet new challenges with the repertoires they have at hand. Thus, although the guidelines of Project Head Start provided two innovations, one in limiting classes to 15 children for each teacher and teacher-aide, and a second in involving parents in the planning of the program, for the most part the curricula have been those of traditional nursery schools.

While none of the Head Start programs appears to have done any harm other than disappointing those adults who hoped for too much, some have apparently achieved considerably more with children than others. The limited evidence from the evaluative studies of the various programs of compensatory education, both those outside and within Project Head Start, appears to indicate that success in improving measures of language skill, number skill, and tested intelligence is a matter of how much deliberate effort has been made to teach these skills, to interest children in scholastic matters, and to inculcate concern for achievement. Such appears to be the import of observations and studies by Martin Deutsch (1964) and his collaborators in New York, the studies of David Weikart and his collaborators (1967), and of the evidence summarized by Weikart (1967b) in his review of efforts at compensatory preschool education. Those children who get these skills seem to be better able to succeed in schools. From comparisons of their own performance with that of their peers from more fortunate backgrounds, they appeared to gain some of the self-respect and motivation required for continued participation in schools. Moreover, as they succeed, they seem even to imbibe the values and standards of conduct which are required to participate in the mainstream of society directly from success in the school situation. This appears to be especially true where the disadvantaged child also gets the impression that the teachers and the other personnel of the school care (Krugman, 1961).

From the evidence available, soft as much of it is at this stage of the history of compensatory education, considerable success appears to come from innovative programs which differ quite radically. One continuum along which these programs can be said to vary is that of teacher-versus-materials centeredness. Related to this is the continuum based on the degree to which the teacher keeps the attention of the child focused upon himself and his own talk in order to keep his attention on the curricular subject matter versus the degree to which the teacher employs the format of games carefully planned to call upon the child to acquire and to use the skills and concepts constituting the curriculum. A third continuum is the degree to which the program depends upon teacher-directed participation in prescribed curricula versus the degree to which it depends upon the spontaneous interests of the children but is teacher-guided by the means of careful preparation of the school environment. A fourth continuum is the degree to which teachers focus on a set curriculum and omit consideration of the motivational concerns and ready-made abilities of their pupils versus the degree to which they focus on matching the curricular activities to the idiosyncratic interests and abilities of individuals. These several continua are very much mixed. At the present time the best that can be done in investigation of their effects is to attempt to indicate all the various factors in the teacher-student and student-curriculum relationships which make a difference.

At the teacher-centered end of the first continuum are those approaches wherein the teacher attempts, except during periods of free play, to keep the attention of her pupils focused on their own personal presentations of various problems and materials of the curriculum. Teacher-centered approaches always have definite curricular materials and activities designed to inculcate specific skills, and in this sense they resemble Procrustean beds. The program of Bereiter & Engelmann (1966) is one such. Another is a program for three-year-olds and four-year-olds run within the public schools of a county in Georgia by a Regional Laboratory from the University of Georgia. These programs differ substantially, however, in that Bereiter and Engelmann use a teacher-student ratio of 1:5 while the Georgia program uses a ratio more like 1:15. If my observations are correct, no teacher-centered program of this sort can hold the attention of such young children for a major share of the time if the teacher-student ratio is more than about 1:5. A very interesting mixture of teacher-centeredness and materials-centeredness is to be found at the Demonstration and Research Center in Early Education (DARCEE) at the George Peabody College for Teachers under the direction of Susan Gray. The colorful and intriguing materials of this program do a great deal toward holding the attention of the children. Even so, the program employs a teacher-student ratio of 1:5, and the teachers are continually posing questions, praising, talking, and evoking talk in the children as do the teachers in the Bereiter-Engelmann program. In the teacher-centered programs, be the classes small or large, a visitor almost always distracts the children. An exception sometimes occurs when the teachers employ a token-reward technique, suggested by the work of Skinner (1953). In Tucson, Arizona, I observed a class of about 30 first and second graders in which the teacher had learned to use the token-reward technique under the direction of Professor Ralph Wetzel. Despite a high student-teacher ratio, the distraction of visitors was but momentary. In conversation with the children in his group, however, it was no easy matter to elicit a discussion of curricular matters. What the children were most ready to talk about was the rewards they were winning for complying with the system.

At the materials-centered end of this first continuum are the Montessori schools. In these, dependence on the comparative spontaneous interests of children usually goes with this centering on materials. The teacher prepares the materials. The child chooses the materials with which he will work at any given time. The child must use them in prescribed fashion, however, and this is supposed to lead the child step-by-step to the motives and skills required for academic competence. In such schools, if my observations do not deceive me, keeping the attention of children on the lessons incorporated into the use of the materials is hardly a problem. The materials-centered approach can make what is essentially spontaneous play of school work, for the children are motivated by their ready-made interests in the use of the materials. Some Montessori teachers, however, become highly directive and even rigid about each child taking every step described by Montessori. Even when children are allowed to use materials spontaneously, their self-directed use may provide insufficient opportunity to develop language skills to compensate children of poverty for the language deficit typical of them. The talking typewriter, developed by O. K. Moore (1963) and Richard Kobler of McGraw-Edison and now marketed by the Responsive Environments Corporation, fits nicely into the Montessori philosophy of materials. It is, moreover, focused directly on the learning of language skills. It represents an extreme of the materials-centered continuum with a gadget, albeit an expensive one, which does interest young children and which can be utilized with a wide variety of curricular materials enabling them to act and to get feedback in both heard and seen language.

Another of the programs at the materials-centered extreme of this continuum is the New Nursery School at Greeley, Colorado, developed by Nimnicht, Meier, & McAfee (1966). This program also uses a typewriter, but not the talking typewriter (Nimnicht, Meier, & McAfee, 1967b). Space at the New Nursery School is arranged to provide areas for activities which range from "dress up" to the "reading" corner. Each child is given a choice of what he will do at any given time. To make the human environment responsive, only the head teacher can initiate interaction with a pupil, but each of the various teacher-aides is instructed to respond accordingly to any child's request for conversation, for tutorial help, for being read to, etc. According to the observations reported, as a school year progresses, the children spend progressively less time in the sand box and the dress up corner and progressively more time with the language-training, number-training, and reading materials. Moreover, the children get what amounts to teacher-centered instruction individually or in small groups from the teacher and her aides at their own request (see Nimnicht, Meier, & McAfee, 1967a).

Along the second continuum, that of teacher-centered direction versus teacher-planned games designed to get children involved with materials in learning academic skills, there are several alternatives to the Bereiter-Engelmann extreme of teacher-centeredness. At the University of Illinois, for instance, Merle Karnes has developed what she describes as "a highly structured preschool program." In certain ways, the Karnes program resembles in its use of a large variety of materials that of the Demonstration and Research Center in Early Education (DARCEE) at Peabody College. It differs, however, in providing greater emphasis on games. Despite the use of games, the teacher-student ratio is kept very low, i.e., 1:5. Social studies–science goals were to teach vocabulary, to develop classification skills, to provide sensory discrimination experiences and basic observation of natural phenomena. The arithmetic portion of the program stresses a useful vocabulary combined with basic manipulative skills, the naming of five geometric shapes, one-to-one matching in the copying of patterns, counting as a functional concept incorporated in a variety of games, beginning addition and subtraction combined with a manipulation of such objects as popsicle sticks, bottle caps, poker chips, and peg boards. The curriculum of the language arts and reading readiness

used books and pictures for naming and identifying objects, for establishing descriptive properties, for introducing the idea of story continuity and sequenced events, for establishing logical and causal relationships and associations, and for providing opportunities to practice both short and long-term recall. Inexpensive books in sets of six were an important aid in fostering reading readiness. Children learned to hold a book right side up, to turn pages singly and in sequence, to associate the pictures with the progression of the story being read, to develop left-to-right progression. In addition, the small-group storytime provided opportunities for reinforcing vocabulary which had been introduced during the other learning periods and for exposing the children to acceptable syntactical models and to the familiar rhythms and stresses of standard, informal English (Karnes, Hodgins, Stoneburner, Studley, & Teska, 1968, p. 408).

Each of the Karnes programs has been evaluated in terms of changes of IQ between pretests and post-tests with forms L and M of the 1960 Stanford-Binet Scale and the Illinois Test of Psycholinguistic Abilities (Kirk, McCarthy, & Kirk, 1968). In the first of these studies with four-year-olds, the gain in mean IQ was from 96.96 to 110.26—a gain of 14.30 points (Karnes & Hodgins, 1969). A later study with three-year-olds employed a control group, and the examiners did their testing without knowledge of who was about to enter preschool or who had been through preschool. During the seven months of preschool, those in the preschool gained in Stanford-Binet IQ from 94.5 to 111.4 (a gain of 16.9 points) while the control group dropped from a pretest mean IQ of 91.3 to a post-test mean of 88.5 (a drop of 2.8 points). The three-year-olds in the preschool also gained more than did the controls on several subtests of ITPA (Karnes, Hodgins, Stoneburner, Studley, & Teska, 1968).

In Tucson, Arizona, where a large share of the poor are Mexican-American families whose children start in the first grade with little or no English, Marie Hughes, Director of the University of Arizona Center for Early Childhood Education, has organized a highly ingenious amalgam which incorporates the curriculum in games and projects in which children have a natural interest and has adapted it for the elementary grades in the public school. The first-grade classes of 30, or somewhat more, are allowed only a teacher and an aide, so that the teacher-student ratio is high (of the order of 1:15+). These large classes are broken down into informal groups. These groups are encouraged to play games and plan the projects. In the planning, which is done in English, the teacher and her aide ask questions which encourage the children to express their wishes and attitudes concerning the project to be carried out sometime hence. During the project, the teacher or teacher-aide asks questions which encourage the children to note the perceivable characteristics of things, persons, and places, and the relationships among them. Answering these questions calls upon the children to formulate these characteristics and relationships in language, also English. After the project itself is over, each child in the group draws from memory a picture of the project and dictates his story of it. His dictation is tape-recorded and is also typed. On a later day, when other groups are planning projects, these children go to the "listening post," where each of the six has a pair of earphones plugged into a tape recorder. There each child hears his own dictated story and that of each of the other five in his group while he reads his own and the other five stories in large poster typescript.

The arrangement of the Hughes program for planning projects in the future, conducting them, and then describing them in retrospect followed still later by listening to and reading about the projects is calculated to expand the span of time in which these children organize their lives. The questions which call for expressions of wishes, which focus attention on the characteristics of relationships among observable things, and which call for the child to formulate his observations in language, combined with the later experiences of listening and reading at the "listening post" are all calculated to encourage development of functional language. At the "listening post" the groups of children need little attention from teachers and teacher-aides.

The Hughes program provides also for short tutorial sessions for these groups in which the teacher helps the children to learn phonics as a method of getting sounds from written material, to learn how various things are the same and different, to learn number skills, and the various other matters incorporated within the curriculum. In this program, holding attention is no problem. One observes that the children are clearly involved almost continually in what they are doing. A visitor disrupts their attention only momentarily; they return almost immediately to their work. The teacher and her aides are seldom called upon for any disciplinary action. They are quite free to praise their pupils for achievements of all kinds. At times near the end of the first-grade year, the children I saw in two consecutive years were fluent in English. They spoke it with little trace of the Spanish accent even though they still spoke Spanish. They still took pride in their Spanish background which had been encouraged by several of the projects which had taken them into their home neighborhoods and into the places where their fathers worked.

Neither Marie Hughes nor Merle Karnes have employed the traditional equipment of the nursery school and kindergarten—the outdoor play equipment, the toy appliances, the toy trucks, dolls, and the materials for playing house. Although I have referred repeatedly to the curricula of the traditional nursery schools as if they were all alike, they actually differ consider-

ably. Some of them long ago introduced considerable conceptual content concerned with language, numbers, and abstractions by incorporating them into the games used in group play.
Since it has become evident that children of the poor gain little
from programs without such content, innovators within the
nursery-school tradition of play have been developing a variety
of new and ingenious ways to incorporate school skills into
games in which nearly all children are readily interested. Thus,
they prepare the social environment as well as the materials
environment for utilization in the teaching-learning process.

In several programs, innovators have developed one-to-one
tutorial relationships of short duration which they incorporate
into more traditional nursery-school programs. Marion Blank of
the Einstein Medical School of Yeshiva University has developed
what one might characterize as an individual tutorial program
for disadvantaged four-year-olds to help them function in terms
of increasingly complex combinations of information in the instructions and questions they hear. This tutorial may begin with
showing the child an object which is highly familiar to him, say
an orange or a ball. The object is then withdrawn from view
and the child is asked: "What was it?" If the child does not
immediately say the name of the object, the first presentation
is followed by a second, and then if the child fails to say what
it was after the second presentation, the issue is brought to
closure without frustration by holding the object before him and
saying: "What is it?" The materials and the verbal directions
and questioning are gradually made more and more complex.
No single session, however, is continued after a child's interest
flags. Moreover, no such tutorial session is extended beyond
10 minutes. These disadvantaged children, who typically start
15 to 30 points below the IQ norm of 100, gradually gain, at
their own pace, in the complexity of the questioning and directions to which they can listen and respond appropriately. When
they can correctly select three or more objects on the basis of
some three or four defining aspects or characteristics of each
in the instructions heard, they show substantial gains in IQ.
Gains up to 30 points have been associated with a total of only
40 or 50 hours of such brief tutorial sessions (Blank, 1967).

Among these various combinations, moreover, is at least one instance where a Montessori school for disadvantaged children has provided opportunities for groups of five disadvantaged children at a time to participate for 20-minute sessions in the teacher-centered program of Bereiter and Engelmann in order to foster their acquisition of language. Such combinations can be extended indefinitely where the conception of the teaching-learning process is sufficiently flexible.

So far as I can glean from the evidence picked up in my observations of 20-some programs of compensatory education over the country, all of those which are academically oriented produce gains in the academic skills of young children. Thus far, however, those who are presumably experts in early childhood education have ardent differences in their views of such varied approaches to compensatory education as I have outlined. Those who believe in harnessing the intrinsic motivation of children for learning by getting academic skills incorporated into children's play, and I am very much one of these (Hunt, 1965a), are likely to be highly critical of what appears to be teacher-directed drill in the efforts of such innovators as Bereiter & Engelmann (1966) to teach standard English, arithmetic concepts and skills, and reading readiness after the model of teaching a foreign language. Bereiter and Engelmann have not played up what appear to me to be some of their most effective motivating techniques. Engelmann and his teachers often preface the posing of a "problem" with such statements as, "Oh, this is too hard, I shouldn't ask you such hard questions." When the children request the question, they get one which stretches them but which is also well within their limits. They thereby experience quite directly *success* with something the teacher has said is hard. Moreover, they make nothing in discussions of their method of the characteristics and the skill of the teachers. Nothing is said about the fact that Engelmann himself is a 230-pound athletic man with a voice which can range readily from a whisper to a hundred decibels without his feeling any special inhibitions or qualms. Such a vigorous man can hardly be anything but a highly helpful model for the little boys in these classes. Moreover, Mrs. Osborn, his innovative collaborator in the teaching, is exceedingly bright and highly adept as a teacher. She could probably make any kind of curriculum and materials hold the attention of children.

Despite the theory-based qualms which have been widely expressed about this program, the evidence available shows indications of considerable success. The 15 four-year-old children with whom Bereiter and Engelmann started in the fall of 1964 all came from families near or at the bottom of the socioeconomic scale. All but two of these families were selected because older siblings had been unable to succeed in regular classes and had been put into special education for those who were handicapped in some fashion. When these 15 four-year-olds started, about half of them tested below the 2.5-year limit in the range of language ages, analogous to mental ages, on the Illinois Test of Psycholinguistic Abilities (Kirk & McCarthy, 1961). During the first six months of three 20-minute sessions (one for standard English, one for arithmetic concepts and skills, and one for reading readiness) in two hours of school each day for five days a week, these children gained two years in psycholinguistic abilities as measured by the ITPA. During the course of the year, two of the original 15 left the group. One moved away; the other was judged unable to continue with the group and was put in a class for the retarded. Three new children were added for the second year. One came from a family of middle-class background, and the other two were judged to be able to learn readily, but otherwise met the criteria for selection of the original group. During this second year, beginning in the fall of 1965, the children continued to gain in terms of scores on standard tests.

Such is the nature of the evidence which has usually been available for the success of the various efforts in early childhood education. The evidence for the Bereiter-Engelmann program, although without controls, goes somewhat further. In the fall of 1966, these 16 children were put into regular first-grade classes. Of the 13 composing the two top tracks for the second year, one ranked, at the end of the first grade, in the middle ability-track at a school attended almost exclusively by children of professional people. The second was at the top of his class, and a third was doing very well in a class for children of high ability in a program of Project Promise. Children four and five were at or near the top of their classes in a former ghetto school where the majority of their peers were now children of graduate students and the younger staff of the University of Illinois being bussed to that school. Children six and seven had done at least average work in these same classes, and child eight was doing well enough to hold on there. Child nine was doing well in the top track at a school for the children of parents of working-class background. Child ten was leading his class in a ghetto school. Children eleven and twelve were considered to be conduct problems at a school attended chiefly by children of the laboring class, but these two children were not in academic difficulty. Their conduct problems may well have been school-made. Child thirteen was in this same school, had been somewhat less of a behavior problem, but he was doing only marginal academic work.

Of the three children who were in the bottom group during the second year for Bereiter and Engelmann, all had to repeat the first grade. This means that, of the total of 18 children involved in the first trial of this program, five failed. One had to be put into a class for the retarded during the first year, and four lacked the skills to enable them to cope with first grade. The outcome of that one who moved away is unknown. I suggest that this constitutes what might be called failure with approximately a quarter of the children involved. It may well be that the Bereiter-Engelmann program provided an improper match for the skills of these five with whom it failed. Whether any other remedial or compensatory program would have enabled them to cope with regular first-grade curricula is a matter of conjecture. It does appear that 12 of these 18 children have performed with fair to fine success in the first grade. In the absence of a control group or contrast group, one can only say that this is a larger proportion of the 18 than one could possibly have expected to succeed in the first grade.

The very notion of compensatory education as conceived by program Head Start begins with disadvantaged children who are already four years old. Thus, compensatory education must be remedial in nature. It is entirely conceivable, therefore, that compensatory education may have to employ some of the "pressure-cooker" methods employed by Bereiter and Engelmann. We lack certainty of this, as yet. We very much need studies of the comparative effects of these different kinds of programs, and we need to know these comparative effects over a longer period of time than the first grade. We very much need studies that follow up groups of children who have had compensatory education of various kinds through the drop-out age of 11 to 14 with the same evaluative criteria employed with children from similar backgrounds without the presumed advantages of the compensatory education. It will also be highly important to revise the programs of our traditional schools to take into better account both the wide range of abilities and preparation in children and the goals of community mental health.

Comparative Evaluative Studies

We are beginning to get from at least two sources, Merle Karnes at the University of Illinois and David Weikart in the public schools of Ypsilanti, Michigan, the beginnings of comparative evaluative studies. Weikart (1967b) has published a review of the gains made in scores on various tests in various preschool programs. From these comparisons he has gained the impression that those which utilize curricula aimed at teaching cognitive abilities (conceptual, linguistic, and numerical) are substantially more successful than those utilizing the traditional curricula of the nursery schools developed for children of the middle class. In a still far-from-finished review of these studies by Roslyn O'Brien and myself, we have gleaned this same impression. We have also gleaned the impression that a rather large variety of factors appear, at least in some studies, to have made a difference (O'Brien & Lopate, 1968).

So far as I know the first experimentally designed evaluative comparison of preschool programs to be published is that of Merle Karnes of the University of Illinois and her collaborators (Karnes, Wollersheim, Stoneburner, Hodgins, & Teska, 1968). This study compares the increases in Stanford-Binet IQ in language development, as measured by the Illinois Test for Psycholinguistic Abilities (Kirk & McCarthy, 1961), and in scores on a developmental test of visual perception constructed by Marianne Frostig (1964) made by four-year-old-children in the course of a year in a traditional nursery school or in the Karnes highly structured preschool. The study started with 60 four-year-olds from economically depressed neighborhoods of Champaign-Urbana, Illinois. Karnes made a special effort to obtain children from families judged by authorities of Public Aid and the schools to be economically and educationally deprived and also to locate children from acutely disadvantaged sections which might be new to the community. The Stanford-Binet scale was administered to the 60 eligible children by qualified examiners. The children were then stratified into three groups (IQ scores of 100 and above, 90 through 99, and 70 through 89) and assigned to class units ($N = 15$) in which one-third of each class consisted of children with the high IQ's, one-third of the middle range, and one-third of the bottom range. Consequently, the mean IQ of those 30 children committed to the traditional program was 94.5, and the mean IQ of those to the highly structured preschool was 96.0. The 30 children committed to each kind of program were divided into two classes of 15 so that there were approximately two black children for one white child in each class and so that the sex ratios were approximately equal.

In this experimentally designed evaluation, the major goals of the traditional preschool were to promote the personal, social, and general motor development of the children. The teachers endeavored to capitalize on opportunities for incidental and informal learning to encourage the children to talk and to ask questions and to stimulate their interest in the world around them. An effort was made to interest the children in books, music, and stories, and art activities were regularly scheduled. When weather permitted, outdoor play on appropriate equipment was routine. Play indoors was focused on a center for dolls and housekeeping, a center for vehicles and blocks, and a center for small toys. The curriculum included juice time, rest period, and show and tell along with routine supervision of toileting and outdoor wraps.

The program of the highly structured preschool has already been synopsized. Each class ($N = 15$) was divided into three tracks, on the basis of Binet IQ's, with a teacher for each track of five children (a teacher-pupil ratio of 1:5 for both programs). The Binet test was used for diagnostic and evaluative purposes to help solve the problem of the match by indicating the kinds of curricular activities each child was most likely to profit from. Neither Karnes nor any of her teachers used the Binet IQ to indicate future levels of ability. Moreover, the track groupings were flexible. Children who did not perform according to test indications and needed extra supervision and instruction were appropriately replaced on the basis of performance in the tracks.

It should be noted that this study was quite nicely designed to remove some of the usual confounding between teacher-skill and program effectiveness, for there were six teachers operating with the 30 children in each of the two kinds of programs. It is possible, however, that Professor Karnes may have communicated her prejudice in favor of her highly structured program to the teachers of the traditional program. This is one qualm to be considered.

The findings confirm the impressions derived from examining the results of various preschool programs by Weikart (1967b) and by O'Brien and myself. Children in the highly structured preschool changed in Binet IQ from a mean of 96 to a mean of 110.3, a mean gain of 14.3 points of IQ. On the other hand, the children in the traditional nursery school, who also showed an improvement, gained from a mean Binet IQ of 94.5 to a mean Binet IQ of 102.6, a gain of 8.1. Since the examiners did their pretests and post-tests without knowledge of who was to go into which program or who had been submitted to which program, this difference of 7.7 IQ points of gain is a fairly solid piece of evidence in favor of the proposition that compensatory preschools should concern themselves with teaching the cognitive abilities that disadvantaged children lack. The fact that the gains in scores on the ITPA and in Frostig's (1964) perceptual quotients are also substantially larger for the children in Karnes's structured preschool than in the traditional preschool lends further support to this proposition, as does the fact that the children in the structured program had higher scores on Metropolitan School Readiness Tests than did those in the traditional preschool at the end of the year.

In another still-unpublished study employing a similar strategy, Karnes, Teska, & Hodgins (1969a) have compared the gains in test scores on the Binet IQ and on tests of language development of disadvantaged four-year-olds in four preschool programs. The first of these is again the traditional nursery school, the second is a community-integrated program providing a traditional nursery school also, the third was a Montessori preschool administered by the local Montessori Society utilizing staff and classroom materials which met the standards of the National Montessori Society, and the fourth the Karnes preschool. These four preschool programs were presumed by Prof. Karnes to represent points along a continuum of structure, a kind of continuum differing from any of those that I have attempted to describe above. On this continuum, Prof. Karnes considered her own preschool to represent the maximum of structure in the four groups concerned. The two traditional programs represented the least structure, but she expected some advantage to fall to the community-integrated program because it attempted to place special emphasis in the domain of language learning. The Montessori program represented a degree of structure intermediate between her own preschool and the two traditional nursery programs. Karnes expected the size of gains to be positively associated with the degree of structure. As she writes: "such was not the case." The children in the Karnes program did show the greatest gains. The children in the traditional program manifested more modest gains, but they were substantially greater than the gains obtained by the community-integrated program. Finally, the children who participated in the Montessori program showed the smallest average gain. Karnes argues that the failure of the Montessori children to show appreciable gains in the various cognitive skills need not invalidate her hypothesis that structure is essential for maximum progress in the compensatory education of disadvantaged children. Although the Montessori program provides a high degree of structure in the kinds of sensorimotor activities required for the development of an adequate base for cognitive and language skills, it does not provide for a high level of the teacher-child interaction required to coordinate heard verbalizations with sensory discriminations and motor performances.

In the case of the programs of both Merle Karnes and Marie Hughes, a great deal of teacher talk is coordinated directly with what the children are doing. Teachers thereby supply the verbal model, and the repetition involved in the format of the games and projects helps the child to establish coordination between the language he hears the teacher verbalizing and the actions in which he is engaged. The actions are well devised to foster the formation of concepts. Such evidence confirms the intuitive opinions of such preschool experts as Millie Almy of Teachers College and Lois Murphy of the Menninger Foundation in Topeka. Both considered my own suggestion in 1962 that we start with the Montessori program in compensatory education of disadvantaged children (see Chapter 1) to be ill advised. Even though the evidence remains strong that the acquisition of language consists in a coordination of the imagery of objects, actions, persons, and places with the verbal signs for these, Bereiter & Engelmann (1966) are apparently correct in their contention that by the time disadvantaged children are as old as four years, they need experience with language more than they need sensorimotor experience. It is clearly of the utmost importance that compensatory education involve experience with language and with its syntactical organization. I would still contend, however, that the disadvantaged child is also so limited in his experience with the identification of objects, actions, and the abstractable characteristics of objects that it is highly important to have both the sensorimotor and the verbal combined. This is typically what the programs of Karnes, of Hughes, of Weikart, and the other academically oriented preschools attempt to achieve whether or not they incorporate the curricular content into games.

In another still unpublished investigation, David Weikart (1969) has compared, in the public schools of Ypsilanti, Michigan, the gains in IQ obtained through a year of preschool by groups of disadvantaged three- and four-year-olds in each of three kinds of academically oriented programs: (1) the Bereiter-Engelmann program, (2) the Weikart program which is based on the teaching of Piaget-like structures with verbalization, and (3) the more traditional, play-based approach attributed to Patricia Sears of Stanford University which ingeniously incorporates the utilization of conceptual, linguistic, and arithmetic skills in games not unlike those of the traditional nursery school. Here the teachers of the play-based approach worked out lesson plans just as explicit as did the teachers utilizing the other two programs.

The three groups of 16 disadvantaged children were so selected as to have mean IQ's within the range of 76 to 82 at the beginning in the fall of 1967. Each of these groups had two teachers, both considered to be excellent (teacher-student ratio of 1:7.5). Each pair of teachers started as advocates of the program they attempted to use. As of February, 1968, the gains in IQ made by those under the Bereiter-Engelmann program were substantially the largest; the gains of those under Weikart's program came next; and those of the children under the "more traditional" preschool program were the smallest. By June of 1968, however, the mean gains for the various programs had essentially evened. The average for the Bereiter-Engelmann program was 30.4 points. That for the Weikart program was 28 points and that for the "more traditional" program 27.5 points.[3] Had there been substantial differences among the gains in this investigation, they would have been hard to interpret because the design confounds teacher-skill with curriculum and program. The resources required to have an appropriate number of teachers of each kind and an appropriate number of classes to avoid such confounding are typically beyond the limits of most individual school systems. The absence of substantial differences in such an index of effectiveness suggests that substantial gains of ap-

[3] Since this was written I have visited Weikart's program (1967a, 1967b, 1969; Weikart & Wiegerink, 1968). It is interesting that these are the largest gains of which I know. Two factors may be important. First, the gains cited are mean gains for the eight three-year-olds in each curriculum-class of 16 and are roughly 10 points higher than those for the eight four-year-olds. Second, Weikart involves the parents of these children in their education through a home-visitor program (Weikart & Lambie, 1967).

proximately the same degree can be obtained with approaches and curricula which appear, at least superficially, to differ markedly. These findings suggest also that many of the differences the experts talk about may be considerably less important than they are considered to be and that these comparative investigations should be focused on the commonalities and on determining what the important factors are. As of now, I am inclined to believe that what is most important in the compensatory, remedial education of disadvantaged four-year-olds is the opportunity to see and to act in contemporary conjunction with language which describes with standard syntax the actions and operations that underlie many concepts and that which is perceived and abstracted about objects, persons, places, and the relations among them.

One more comparative study, this one coming again from Karnes, Teska, & Hodgins (1969b) at the University of Illinois, should be considered here because it does compare the longitudinal progress of disadvantaged children who participated in three different kinds of compensatory education for four-year-olds. The three kinds of programs include (1) a "direct, verbal program" which was actually the Bereiter-Engelmann program, (2) an "ameliorative preschool emphasizing language development" which was actually the structured program of Karnes, and (3) the Karnes version of a traditional preschool. Subjects were assigned to five class units of 15 children each. All but traditional classes were divided in tracks of five (a teacher-student ratio of 1:5) with a single teacher in charge of each track at any given time. The Bereiter-Engelmann program endured for two consecutive years; then the children were followed with testing through the first grade. The Karnes program endured for a single year. During the second year, the children under this program attended public kindergarten in the morning and then participated, for one hour each afternoon, in an additional session divided into two periods, one concerned with language development and reading readiness, and the other concerned with arithmetic concepts and skills. This schedule was broken for field trips and art projects, but these diversions were only occasional. In this additional supportive program, an effort was made to avoid re-

Figure 2. Binet IQ: Three groups for three years.

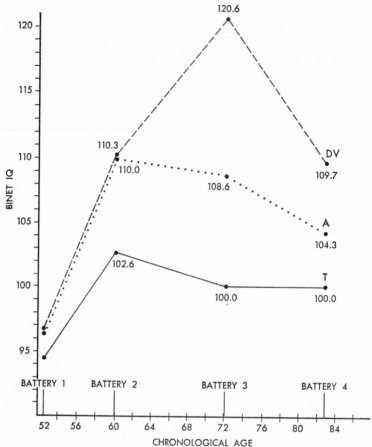

Note: The times of the four batteries are plotted at the mean Binet chronological age of the three groups.

peating activities which had already been provided in the morning by the public kindergarten. It emphasized, rather, activities quite directly related to success in the first grade. Those children in the "traditional" preschool, designed to promote their personal, social, motor, and general language development, enrolled during the second year in kindergartens and were solely under the supervision of the public school.

Examiners tested all the children in each of these three preschools without knowledge of who was in which, at four different points in time: (1) before the children entered preschool, (2) at the end of the preschool year, (3) at the end of the kindergarten year, which in the case of the Bereiter-Engelmann program was at the end of the second year of their program, and (4) at the end of the first grade. The outcome in terms of the highly familiar Binet IQ appears in Fig. 2.

Fig. 2 shows that the gain in Binet IQ from 96.2 to 110 for Karnes's preschool was almost identical with that from 96.6 to 110.3 for the Bereiter-Engelmann program during the first year. These two gains in mean IQ of approximately 14 points are considerably larger than the one of about 8 points from 94.4 to 102.6 for the "traditional" preschool. During the second year, substantial differences appear. The children in the Bereiter-Engelmann program go up another 10 points to a mean IQ of 120.6, while those in the Karnes program drift slightly downward despite the hour of supplementary teaching each afternoon. The mean IQ of the children in the traditional nursery school also drifts slightly downward to a mean of 100. At the end of the second year, the mean Binet IQ of 121 for the Bereiter-Engelmann class is definitely superior to that of the other two. During the third year, in the first grade in the public school, the Bereiter-Engelmann class shows a loss of 11 points, the Karnes class a loss of 4 points, while the "traditional" class holds steady at a mean IQ of 100. At the end of the first grade, the variation of the mean IQ's for the three groups is no longer statistically significant. In terms of language age gains (ITPA) the Bereiter-Engelmann children achieved a degree of superiority at the end of their second preschool year and at the end of first grade, and both the Karnes and the Bereiter-Engelmann groups retained their superiority in performance on the Frostig developmental test of visual perception through the first grade. On the California Achievement Tests, the reading scores for the Bereiter-Engelmann group were identical to the scores obtained

by the Karnes group, and these in turn were superior to the
scores obtained by the group in the "traditional" nursery school.
These findings constitute further evidence of the importance of
language training in the curricula of compensatory education for
disadvantaged children.

The Case for Preventive Measures

The evidence outlined here indicates quite clearly that compensatory education is remedial in nature even when it is given
to the disadvantaged children of the poor at four years of age.
Moreover, from the fact that successful compensatory programs
call for high teacher-student ratios, typically of the order of 1:5,
it is abundantly clear that compensatory education is expensive.
Moreover, expensive as it is, it may all too often be too little and
too late, even at best, to overcome sufficiently the incompetence
inculcated during the first four years to enable perhaps a fifth
or a fourth of these children of the persistent poor to compensate
sufficiently in order to succeed in the public schools and to enjoy
full participation in the mainstream of our highly technological
culture. In the tradition of the Public Health Service, we need
measures to prevent incompetence. We need something which
is, at least at the superficial verbal level, analogous to innocula-
tions against smallpox. We need to develop a way to intervene
in the lives of families of poverty to enable the parents to help
their children acquire the cognitive skills, motivational systems,
and the values and standards of conduct required, first for success in school, and ultimately for full participation in the mainstream of society. We need also to intervene in the organization
of neighborhoods within the inner cities to enable these parents
of poverty, who have migrated from marginal farms during the
last 20 years, to enrich their own lives now. Again, recent investigations in attempts at innovation in early childhood education provide suggestive evidence for a promising approach to
the prevention of incompetence. The suggestion comes, first, from
considering the failures of certain kinds of innovative interventions in conjunction, second, with at least the initial promises
of success in others.

On the side of failure, clinical psychologists, psychiatrists, and social workers have attempted in a number of instances to improve the child-rearing practices of parents from chronic poverty by counseling them individually or in groups. So far as I can ascertain from the evidence I have seen, attempts to intervene by means of these psychotherapy-like approaches have failed completely to help the children of these parents.

On the other hand, Rupert Klaus & Susan Gray (1968) and their colleagues associated with the "Early Training Project" at the George Peabody College for Teachers in Nashville, Tennessee, have taken quite a different kind of attack. They developed first a special summer nursery school for disadvantaged children of poverty. The curriculum of this nursery school aimed to teach children the language skills, attitudes, and motives required for coping with the elementary school, and to serve in teaching their mothers. During the summer, home visitors brought each mother to the nursery school where the mother could see for herself not only what the teachers were doing with her child, but also the results of the teachers' approach in the behavior of her own child and of other neighborhood children familiar to her. These home visitors were certified teachers with a background which made them well acquainted with the views and attitudes of these mothers of low socioeconomic status. They interpreted for the mothers, sometimes while the mothers were observing the teachers with their children, what the teachers were doing and why. The home visitors attempted also to relate the teachers' efforts to what each mother did with her own children at home. During the periods between the summer sessions of nursery school (September to May), moreover, the home visitors saw each mother every week. During these visits, the home visitor undertook to demonstrate for each mother such matters as how to read a story with enthusiasm to a two-year-old, how to reinforce very young children for acquiring such new skills as the ability to get dressed, how to talk with them about such homely operations as peeling potatoes while in the process of peeling them. These home visitors also let the mothers discuss their own problems and helped them find new ways of coping with these problems.

At regular intervals, the examiners tested the two groups of 19 children attending the nursery school and also the two other contrast groups of children. One of the former two groups attended nursery school for three successive summers (1962, 1963, 1964) and got weekly visits during the course of three successive periods of fall-winter-spring. The other group of 19 children attended nursery school for two summers (1963 and 1964) and got weekly visits during two winters (1963-1964, 1964-1965). The two contrast groups consisted of children of families of socioeconomic education status comparable to the children in the nursery school. One of these groups lived in the same ghetto neighborhood as the families of the children in the nursery school. The other families lived in a community some 60 miles from Nashville. The examiners tested all groups at approximately the same time. The pretests were made with the 1960 edition of the Stanford-Binet, and later testings included the Wechsler Intelligence Scale for Children, the Peabody Picture Vocabulary Test (Dunn, 1959, 1965), and the Illinois Test of Psycholinguistic Abilities (Kirk & McCarthy, 1961). Once the children got into the public school, the regular tests of readiness and achievement were included.

The performances of the children on these tests showed spurts of improvement between the testings made before and after the summer sessions of the nursery school. These improvements clearly separate the children who got the nursery school and home visits from those who did not. The superiority of their test performance continued through the first grade. The results also showed two other phenomena of highly significant promise. First, the younger siblings of the children in the two nursery-school groups proved to be significantly superior on test performances to the younger siblings of children in either of the two contrast groups. This finding implies that what the mothers learned about child rearing improved their management of their younger children as well as of those attending the nursery schools. This finding Klaus and Gray call "vertical diffusion." Second, the children of the contrast groups who lived in the same ghetto neighborhood as those attending the nursery school and receiving the home visits gave performances on the tests significantly superior to the performances of children living some 60 miles away. This finding, termed "horizontal diffusion" by Klaus and Gray, suggests that these mothers who had learned new child-rearing practices were somehow communicating them to their neighbors to a significant degree. Other innovators, like Ira Gordon (1969) and Ronald Lally of the University of Florida, also appear to be finding evidences of both "vertical diffusion" and "horizontal diffusion." Moreover, the Demonstration and Research Center for Early Education has underway another project not unlike the "Early Training Project" of Klaus & Gray (1968) in which the evidence of improved test performance is even more substantial. This has been reported in preliminary fashion by Miller (1968).

Another innovative program of intervention at the University of Illinois, under the direction of Merle Karnes and her associates, has demonstrated that the mothers of highly disadvantaged preschool children can be taught to be effective teachers of their own children. In one of these studies, Karnes, Studley, Wright, & Hodgins (1968) selected as subjects 30 children between the ages of three years and three months and four years and three months from families known to the school authorities to be among the most economically and educationally deprived in a neighborhood with the lowest socioeconomic status of the community. The 30 children were divided into a control and experimental group. Subjects in neither group were enrolled in a preschool. The mothers of the control children were not enrolled in any program while the mothers of the experimental children attended a short-term training program where they made instructional materials and learned to use them to teach their children at home. The mothers of these children were paid $3.00 a session. This hourly rate of $1.50 was selected to approximate the usual wage of such working mothers to prevent economic loss. The mothers attended 11 weekly two-hour sessions in the neighborhood elementary school. These sessions were led by three preschool teachers each of whom was responsible for a group of five mothers. The teachers encouraged the mothers to believe that their assistance was highly needed in order to develop and test educational activities for preschool children.

In the first portion of each session, the mothers made such inexpensive educational materials as a sock puppet; a homemade flannel board; lotto and matching games made with gummed seals, with geometric shapes, and with color chips; counting books made from magazine pictures; sorting and matching activities utilizing miscellaneous household items and an egg carton for a sorting tray; and classifying activities based on pictures cut from furniture and clothing catalogs. The teachers also taught the mothers appropriate songs and finger plays, and distributed copies as a teaching aid at home. Finally, books were made available for the mothers to take home for use with their children during the following week.

After these materials had been made, groups discussed appropriate ways to use them at home during the following week. The teachers repeatedly emphasized the importance of combining language with all of the activities planned. They also involved the mothers in role playing to demonstrate for each other the various ways of using the materials. Finally, each teacher visited each of the mothers in her group at two-week intervals in order to become acquainted with the child, to offer further teaching suggestions, and to help evaluate the appropriateness of the activities for the particular children.

Pretests and post-tests with the 1960 Stanford-Binet Scale and the Illinois Test of Psycholinguistic Abilities (ITPA) were given by trained examiners who knew nothing about the study or the circumstances of each child. What is especially interesting for our discussion here is the fact that these mothers, as teachers, obtained gains in Binet IQ over the relatively short period of 12 weeks averaging 7.46 points. This gain is to be compared with the mean gain for the control group of .07 points of IQ (P < .05). The mothers also effected statistically significant gains on three of the subtests of the ITPA, namely, visual decoding, auditory-vocal association, and auditory-vocal sequential.

In another study of the feasibility of teaching mothers of poverty to become effective teachers of their children, Karnes (1969) has compared the test gains of four-year-olds taught by mothers who received inservice training and supervision with the test gains made by children matched for age, intelligence, sex, and socioeconomic status and taught by professional teachers. Both groups implemented the Karnes structured preschool program. Those children taught by mothers gained in mean Binet IQ from 93.4 to 105.9 (a gain of 12.5 points); those taught by professional teachers gained from 96.0 to 110.3 (14.3 points). The difference between these two gains in mean Binet IQ of 1.8 is both negligible and nonsignificant. The other tests given in this study included the ITPA, the Frostig (1964) developmental test for visual perception, and the Metropolitan Test of School Readiness. Although the gains in the scores on each of these tests obtained by the mothers was slightly less than that obtained by professional teachers, none of the differences even approached statistical significance. When this same kind of study was repeated and teen-agers, enrolled in a high school work-study program, served as preschool teachers in the Karnes program, the children obtained gains on the various tests similar to those made by children taught by professional staff.

Inasmuch as the parents of children promise to be the least expensive teachers and the most appropriate teachers of their children during the early years, these findings are highly promising.

These investigations have also turned up evidence that when parents become actively involved in such projects concerned with the education of their own children, the experience enriches their own lives. Miller (1968) points out that over half of the mothers participating in the repetition and extension of the "Early Training Project" have been encouraged to complete their high school education or have enrolled in courses to upgrade their vocational skills. About one-fourth of the mothers in this project have enrolled in or completed the training to become licensed practical nurses, and several have completed courses in cosmetology. None of the mothers who have participated in the nursery school and home-visiting program are now employed as domestics, and half of those who were originally employed as domestics have upgraded their employment status. Two of these mothers who were originally illiterate have now gained reading skills at the third- or fourth-grade level. The experience appears also to have led to a greater concern with community affairs. One of the mothers in this project has joined in the elections of the Metropolitan Action Council of Nashville; two others have served on the Council's board for the Head Start program, and several have served on their church boards. On their own initiative, the families in this project have developed a parent organization which plans cooperative picnics, outings for the families on weekends, has developed a rotating book library, and even organized a mother-father bowling league. Increases in savings accounts and checking accounts are also demonstrable. One family of most desperate means has shown such improvement in the furnishing of their home and in the care of the grounds around their apartment that neighbors have remarked to the home visitor of this family's progress through involvement in the project. As further evidence of the horizontal diffusion, the home visitors in this project have repeatedly been asked into the homes of nonparticipating families to observe and to evaluate the educational experiences which these nonparticipating parents are providing for their own children. Clearly, such evidence, while it is difficult to quantify, is highly important. It attests that the lives of these parents have been enriched by their participation in these programs aimed at improving the educational opportunities of their young.

Similar evidence of enrichment in the lives of the parents was found in the Karnes program. There was observable improvement in the organization within the families and homes of many of the 20 mothers of infants who participated in a training program. Interestingly, these mothers agreed that if they were to be proper teachers of their young, they dare not have a new child each year. They therefore sought the aid of the Association of Planned Parenthood "to get on the pill."

If taken in conjunction, failures of professional psychotherapy-like counseling and the promise of illustrative demonstrations combined with explanation and participation are highly instructive. Attempting to modify the child-rearing practices of parents by means of professional talk alone fails. Perhaps this should not surprise us inasmuch as one of the chief characteristics of such parents is their lack of facility in linguistic communication. On the other hand, these same parents of poverty can learn im-

proved ways of child rearing from opportunities to observe the
ways of relatively expert teachers and to observe the effects of
the experts' approaches on the children's behavior, especially
when these effects are then explained in language which they
can understand. Moreover, these parents are able to communicate through demonstration and talk these improved practices
in child rearing to their neighbors. In Nashville, this communication can often be observed in informal back-porch gatherings
through a process of demonstrations which imitate those of the
home visitors. This finding, combined with the evidence of the
enrichment in the lives of the participants, provides a substantial
hope of preventing the incompetence almost universal now in
the children of families living in slum neighborhoods.

Centers for Parents and Children

Such findings, coupled with observational evidence that parents from a background of poverty love their children quite as
much as any parents, suggest a mode of intervening in community organization which fits well with the tradition of the
Public Health Service and with what is now called Community
Mental Health. This mode of intervening promises not only to
serve as an effective way of preventing incompetence; it also
promises to have a salutory side effect in reducing the fearful
impersonality of the newly formed slum neighborhoods of the
inner cities of our megalopoli.

The intervention suggested would take the form of Parent
and Child Centers. Such Centers should provide an open door
where the families in a region, numbering perhaps two or three
thousand, could obtain the full range of services available within
their communities either directly or through informed and skilled
referral. Moreover, the Centers would mobilize the concern of
these parents for their children's welfare by providing the leadership required to develop day-care facilities for infants and toddlers, and Head-Start-like facilities for children of three, four, and
five years within the more limited neighborhoods. These Centers
should provide not only the professional personnel for these
facilities, but also the leadership required to get the fathers,

the older siblings, and the older children to take their turns as teachers' aides in conducting these facilities. The professional persons in charge would thereby serve as models for these parents and for the older children. Moreover, demonstrators for child-rearing and educational practices should be sent into the homes to show mothers and fathers how to apply these new practices, illustrated within the day-care facilities, within the home situation. These home demonstrators or visitors should, following the lead of Klaus & Gray (1968), of Karnes (1969), and of Weikart & Lambie (1967), demonstrate such down-to-earth matters as how to reinforce behavioral evidences of new competence, how to tell stories about pictures to children as young as 18 months, how to read a story with enthusiasm to a two-year-old, how to talk to children about the various home-making operations while engaged in them, how to ask questions which prompt the child to note the observable characteristics of objects and their relationships, and how to ask questions which require children to verbally describe those characteristics and their relationships. In addition, for the benefit of the older preschool children, these professionals should show both the parents and the older siblings how to conduct a field trip while talking about the sights and sounds of the resources of the community, the parks, the museums, and even the industrial operations.

If I have properly understood the basis for the highly promising results of such successful innovations as that of Klaus and Gray and that of Karnes, children reared under such a regime should be much less incompetent and much better able to cope with the traditional schools than those now coming from our slum families. As a side effect, Parent and Child Centers should yield a basic security and enrichment for the lives of the parents themselves. In utilizing the love of these parents for their children in order to help motivate them to cooperate to create and to operate the children's facilities, it is very likely that the parents and older siblings of the infants and young children will form warm friendships and will develop something of a future orientation. It is likely that they will develop a new level of pride in their neighborhood which will foster that interdependence which should do much to damp the hostility which has grown out of the existing frustration of life in the slums of our megalopoli.

This is but the barest outline of what looks hypothetically like a promising prescription that fits nicely the tradition of the Public Health Service. It might equally well become a new function of our educational system. It utilizes the findings of behavioral science rather than biological science to cope with the major problems of living. It is a prescription which needs trying.

This prescription will take considerable trial and error before we become skilled in the creation of such Centers. As we learn how to produce and to conduct them, spreading them widely will call for a new kind of education and create new kinds of employment opportunity. These opportunities can be expected to range in educational level from the high school for various paraprofessionals, through junior college and college for various professional administrative groups, to the doctoral level for those who will investigate the operation of such programs and formulate the principles whereby they best succeed.

In his message to Congress of 8 February 1967, President Johnson recommended such an approach. The Office of Economic Opportunity has been authorized to establish approximately 25 such Centers on an experimental basis in order to enable us to learn how to organize them before any attempt is made to deploy them generally across the nation if their hypothetical promise is realized.

In conclusion, let me say that the new evidence makes it no longer sensible to consider the incompetence of the children of parents from a background of poverty, be they black or white, as an inevitable consequence of their biological constitution and inherited nature. This new evidence is the basis for a justified hope that much of this incompetence and much of the fearful frustration and impersonality of the inner-city slums within our megalopoli can be changed. We of the behavioral sciences and their applications in education and mental health still have a long way to go. Perhaps, however, our investigations and innovations have at least produced a start toward some guidelines for the immediate implementation of a program in early childhood education which corresponds in many ways to the traditions of the Public Health Service.

7

Poverty Versus Equality of Opportunity

Poverty is coming to be viewed in a new perspective. As recently as two decades ago, those persistently poor were typically seen as just naturally inept, stupid, lazy, and irresponsible. The children of those persistently poor were observed to manifest a combination of such characteristics when they entered school at only five or six years of age. On tests of intelligence, they had low IQ's (see Anastasi, 1958). Once in school, they gave poor attention to school tasks and to teachers' utterances. Moreover, they were often hard to control. In short, these children already manifested the signs of that incompetence characterizing their parents. Because these various indicators of incompetence were already present so early in the children of the poor, they were presumed to be inherited from their inept, stupid, lazy, and irresponsible parents.

In a sense these indicators of incompetence are inherited, but less through the genes of these children than through their interaction with their parents and with the circumstances of their poverty. Our conception of the role of the circumstances which a child encounters, especially during infancy and very early

This paper, now somewhat modified, was originally prepared for presentation on 22 June 1967 at the Institute for Research on Poverty organized by Vernon L. Allen at the University of Wisconsin in Madison. Reprinted by permission from V. L. Allen, ed., *Psychological Factors in Poverty* (Chicago: Markham, 1969).

childhood, in the development of intelligence, of motivation, and of those values and patterns of conduct required for an organized society has been changing. This newly recognized role of circumstances in early psychological development has obvious implications for our beliefs about the basis for the deficits in intellectual skills and in motivation so prevalent among the children of the poor when they start to school. It now appears very likely that these children arrive at the public school with their various defects because in large part they have not had the opportunities required to develop the linguistic and numeric skills basic to normal performance on intelligence tests, or the motivational systems required for attention to teacher talk, or the habits of conduct required for teacher control and approval. Let me summarize the background of the problem.

Historical Background

When our forefathers declared it to be self-evident that "all men are created equal," they uttered biological and psychological nonsense. But they were not thinking in terms either biological or psychological. Their concerns were ethical and political. In these latter terms that equality of opportunity, which is the essence of their declaration, is the basic foundation for a democratic society.

So long as biological and behavioral development were believed to be programmed, and intelligence was believed to be fixed by each individual's heredity, those persistently poor of the bottom socioeconomic class could readily be accepted as just naturally inept, lazy, and irresponsible. In the light of these too widely held beliefs, any improvements in this class of human beings had to look entirely to eugenics and to Francis Galton who founded the eugenic movement (see Hunt, 1961, Ch. 2). So long as the beliefs in predetermined development and fixed intelligence prevailed, no reason existed to extend the ethical implications of the equality of opportunity to those condemned by the accident of their birth to develop in the circumstances and the child-rearing practices of parents in poverty.

These beliefs in predetermined development and fixed intelligence never went unquestioned. They were questioned by those sociologists who took their lead from the thought and writings of Lester F. Ward (1883). They were also questioned, and ironically, by Alfred Binet (1909), whose tests became standard in the intelligence testing movement whose American leaders came, largely through the influence of Sir Francis Galton and G. Stanley Hall, to consider intelligence to be essentially fixed. Finally, they were called into question by Freud (1905), at least for the origin of emotional and motivational characteristics. Nevertheless, these beliefs in predetermined development and fixed intelligence dominated thought among a preponderant majority of the leaders of psychology and education and among a major share of the intellectual leaders of America from the latter days of the nineteenth-century debates over Darwin's theory of evolution through World War II.

Even before World War II, bits of suggestive evidence dissonant with these beliefs began to appear, but the beliefs were so firmly held that the leaders of educational and psychological thought made every effort to discredit the dissonant evidence. The evidence in a study by Skeels & Dye (1939) is an example. In this study, every one of a group of 13 retarded infants, who were transferred from an orphanage to a women's ward in an Iowa State School for the Mentally Retarded where the women doted on them, showed gains in IQ ranging from 7 to 58 points during periods ranging from 6 to 52 months. Another group of 12 somewhat less retarded infants who were allowed to remain in the orphanage showed decreases in IQ varying from 8 to 45 points over periods ranging from 20 to 43 months. These findings met with derisive skepticism (Goodenough, 1939) and methodological criticism (McNemar, 1940) which deprived them of the suggestive, corrective value that they deserved to have. But this state of affairs was only temporary. After World War II, evidence clearly dissonant with beliefs in preprogrammed development and fixed intelligence began accumulating. Let me synopsize at least the nature of these various kinds of evidence.

Evidence Dissonant with the Beliefs in Preprogrammed
Development and Fixed Intelligence

First, within genetics, the work of Johannsen (1909) has been given recognition equal to that of Mendel (1865). Johannsen distinguished the observable *phenotype* from the *genotype*, which consists of the genes comprising an individual's hereditary constitution, and did the pioneering demonstrations that the phenotype is a product of the genotype's interactions with the circumstances encountered. These demonstrations served to correct the misinterpretation of Mendel's work in the view that observable, measurable characteristics are predetermined by heredity. Thus, when even the sexual anatomy of genotypic male, snowpool mosquitoes have been shown to develop female parts when the eggs and larvae undergo their embryonic maturation in unusually high temperatures (Anderson & Horsfall, 1963; Horsfall, Anderson, & Burst, 1964), it becomes hardly surprising that the developmental quotients and intelligence quotients of infants or young children change markedly with the circumstances they encounter (see Jones, 1954). This concept of interactionism, deriving originally from Johannsen's work, has the important implication that children of different genotypes may need different kinds of circumstances to enable them to achieve their potential of competence.

Second, studies of the effects of dietary deficiency and emotional stress in both animal and human females at the time of conception and during gestation have yielded evidence suggesting that these conditions tend to produce disorders of pregnancy and premature delivery. These disorders of pregnancy hamper the embryonic and fetal development of infant organisms and result in what Pasamanick & Knobloch (1960) term minimal brain damage (see also Bell, 1965, pp. 4-6).

Third, the theorizing of Donald Hebb (1949) has inspired a variety of investigations which indicate that the problem-solving ability of animals is far from fixed by their genotype. Hebb (1947) himself and such colleagues as Forgays & Forgays (1952), Forgus (1955a, 1955b), and Hymovitch (1952) have found that rats reared under various kinds of enriched perceptual circumstances are better solvers of maze problems as adults than littermates reared in opaque laboratory cages. Moreover, Thompson & Heron (1954) have found superiority in the problem-solving ability in pet-reared Scottie dogs over their cage-reared littermates that is, if anything, more pronounced than the degree of superiority that Hebb (1947) found for pet-reared rats over their cage-reared littermates. Such evidence, of which this is but a sample, suggests that the importance of early experience for later problem-solving ability probably increases up the evolutionary scale. Against this suggestion, perhaps, is the evidence from studies of the effects of rearing monkeys in solitude (Angermeier, Phelps, & Reynolds, 1967; Griffin & Harlow, 1966). Such monkeys are deficient in social skills, but they acquire the learning-set to use pattern cues as readily as monkeys reared by their mothers. Whether the number of trials required to use a pattern cue instead of a place cue should be the criterion of problem-solving ability is a matter of both definition and investigation. It is quite conceivable that such a learning-set requires the acquisition of no others below it in the hypothetical hierarchy of abilities constituting intelligence whereas the detour tests (Hebb & Williams, 1946) do require rats and dogs to learn subordinate abilities if they are to solve the detour problems readily. This question of the operational criteria for problem-solving ability in animal subjects calls for much more careful analysis than it has so far received.

Fourth, at least three different lines of investigation indicate that encounters with circumstances appear to influence the maturation of new anatomy as well as the development of behavior. Studies of the histological and histochemical effects of rearing young animals in the dark has shown that glial cells and retinal-ganglion cells fail to mature properly and that the production of ribonucleic acid (RNA) is deficient in chimpanzees (Rasch, Swift, Riesen, & Chow, 1961), in kittens (Weiskrantz, 1958), in rabbits (Brattgård, 1952), and rats (Liberman, 1962) reared in darkness. Conversely, evidence of increased growth in cortical tissue and of higher total acetylcholinesterase activity of the cortex has been found in rats reared in complex environments than in rats reared in the simpler environments of laboratory cages (Altman & Das, 1964; Bennett, Diamond, Krech, & Rosenzweig, 1964). Some of these studies have stemmed from the theorizing of Donald Hebb (Rasch, Swift, Riesen, & Chow, 1961). Those of Bennett, Diamond, Krech, & Rosenzweig (1964) have shown with the increased complexity of the environment not only the anatomical and biochemical changes in the brain but also increased ability to solve maze problems. The study by Brattgård (1952) stems from the biochemical theorizing of Hydén (1960), and the work of Hydén & Egyhazi (1962) has also indicated increased production of ribonucleic acid in brain tissue following learning which contrasts with the depression of RNA production in the retinae of rabbits reared in the dark.

Fifth, bits of evidence uncovered by various investigators indicate that the rate of psychological development in human infants is far more plastic than has been believed. White & Held (1966), for instance, have reduced the median ages of the appearance in two landmarks in the development of eye-hand coordination very substantially. Fisted swiping at objects presented to view has appeared at median ages of 72 days, 75 days, and 55 days, depending upon circumstances. Top-level reaching for objects presented to view, that is to say, reaching with the hand shaped in anticipation for grasping, has appeared at median ages of 145 days, 105 days, and 87 days. They achieved this hastening by means of a program of enrichment which included handling the infants some 20 minutes a day, turning them on their stomachs for 15 minutes after each of three feedings a day, and arranging a complex stabile for the infants to view and to feel with their hands. Inasmuch as the difference between 105 days and 87 days for top-level reaching involved a change in the opportunity for looking with no change in other enrichments, the looking is probably the most important of the three elements in their enrichment program. In the familiar terms of the IQ ratio, this change from 145 days to 87 days in the median age for top-level reaching is an increase of the order of 67 points. In my own laboratory, David Greenberg, Ina Uzgiris, and I (1968) have found that infant children of middle-class parents in Champaign-Urbana who were provided with an opportunity for looking at a stabile hung over the cribs, beginning at five weeks of age, manifested the blink-response to an object rapidly approaching their eyes at an average age of seven weeks, while other comparable infants, whose mothers agreed not to put anything over their cribs, failed to show this blink-response until an average age of 10.4 weeks. In the familiar terms of the IQ ratio, this is an increase of the order of 48 points. It should be understood that hastening the appearance of eye-hand coordination and of the blink-response can have in itself hardly any permanent significance for the development of competence, but these findings do illustrate the plasticity of that early development in human infants once considered to be predetermined in rate.

Sixth, a variety of investigations has yielded evidence that the longer organisms live under any given kind of circumstances, whether they foster or hamper development, the harder it is to alter the influence of these circumstances on either anatomy or behavior (Hunt, 1961, p. 321ff, Ch. 6, p. 150). Moreover, Bloom (1964) has assembled evidence from longitudinal studies of the development of abilities, attitudes, interests, and values to show that the stability of measures of these various human characteristics increases substantially with age. For tested intelligence, for instance, about half the variance in IQ's at age 17 is accounted for by test scores given at age four. The plasticity of infancy diminishes rapidly as children grow older. Thus, the longer children live under the stultifying conditions of poverty, the harder it must inevitably be to overcome the deficit resulting.

Seventh, a new hierarchical conception of intelligence is replacing that of intelligence as a fixed dimension of individual persons (see Chapter 3). This hierarchical conception has been proposed on the basis of such radically differing kinds of evidence as the developmental observations of Piaget (1936), the findings of factor analysis by Ferguson (1954, 1956) and by Humphreys (1959, 1962b), and the investigations of adult problem-solving by Gagné (1966b) and Gagné & Paradise (1961). In the light of this new hierarchical conception of intelligence, such increases in the rate of development as are evidenced by hastening the appearance of eye-hand coordinations and the blink-response suggest that the effects of the circumstances encountered may

be cumulative. In this hierarchical conception, such simple sensorimotor organizations become incorporated in more complex
organizations through a process of coordination. When such
simple sensorimotor organizations are hastened, they then become available for coordination with others into more complex
organizations at an earlier age, and these coordinations of coordinations then become available for still more complex organizations at an earlier age. We must investigate this theoretical
suggestion of an accumulative effect from circumstances that
continuously interest and challenge infants and very young children.

Eighth, investigations in the domain of social trends in intelligence indicate increases in tested intelligence where, from the
fact that about 60 per cent of each new generation comes from
that bottom third of the population in socioeconomic-educational
status with a mean IQ of about 85 (see Anastasi, 1958, p. 515),
decreases were predicted. Some 13 years after Cattell (1937)
estimated a drop of a little over three points of IQ for each generation, or of about one point a decade, he published a comparison of the tested intelligence of 10-year-olds living in
the city of Leicester in 1949 with that of those living there in
1936 and found an increase in the mean IQ of 1.28 points (Cattell, 1950a). Other studies have disconfirmed the predicted drop
in IQ with increases substantially larger. A study of children
from a sample of families tested before and then a decade after
the social changes instituted by the Tennessee Valley Authority
uncovered a mean increase of 10 points (Wheeler, 1942). One
of students in a sample of Minnesota high schools, tested first in
the 1920's and again in the 1940's, uncovered gains in means for
the various high schools ranging between 10 and 15 points of
IQ (Finch, 1946). One of children in a sample of schools in
Honolulu, first tested in 1924 and again in 1938, uncovered an
increase in the mean IQ of 20 points (Smith, 1942). Similar evidence of increases has come from comparing the test performances of soldiers of World War I with those of soldiers of
World War II on the military tests of intelligence (Tuddenham, 1948). Perhaps the most dramatic evidence comes from
Puerto Rico where Albizu-Miranda (1966) found children of

seven and eight, who have enjoyed during their early development some of the advantages of the prosperity brought by the
new industrialization, with mental ages as high as or higher than
those of their parents, who had been reared in rural poverty
before industrialization came to Puerto Rico, and who were
tested at the same time as the children.

Finally, recent findings of Wayne Dennis (1966) suggest that
the variations in tested intelligence deriving from the circumstances under which infants and young children are reared are
larger than has been imagined. Dennis has given Goodenough's
(1926) Draw-a-Man Test to groups of typical children, aged
from six to eight years, from some 50 cultures over the world.
Goodenough proposed this test to be culture free, but this assumption was called into question when typical Hopi Indian
children turned up with a mean IQ of 124 (Dennis, 1942). This
mean IQ of 124 approximates the means for samples of children
of the suburbs in both America and England. This same mean
holds for samples of children growing up in Japanese fishing
villages (Dennis, 1966). At the other end of the distribution,
Dennis (1966) finds nomadic Bedouin children with an average
IQ of 52. Here, then, is a range of approximately 70 points in
mean IQ for typical groups of children from these various cultures over the world. It is extremely unlikely that such a range
can have hereditary determination. The most obvious correlate
is degree of contact with pictorial art. Hopi children, like the
children growing up in Japanese fishing villages, and like
the children of the suburbs in both America and Britain, have
continual contact with pictorial art. On the other hand, in the
Moslem Arabic countries where religion prohibits graven images,
the children have relatively little contact with pictorial arts, and
Draw-a-Man IQ's are low. But even among Arabic subcultures
the variation is large. Thus, the nomadic Bedouin children and
the Shilluk children of the Sudan, with almost no such contact,
have a mean Draw-a-Man IQ of 52 and 53. On the other hand,
the children of Lebanon, with a high degree of contact with
Western culture and with the pictorial arts inherent in Western
culture, have a mean Draw-a-Man IQ of 98. Thus the range of
mean IQ's even among samples of Arab children is of the order

of 45 points. Because the complex of abilities assessed with the Draw-a-Man Test is probably simpler than the complex of abilities assessed with the Stanford-Binet or the Wechsler Children's Scale, it may well be easier to modify the Draw-a-Man IQ by means of contact with pictorial arts than it would be to modify in the same degree IQ's from these other tests through encounters with variations in circumstances. Nevertheless, this finding by Dennis suggests that variations in circumstances may alter the intelligence underlying competence to a degree hitherto not suspected.

From the standpoint of longitudinal prediction, clearly the IQ of a child based on a test given at a very early age cannot tell what his performance on such tests will be later without solid knowledge of the circumstances under which he is to live. In the light of these various kinds of evidence, the beliefs in predetermined development and in fixed intelligence are hardly any longer tenable.

Ethical Implications

Now, if the genotype guarantees neither the rate nor the course of psychological development, and if circumstances can have effects of such magnitude on the outcome level of competence, the accident of being born to parents who have themselves grown up under the conditions of persistent poverty may well be, and indeed must be, depriving the children of poverty of the opportunity to develop those intellectual abilities and the motivation which exists within their hereditary potential. In the light of such considerations, the ethical and political doctrine of equal opportunity takes on new implications and creates new ethical obligations for our political system. Such children, by the accident of their birth, become deprived of the opportunity to develop those intellectual abilities and those motivational systems required for coping successfully with our schools. As a consequence, they are deprived, in turn, of the opportunity to participate in the mainstream of our society and to partake of the benefits of our technological advances. If we take seriously the declaration of our forefathers that equality of opportunity is a birthright of all, we are ethically bound to try to do everything in our power to equalize the opportunity of children born to parents in poverty. The new evidence makes of early childhood education an ethical matter and a political issue.

Implications for Two Challenges of Our Day

Two major challenges of our day emphasize the ethical importance of this issue. One of them is our advancing technology. The other is the recognition of the evils of racial segregation in the Supreme Court decision of 1954 which demands desegregation.

These two challenges are intertwined. The consequences of our advancing technology have probably been most evident during the past few years in agriculture. With the industrial revolution coming to the farms, it is said that more people have moved from the farms to the cities during the past 20 years than moved from the farms to the cities since Europeans came to North America until World War II. Most of those moving have been marginal farmers. They have been the rural poor. A large share of them have been black sharecroppers from the South. They have lacked both money and skills, and the new machines have destroyed their livelihood and their way of life. Because they have typically heard of more economic opportunities and bigger welfare allowances in the North, they have flocked to the slums in the centers of our cities. Here is a major source of the dire contemporary plight of our inner cities. Here is also one of the most important instances wherein our advancing technology is reducing, and reducing drastically, the economic opportunities for those with limited competence. At the very same time, our advancing technology is markedly increasing the opportunities of those with high-level competence. Back in the 1930's, even those with newly acquired doctorates were a drug on the market. Now the problem not only for those with new Ph.D. degrees, but also for those with new baccalaureate degrees and with new certificates from courses for mechanical, secretarial, and trade skills, is one of choice. Openings abound for those with technical skills at all educational levels from high school graduation up.

The intertwining of these challenges from our advancing technology and from the Supreme Court decision of 1954 derives from the fact that a major share of our black people have been kept persistently poor ever since they were released from the legal bondage of slavery. Desegregation and integration are necessary in achieving the equality of opportunity for all men that our forefathers declared to be a birthright. But desegregation of schools is not enough. Moreover, in the absence of compensatory opportunities for the children of the very poor, it may actually be harmful.

Let me explain. Although children build their concepts of themselves in part from the way they are viewed and talked about by the adults with whom they come in contact, they build a major share of their hopes for themselves by comparing their own achievements and performances with the achievements and performances of other children with whom they interact and compete (Diggory, 1966). When children ages five and six without the experiences that give perceptual and manipulative familiarity with the things and places that are taken for granted by teachers and with very limited ability to understand verbal directions, numbers, and rules of conduct are put together in our traditionally competitive schools with children who have had these experiences and have considerably higher levels of these abilities, no one has to tell the children of the poor that they are failing. Any light of hope they may have brought to the school is all too quickly dimmed or extinguished by their sense of failure from their encounters with children of another world who are obviously, to them, their betters. If frustration instigates aggressive behavior, as we psychologists have long contended (Dollard *et al.*, 1939), it is hardly surprising that aggressive behavior becomes common among these children of the poor when they enter such schools. As their own hopes become extinguished, neither is it surprising that they tend to drop out of school at the earliest opportunity. Until something is done to change the traditional use of the lockstep and of competition in our schools, merely putting those culturally deprived, be they white or black, together with those culturally privileged can only make matters worse for those deprived. Where most of those culturally deprived are black, desegregation may actually exacerbate *their* problem.

Opportunities Lacking for Children of the Poor

Ever since Francis Galton (1869) published his studies of hereditary genius, and perhaps long before, the existence of a substantial positive correlation betwen socioeconomic status and competence has been abundantly clear. Evidence continuing to confirm this association has continued to accumulate. The soldiers of World War I from the professional classes averaged substantially higher scores on the Army Alpha than did skilled manual workers, and the latter averaged higher scores than did the unskilled (Fryer, 1922). In World War II, the Army General Classification Test revealed the same relationship. Accountants and teachers had average scores in the 120's while such laboring groups as miners and farm workers had average scores in the upper 80's. Moreover, when the children who served in the standardization of the revision of the Stanford-Binet were classified according to parental occupation, the preschool children of semiprofessional and professional families had mean IQ's between 110 and 115 while those preschool children from the families of day laborers had an average IQ of only approximately 94 (McNemar, 1942). Children of both rural and urban poverty have typically shown mean IQ's substantially lower than those of day laborers. Sherman & Key (1932) have found children living in the hollows of the Blue Ridge Mountains averaging in the low 80's at age 6-8 years and decreasing with age so that those aged 10-12 were averaging in the 50's and 60's. Similarly, Gordon (1923) found the English canal-boat children with mean IQ's of about 90 at age 4-6 and decreasing to a mean of about 60 at age 12-22 years. Klineberg (1935) found the average IQ's of various samples of black youths from the poverty of the southern states before World War II to be even lower than 60. It is from such backgrounds that the new poor of our urban centers of the 1960's have come. Their children do poorly in school (Bloom, Davis, & Hess, 1965).

Until recently, Galton's causal interpretation has been the one most commonly accepted. That lack of competence found in those of low socioeconomic status has been attributed to their lack of hereditary potential. In the light of this traditional interpretation, much of the evidence already described in the earlier papers of this collection is highly puzzling. More puzzling evidence appears in a recent study by Lesser, Fifer, & Clark (1965). These investigators tested a large group of first-grade children who were divided according to both socioeconomic and ethnic background. They compared the subgroups both in terms of average scores across the several kinds of tests and in terms of patterns of scores in the several kinds of tests. Social class was associated chiefly with average score across all tests, the higher the socioeconomic class the higher the general level of ability as measured by the test. Ethnic background was associated, however, with the pattern of scores on the several tests. Chinese, Jewish, Negro, and Puerto Rican children differed substantially in terms of the several tests on which they showed high scores and on which they showed low scores. These ethnic differences in pattern were consistent, moreover, across levels of socioeconomic status. Thus, even though the children of low socioeconomic status from each ethnic background had average scores for all the various tests below the average scores for those of higher socioeconomic status from the same ethnic background, lower-class Jewish children manifested the same pattern of abilities as did higher-class Jewish children, and lower-class Chinese children showed the same pattern as higher-class Chinese children, etc. Unless one presumes that these ethnic patterns are based on hereditary patterns of potential in these cultural and racial groups, it is hard to explain such variations in pattern without appealing to cultural differences in the circumstances provided for developing children. The question is: are there variations in circumstances and in opportunities associated with poverty which could account for the generally low levels of tested abilities so commonly found in children of poverty from all cultural backgrounds?

BASIC BIOLOGICAL REQUIREMENTS

First of all, many of the children of the poor lack even the basic requirements of their biological well-being and growth. Nutritional deficiencies and emotional stress in mothers of poverty at about the time of conception and during pregnancy may well hamper the development of their infants in utero during the embryonic and fetal phases (Cravioto, 1964; Pasamanick, 1962). McDonald (1966) has reported incidents of chronic health problems almost four times as high among the families of the poor (incomes under $2,000) as they are among families with average or higher incomes (from $7,000 up). These nutritional differences sometimes lead to strange cravings. Liebow (1967) has reported that pregnant women of the poor sometimes crave starch and some have been known to eat as many as four boxes of Argo laundry starch a day. Inadequate diets, especially for pregnant women, are a likely cause of higher infant mortality, prematurity, and birth defects among the poor. When the fetus survives birth, the result is all too commonly an infant of high vulnerability (Pasamanick, 1962). The later fate of these infants of high vulnerability is, however, in considerable measure a function of the circumstances that they encounter during the first months and years after birth (Lois Murphy, 1961, 1968). Unfortunately, in families of poverty, these vulnerable infants typically encounter circumstances which further compound their vulnerability and tendency to defect.

COGNITIVE SKILLS

These children of poverty lack, second, many opportunities to develop cognitive skills. They lack especially the circumstances which foster linguistic skills, numerical skills, and the syntax of standard language in which the abstractions of cognitive content are couched.

During their first year, these children are often reared in crowded quarters where loud voices and the blare of television or radio are jumbled continuously. At a time when I thought amount of stimulation itself might help to foster psychological development, I thought this might possibly be to the advantage of the children of the poor during the first year (see Chapter 1). On the other hand, as Clark & Richards (1966) have found, the children of the poor do a poorer job of discriminating vocal patterns of sound than do children of the middle class. In this connection, Cynthia Deutsch (1964) has suggested some similar findings that children of the poor learn to "tune out" the noises they hear. I am inclined to agree that an attentional factor is involved, but I now suspect that it is not an active "tuning out." Rather, I suspect that continual exposure to loud, vocal sounds sequentially unassociated with such significant events as the smiling face of a mother, being picked up, and/or being fed, leads to an habituation of the arousal aspect of the orienting response to loud vocal inputs such as that demonstrated experimentally by Sharpless & Jasper (1956) in cats. Maltzman & Raskin (1965) have found that kinds of input for which the orienting response is weak or absent served poorly as conditional stimuli in classical conditioning and as cure in more complex learning tasks. This finding strongly suggests that habituation to loud vocalization in infancy may serve indefinitely to damp the capacity to attend to vocalizations, to discriminate among them, and thereby to learn language efficiently.

But these infants of the poor lack several other kinds of opportunities to acquire these cognitive skills (McCandless, 1952). Their parents typically spend less time in verbal interaction with them than do the parents of the middle class (Keller, 1963; Milner, 1951). When they are communicating with their children, these parents verbalize in sequences substantially shorter than those of middle-class parents (Cynthia Deutsch, 1964). It is this relative paucity and impoverishment of communication between mothers of poverty and their children, as compared with mothers of the middle class and their children, which Hess & Shipman (1965) have considered to be at the heart of the lack of language and number skills in children of poverty.

What parents of poverty talk about may be another factor. Their talk may be rich in emotional content and in the similes of such content, but highly lacking in what calls upon the child to abstract such aspects of objects as their color, their shape, and their size in relation to other objects. What these parents talk about is also lacking in such conceptual constructions as prepositional relationships, causal explanations, and concepts of space, time, and justice (my own unsystematic observations combined with the reports of Deutsch, 1965; and Hess & Shipman, 1965). The parents of the slums not only talk less with their children than do parents of the middle class, but they seldom undertake to discuss with their children matters which prompt them to discern various kinds of relationships among things and people or to use language to describe these relationships. Similarly, these parents seldom discuss with their children the whys of decisions or the outcomes of various courses of action. Such elements of parent-child communication are components of the warm democratic atmosphere found by Baldwin, Kalhorn, & Breese (1945) to be associated with rising IQ's (see Baldwin, 1955, p. 523). On the contrary, when the children of the poor ask questions or talk out, their parents typically respond with "shut up" without saying why (Bronfenbrenner, 1958; Chilman, 1965). Incidentally, there is a world of difference between a simple "shut up," and a statement such as: "shut up, can't you see I'm talking on the telephone." In view of such considerations, it is hardly surprising that recognition vocabulary, vocabulary of use, length of remarks, and complexity of sentence forms in the children of poverty fall substantially below the norms for the tests of these abilities (Jones, 1966).

Finally, parents of the slums have seldom learned the syntax of standard language, so they serve as poor imitative models for their children (Bernstein, 1960, 1961; John & Goldstein, 1964). Thus, the children of poverty come to school age all too often after having become habituated to loud vocal sounds as meaningless aspects of their circumstances, with little environmental pressure to note and to abstract such characteristics as the color, shape, and size of objects and persons, with little opportunity to hear extended conversations directed toward themselves, with little call upon themselves to formulate the characteristics of objects and relationships among them and persons in language, with little opportunity to discuss the whys of decisions and the outcome of various kinds of action, and with poor models of syntax for that discussion which does occur.

Students of linguistics may quarrel with some of these statements in the preceding paragraphs (see Cazden, 1968). Some contend that the language of poor children of the slums is as complex syntactically as that of children in the middle class. I suspect that these students of linguistics confuse their concepts of syntactical complexity, about which there is genuine disagreement, with communication. The evidence for the statements I have made in the preceding paragraphs is becoming increasingly systematic and compelling. Moreover, a still quite incomplete study by Schoggen & Schoggen (1968) of the Demonstration and Research Center for Early Education at the George Peabody College for Teachers in Nashville, Tennessee, promises to be especially illuminating. The Schoggens have selected three samples of eight families, one of professional people, one of the rural poor, and one of the urban poor. Each of these 24 families contains a three-year-old who is the target child of the study. Investigator-recorders, after becoming very well acquainted with these families, record all the instances of social interaction, physical and verbal, initiated by the adults and the older children of the family with the target child in such functionally equivalent situations as mealtime, bedtime, and the time when the older children return from school. These units of interaction they term "environmetal force units." In the sample of data available, not only do the adults and older children of the professional families initiate more than twice as many such units with their respective three-year-olds as do the adults and older children of both the urban and rural poor families (40 versus 17 and 18 respectively), but what the Schoggens call "the quality of interaction" also differs radically. Although restraining commands like "stop that" or "don't do that" in one form or another are common to all families, they constitute much the larger share of the total of the "environmental force units" to be found in the families of the rural and urban poor than in those of the professional families. In the families of professional status, a substantial portion of these "environmental force units" call upon the child to discern various kinds of relationships among things and people and to use his own language to communicate his impressions (personal communication). This still unfinished investigation is bringing out more

clearly than any other of which I know the tremendous difference of the ecology of children of poverty from the ecology of
children growing up in the professional class. The small samples
of families concerned in this study probably represent fairly
marked extremes. One would probably find a continuum for any
of the measures used existing between the persistent poor, on
the one hand, and professionals with maximum concern for the
early development of their young.

MOTIVATIONAL OPPORTUNITIES

The children of poverty lack, third, a variety of opportunities
in which to develop the motivational systems inherent in competence. Children must learn to take initiative and to control
their own impulses and actions, to postpone momentary gratification in the hope of more enduring forms of gratification in the
future, and to sustain effort in order to complete tasks once
started. In each of these aspects of motivation, the children of
the poor suffer disadvantage as compared with most children
of middle-class background.

Seldom do the children of the poor have an adequate opportunity to learn the taking of initiative and self-control. To the
troubled parents of the slums, a good child is all too often a
quiet child who does not bother them. It is not that these
mothers fail to love their children. They often show their affection by sending them off to school overdressed when the overdressing calls for large amounts of effort at washing and ironing (Gray & Klaus, 1963). With this overdressing, however, goes
the command, "you be good, keep clean, and do like the teacher
says." Since being "good" is defined as being quiet and inactive,
such treatment hardly encourages the taking of initiative.

Seldom do the children of poverty have an opportunity to
develop motivation directed toward future goals and toward
social status. The parents of the slums have themselves seldom
had an opportunity to learn such motivation (Bronfenbrenner,
1958; Chilman, 1965; Davis, 1948; Davis & Havighurst, 1946;
Lewis, 1961, 1966a). Their responses to their children's actions
and efforts at communication tend to be dictated largely by
their own immediate impulses and needs, not the child's. Since

there is never enough of anything, and little hope that there ever will be enough of anything, the child is reinforced repeatedly for taking all he can get while he can get it. As a consequence, these children all too seldom develop far beyond the motivational status of infants who "want what they want when they want it." Rarely, except in the domain of fighting, does a child have an opportunity to gain much for acquiring skills. Thus, it is not surprising that children of the poor are found to prefer concrete rewards over more abstract reinforcement in the learning of laboratory tasks, while the children of the middle class perform at a higher level and prefer the reinforcement of social approval (Terrel, Durkin, & Wiesley, 1959; Zigler & de Labry, 1962). The ecological conditions I have attempted to describe here also tend to explain the finding that children of poverty tend to prefer immediate reinforcement over delayed reinforcement even when the rewards obtained are palpably larger under the condition of delay whereas the children of middle-class and upper-class background prefer to wait for a larger but delayed reinforcement (Maitland, 1966; Mischel, 1961; Mischel & Metzner, 1962; Steen, 1966; Strauss, 1962). Such motivational preference for delayed gratification is typically found to be associated with not only the higher levels of socioeconomic status, but with higher levels of intellectual functioning and with the absence of various conditions of family disorganization. Here again is evidence of the interrelatedness of the cognitive and motivational aspects of psychological development. Certainly there is little to gain for children of the slums in acquiring linguistic and numerical skills or even in working skills. Seldom do these children of poverty, moreover, see books and magazines or see their adult models reading them. Seldom do these children have an opportunity to see adults at work until they are already old enough to leave their neighborhood. Insofar as motivational systems permitting the delay of gratification depend upon the opportunities to imitate such activities and partake of the satisfactions they yield, the children of poverty lack the opportunity.

Persistence of effort toward the completion of tasks once started and a sense of inner control probably depend upon having had appropriately graded sequences of experiences (see Hunt, 1963a, pp. 92-93). The sequence must probably begin with actions fairly consistently followed by the reinforcement from interesting feedback or events. This should probably then be followed by intermittent reinforcement (Humphreys, 1939) in which the infant or young child must persist in his effort to achieve the anticipated feedback of interest. It is likely that repeated encounters with the sense of effort associated with attaining the interesting feedback is the source of the sense of inner control which, at least introspectively, appears to underlie the feelings of responsibility. Slum parents seldom have any appreciation of such matters in the lives of their young. It is hardly surprising that this feeling of responsibility for what happens has been found to be considerably less evident in children of the poor than in children of middle-class background (Battle & Rotter, 1963). Moreover, in school-related tasks, boys from a background of poverty show much less persistence and much less evidence of a sense of control over the environment than the boys from middle-class backgrounds. Also, children from backgrounds of poverty show a substantially greater discrepancy between actual performance on test tasks and expressed levels of aspiration on these tasks than is found among children of the middle class (Hieronymus, 1951; Keller, 1963).

Another line of evidence consonant with such an interpretation comes from investigations of that dimension of personal style which Kagan (1965) has called "impulsivity-reflectivity." Reflectivity involves a delay in response which appears to indicate attention to internal processes which require some time. The tendency for such reflective delay of response has been found to be positively correlated with measures of reading achievement and of intellectual ability, and also to be positively associated with socioeconomic status (Kagan, 1965; Miller & Mumbauer, 1968).

Temporal conceptions and concerns for those of poverty differ from those with middle-class background. In a study by LeShan (1952) children of poverty were more concerned with matters in the present and less concerned with things of the future than children from the middle class. This difference in

temporal orientation can readily be understood from the differing social ecologies of poverty and middle-class status. In her
ecological studies of slum homes, Maxine Schoggen (1967) has
reported that the disorganization of these homes can best be
characterized in terms of a lack of regular temporal and spatial
organization. In the poorest homes, families seldom have regular
times for meals. Regular mealtimes represent perhaps one of
the most basic time-ordering circumstances through which a
child can begin to develop his temporal concepts and an orientation toward the future. Thus, children of poverty lack not only
opportunities to develop their cognitive skills, but they also
lack opportunities to learn how to take initiative and to control
their own actions, to relinquish immediate and concrete gratification for future abstract forms of gratification, to persist in their
efforts to complete tasks once started, and to develop an orientation toward the future.

OPPORTUNITIES TO DEVELOP VALUES AND STANDARDS OF CONDUCT

The children of poverty lack, fourth, an opportunity to develop those values and standards of conduct which are required
for participation in a technological society that operates con-
structively and relatively peacefully. As the troubled mothers of
slum children respond to most of their requests with "shut up"
and "leave me be," despite clear evidence of love for their children such as the washing and ironing of clothes for school,
these children turn very early to their peers for acceptance,
companionship, and human contact. With both parents absent
from the home much of the time, moreover, the peer groups
go unsupervised. Despite the affluence of America, hundreds of
thousands of her children under five years of age spend a large
share of each day with little or no adult supervision (Reid,
1966). From these unsupervised peer groups, then, the children
of the poor learn their values and standards (Short & Strodtbeck, 1965). While still very young, they copy preadolescents in
various kinds of delinquent behavior (Childers, 1936). As preadolescents, they copy the adolescents of the local delinquent
gangs. These gangs vary in the patterns of delinquency which
they inculcate (Shaw, 1929). They vary in their structure (Short

& Strodtbeck, 1965), and in the motivation involved for delinquent behavior. Where the delinquents of a past generation
were typically motivated chiefly by a search for fun and excitement, the delinquencies of contemporary inner-city gangs
tend to be motivated more by frustration and protest (Cohen,
1955; Miller, 1958; Short & Strodtbeck, 1965). Although violence
has always been a part of intergang warfare, this new motivation has, if anything, increased the trend toward violence and
increased also the level of hostility toward the mainstream of
society. Thus, these slum-reared children have little chance to
develop a respect for law, especially for a law which they see
as just, little chance to become concerned for the needs of
people in general, and often little chance to develop even the
habit of basic honesty. Such values and standards are no mere
matters of middle-class taste. They are basic for the constructive and peaceful operation of any society.

Participation in the mainstream of our technological society
probably calls for a positive valuation of self and a tendency to
prize achievement for its own sake. McClelland *et al.* (1953)
have termed achievement motivation a "need for achievement
(*n* achievement)." Various investigations have uncovered evidence that circumstances encountered within families during the
early years help substantially to determine whether a child will
have a high or a low need for achievement. In a study limited
to mothers of the middle class, Winterbottom (1958) found that
mothers of children with high need for achievement differ from
mothers of children with low need for achievement by making
more demands on their children before an age of eight years, by
giving a higher evaluation to their children's accomplishments
and providing more reward, by placing more restrictions on their
children through age seven but allowing them greater freedom
as they achieve the competence to meet the demands of various
situations. Similarly, Rosen & D'Andrade (1959) have found
that fathers of boys with a high need for achievement stress independence and tend to help their sons develop self-reliance by
providing hints for the solution of problems rather than solving
their sons' problems for them. These familial conditions for high
need for achievement contrast sharply with the mother-teaching

styles that Hess & Shipman (1965) have found in their Negro families. Buehr (1965) has reported that boys from this milieu with a high need for achievement manifest less of the dialect in their speech when they are in problem situations. Also, Strauss (1962) has found both need for achievement and ability to delay gratification lower in poor children than in those of middle-class backgrounds. Again, then, the evidence points to the fact that children of poverty have less in the way of opportunity to develop achievement motivation than do children of the middle class, and therefore the lack of achievement motivation in children found by Strauss (1962) should not be attributed simply to a lack of genotypic potential in these children.

Circumstances within families are not the only sources of these values concerning achievement and self. Circumstances within the school situation itself are of importance, for as Diggory (1966), already noted, has shown, children build a major share of their hopes and of their self-esteem from comparing their own performances with those of the other children with whom they interact and compete. It should be noted also that Atkinson & Reitman (1958) find that achievement motivation leads to excellence of performance chiefly when individuals expect that excellence of performance will produce a sense of pride in accomplishment. Such pride comes only with experiences of approval and pride for accomplishment on the part of those significant persons in the lives of children (Krugman, 1961). The children of poverty come into the school situation not only lacking both the linguistic and numerical skills presumed by school curricula, but also with little basis for an expectation that their efforts to achieve can yield even approval, let alone any sense of pride. As a consequence, it is to be expected that schoolchildren of poverty will manifest lower self-esteem than will their schoolmates of middle-class background, and this has been repeatedly found (Coleman, 1966; Keller, 1963; Long & Henderson, 1967). It is therefore no wonder that Battle & Rotter (1963) have found that boys from the slums fail to persist in school-related tasks and tend to feel that circumstances control their fate. Similarly, success in various school subjects is apparently no factor in the value which these children of poverty place upon these subjects (Greenberg, Gerver, Chall, & Davidson, 1965). Thus, also, in risk-taking situations where children with high need for achievement take moderate risks nicely geared to their previous levels of achievement (McClelland, 1958), children from the slums manifest little relationship between their expressed aspirations and their actual performances (Hieronymus, 1951; Keller, 1963). If these evidence-based considerations are accurate, they suggest that integrating the children of poverty in schools with children having had the advantages of middle-class background may compound the disadvantages of coming from poverty. When children of poverty are black while those of middle-class backgrounds are white, such considerations suggest that integration without compensatory education may exaggerate a tendency to give a low evaluation in general to all black people.

Summary

Despite the love that poor parents have for their children, the opportunities they provide for their children fail to foster the intellectual skills, motives, and standards of conduct and values required for coping with the situations in most schools. The early experiences of these children of poverty serve chiefly to unfit them for adaptive coping with the schools. As they fail, it is hardly surprising that they lose hope, become fed up with school, and drop out as soon as they can. Once out, they have extremely little opportunity to gain, in turn, that competence required for anything more than marginal employability in the marketplace of our highly technological economy. Marginal employability not only fails to bring the income required to buy the fruits of our advancing technology that would enable them to participate in the mainstream of our society, it perpetuates the habits, the thought, and the sense of inferiority that tends to produce incompetence in the succeeding generation.[1]

[1] I am greatly indebted to a paper by James O. Miller (1968) for calling my attention to a number of the sources of evidence cited in the foregoing section. Some of these I had missed when I first wrote this paper in the spring of 1967. Others have failed to come to my attention since that time until I found them cited in this very interesting paper.

What to Do

What to do? The answer must include several kinds of things. The first thing is to remove race completely as a barrier to employment at all levels for those who have the competence. Substantial legal strides have already been made toward this end, but we still have a long way to go in winning the hearts and wills of many people in all levels of our society toward the elimination of race as a factor in employment and also in human relations. The second thing is to provide appropriate training and counseling for those with levels of competence such that they can be made employable in existing niches of industry. We have at least begun to do this kind of thing, but we have not done enough of it. The third thing is to create employment opportunities for those with levels of competence too low to make them employable for existing industrial openings. Probably government must be the employer of last resort for those with the lowest levels of competence. The fourth thing is to provide in some way incomes for poor families adequate to permit healthful diets regardless of the region of the country in which they live. It is highly important, moreover, to provide these incomes in such a way as to permit the members of these families to improve their own lot by their own efforts. The existing welfare situation, as both Moynihan (1965) and Rainwater (1966) have carefully documented, operates further to damage what little initiative individuals of poverty may have retained through the lack of opportunity to develop such motivation as they grew up, and also to damage family stability and to promote father absence. Even after such things are done, however, something more must be done if the children of parents from a background of persistent poverty are to have an opportunity to develop their potential competence more nearly equal to that of children born to parents of the middle class. This "something more" is an ethical imperative for that equality of opportunity which our forefathers considered to be the birthright of all.

At least two approaches exist to the "something more." One is to provide compensatory education for the children of the poor before they enter the public schools at age five or six—

depending upon the existing laws of the various states. The second is to develop programs designed to prevent the incompetence which comes now with the accident of being born to parents of poverty. What helps these parents to improve the opportunities of their children to develop is likely also to improve the general quality of their own lives.

Compensatory Education

Compensatory education has already begun. Project Head Start was devised as a large-scale effort to provide early education that would help to equalize the opportunities for children of the poor. The goal of this project is right, perfectly right. Moreover, the audacity of the immensity of the project has been extremely valuable in making known to a wide share of the populace the possibilities which exist. But having a proper goal and knowing immediately how to achieve that goal are highly different matters. Although the behavioral sciences have uncovered evidence that makes the old beliefs in preprogrammed development and fixed intelligence no longer tenable, this evidence is still insufficient to tell us with precision how to provide effective compensatory educational opportunities.

The children who came to the first summer schools of Project Head Start typically had as teachers those who had been accustomed to teaching in the elementary grades. They had a curriculum taken largely from traditional nursery schools, even though it varied with the school concerned. Although the nursery school originated during the first decade of this century through efforts to help children of the poor in the work of Maria Montessori (1909) in Italy, and Margaret McMillan (1919) in the midlands of England, it was adapted in America chiefly for children of the middle class. The factors forcing this adaptation were several. Due to the prevalent notions of predetermined development and fixed intelligence, attempts to improve the intelligence of children of the poor were regarded as nonsense. Moreover, the poor could not themselves pay for nursery schools. The more affluent parents of the middle class and of the upper middle class could pay, so the nursery schools were adapted to their concerns. Froebel's (1826) kindergarten movement emphasized the potential of free play, and the influence of this movement appears to have combined with that of the child-study movement, instigated by G. Stanley Hall and his faith in recapitulation, to base the curriculum on the motivation for spontaneous activity and play. I must confess that my own predilections and prejudices are heartily in favor of this choice (see Hunt, 1965a). The earliest influence of the psychoanalytic movement in America stressed the importance of avoiding neurotic inhibitions. When this psychoanalytic influence coalesced with those streams of influence stemming from Froebel and G. Stanley Hall, American parents of the middle and upper classes began their "experiment" in laissez-faire child rearing. For many of the leaders of child development and early childhood education, one of the major purposes of the nursery school was to release young children from the excessively inhibitive restraints of their middle-class homes. Although a good many of the university-based nursery schools developed ingenious ways of getting children to learn readiness for academic skills through the process of spontaneous play, such practices were very far from universal. When the various kinds of curricula from the traditional nursery school were employed in the schools of Head Start, sometimes quite inexpertly by teachers accustomed to older children, the educational results were often far less compensatory than they might have been. I personally feared that an "oversell" of the gains to be expected in this state of affairs might result in an "overkill" of support for early childhood education, and that this overkill might result in a loss of the support from the public for an opportunity to show what existing evidence suggests could happen if those of us in the behavioral and educational sciences were allowed the time to learn how to manage early childhood education properly and effectively (see Chapter 5).

So far as I can ascertain, none of the programs within Project Head Start has done any harm. Most of them have done considerable good, but some have apparently achieved considerably more in the way of compensatory education than others. Perhaps some of the greatest values of Head Start have been medical and social. A great many medical deficiencies were discovered in young children. They were then corrected early as a consequence of the medical component of the Head Start program. One major social value of this program consisted of involving the parents in these projects concerned with the education of their young children. This involvement of the parents has uncovered latent educational power which should, by all means, be harnessed.

Compensatory educational programs have existed outside of Project Head Start as well as within it. From the limited evidence derived from the evaluative studies of these various programs of compensatory education, both outside and within Head Start (see, e.g., Weikart, 1967b), it appears that improvement in measures of intelligence and school readiness is related to the amount of deliberate effort to teach linguistic skills, rudimentary number skills, interest in school matters, and motivational concern for achievement. Gains of considerable magnitude in several programs, approaching 30 points in IQ during the course of a year, have been reported in programs of compensatory education which differ in curriculum and in method of teaching substantially (see Chapter 6). But those regarded as experts in early child development and early childhood education still disagree on major issues. Since psychologists and educators considered it too softheaded during the preceding half-century to be worthwhile even to try experimentally to increase the competence of children from any background, we shall have to do our experimenting now that the challenge is present. We shall have to try as best we know how. When we fail, we shall have to profit from our failures, and try again. We are now being asked for ready-made solutions that we do not have. We can provide these needed solutions only through an extended program of basic research and educational development. The basic research should be directed toward better understanding of those factors influencing psychological development in all its aspects: intellect, motivation, emotional stability, and values. Those innovations which show promise, we must evaluate carefully for effectiveness. Those innovations which prove to be effective, we must disseminate vigorously. By disseminate, I mean that we must actively help the officials and teachers of Head Start and the officials and teachers of our public schools to implement them widely in practice.

Preventing the Development of Incompetence

Compensatory education even for children who have spent the first four years of their lives under the stultifying effects of poverty is in essence a remedial rather than a preventive process. Moreover, it is highly expensive. It is expensive in the first place because at least one teacher or teacher-aide is required for about every five pupils if the teaching is to be effective. It is expensive, moreover, because even at best it may be too little and too late to enable a good many of the children of the poor to develop their potential sufficiently to succeed in the public schools and later to participate in the mainstream of our society so as to enjoy the benefits of our technology. A way must be found, I believe, to intervene during the first four years of the lives of these children in order to prevent that retardation in the development of their competence which I have already described. But how do we do it effectively?

Parents, at least potentially, should be both the least expensive and the best teachers of their own children during these earliest years. In view of this consideration, various federal agencies have spent, to my knowledge, of the order of two million dollars on projects wherein psychotherapy-like approaches have been used with parents by social workers, clinical psychologists, and psychiatrists. From the evidence I have seen, but which I cannot at this writing document with references, the children of these parents have gained nothing from these attempts to intervene by means of the professional talk involved in such approaches, be the relationships dyadic or group. On the other hand, when parents, and especially mothers, are provided with an opportunity to observe the behavior of their children with skilled teachers, and with the opportunity to discuss the relation of this behavior to the skills of the teacher, there are evidences of imitative change in the behavior of the mothers which are highly hopeful. These statements can be documented in the findings of several pioneer programs.

In perhaps the first of these pioneering examples of such studies, Rupert Klaus & Susan Gray (1968) and their colleagues associated with the "Early Training Project" at the George Peabody College for Teachers in Nashville, Tennessee, developed a special summer nursery school for four-year-old children who had suffered the disadvantages of poverty. The curriculum of this school aimed to teach language and number skills along with the attitudes and motives required to cope with the curriculum of existing elementary schools. In addition, home visitors brought each mother to the nursery school where she could see for herself not only what the teachers were doing with her child and those of her neighbors, but also the results in the behavior of her own child and of others familiar to her. The home visitors, who were certified teachers with a background making them well acquainted with the views and attitudes of the mothers, interpreted what the teachers were doing and why in language that these mothers could readily understand. Through this process, these mothers got not only correctives for their implicit theories of child rearing, but they got to see approaches alternative to their own with the behavioral results of these alternative approaches in familiar children. Thus, one child, with a frequent need for urination that produced obvious restlessness and inattention, was simply taken out of the room and to the toilet frequently. One visiting mother, who held the implicit theory that punishment is what makes children good, presumed that he was, of course, being spanked while he was out of the room. Only after several observations of his trip to the toilet was she finally convinced that it was merely an opportunity to urinate rather than getting spanked that changed his behavior in the classroom.

The home visitors in this project also related the teachers' work to what each mother did with her children at home. During the periods between the summer sessions of the nursery school (September to May), a home visitor saw each mother in the two classes of 20 children every week and undertook to demonstrate for her such matters as how to read a story with enthusiasm, how to reinforce two-year-old infants for acquiring such new skills as finding new ways to cope with the problem of getting dressed, how to talk with children about such homely operations as peeling potatoes while in the process, how to prepare materials that would help the children learn about the seasons and what happens to animals and plants with the seasons. These home visitors also let each mother discuss her own problems and helped her to find ways of coping with them. The evidence of effectiveness in the study comes chiefly from test results. Examiners have tested the children in each of the two nursery classes and also those in other contrast groups with similar socioeconomic status, one nearby, and one removed by some 60 miles. The test performances at the end of each summer session, when compared with those at the beginning of the session, have shown spurts of improvement which do not appear in the test results of those children in the contrast groups who got neither the nursery school nor the home visits. The superiority of the test performances of those children in the nursery school who also got the home visits over those in the contrast groups has continued through the first grade.

These test results have shown two other phenomena of highly significant promise. (1) The younger siblings of the children attending the nursery school and getting the home visits were significantly superior in test performance to the younger siblings of children in the contrast groups. Apparently what these mothers were learning from their observations at the school and from the home visitor had really improved their management of their younger children. Klaus and Gray have called this "vertical diffusion." (2) The children of the contrast groups living in the same neighborhood as those who attended the nursery school and received the home visits got higher scores on the tests than did those children in the contrast group living some 60 miles away. Apparently these mothers who learned new child-rearing practices were somehow communicating them to their neighbors in a significant degree. Occasional observations indicate that their methods of communication consisted in informal demonstrations given to neighbors during back-porch gatherings. Klaus and Gray have called this phenomenon "horizontal diffusion." Other innovators like Ira Gordon (1969) and Ronald Lally at the University of Florida, and David Weikart and his collaborators in the public schools of Ypsilanti, Michigan, are apparently finding success in attempts to repeat these evidences of both "vertical diffusion" and "horizontal diffusion." Moreover, these findings have recently been repeated and extended at the Demonstration and Research Center for Early Education (DARCEE) at Peabody College (Miller, 1968). It remains to be determined whether the children in the intervention programs actually succeed better in the acid test of school performance than do those in the control groups.

One exceedingly interesting outcome of the repetition of the Early Training Project, reported in preliminary fashion by Miller (1968), consists in the various bits of evidence that participation in the project has enriched the lives of the parents. Over half of the mothers participating have gone on to complete their high school education or have enrolled in courses to upgrade their vocational skills. Several have completed courses in cosmetology. Almost one-fourth of these mothers have enrolled in or completed the training to become licensed practical nurses. None of the mothers who participated in the nursery school and the home visiting are now employed as domestics, and half of those who were originally employed as domestics have upgraded their employment status. Two of these mothers who were originally illiterate have now gained reading skills at the third- or fourth-grade level. A concern with community affairs has also increased. Several of these women have served on their church boards; one has joined in the Metropolitan Action Council elections, and two others have served as representatives on the Council's board for the Head Start program. On their own these families have developed a parent organization which has planned cooperative picnics, outings for the families on weekends, developed a rotating book library, and organized a mother-father bowling league. From the standpoint of completing the investigation, one of the problems has been to keep the members of these groups in the housing project until the program of intervention is complete, for these parents develop a strong interest in buying their own homes. Two of the families have actually bought homes while continuing their children in the classroom program by providing their own transportation. Increases in savings accounts and checking accounts are evident. Even a family of most desperate means has shown such improvement in the furnishings of their home and the care of the grounds around their apartment that neighbors have been prompted to remark to the home visitor of this family's progress during involvement in the project. On the side of the horizontal diffusion effect, the staff of the project is being repeatedly asked into the homes of nonparticipating families to discuss and to evaluate the educational experiences being provided for their own children. Although it is no easy matter to put numbers on such evidence of change, it clearly indicates that the lives of parents can be enriched by participating in programs aimed at improving the educational opportunities of their young.

From another pioneering program under the direction of Merle B. Karnes at the University of Illinois comes evidence that mothers of poverty can be taught to be effective teachers of their preschool children. The first of these pioneering studies was designed to determine if the effects of a brief period of training for the mothers of a sample of 30 children judged by the principal of the neighborhood school to be among the most economically and educationally deprived would be reflected in the intellectual and linguistic development of their children. In this study, the emphasis of the training was placed on helping the mother make instructional materials and learn how to use those materials to teach her child at home. Instead of lectures, the teaching, like that at Peabody, involved the individual mothers in interpretive discussions of what they saw teachers doing in a classroom. This training was given in 11 weekly sessions of two hours in the neighborhood elementary school. Three experienced preschool teachers conducted the discussions. Each teacher was responsible for a group of five mothers. The mothers were paid $3.00 a session—the usual hourly wage of $1.50 to prevent loss of income—for each teaching session, but nothing for the time spent with their own children at home. The mothers actually made inexpensive educational materials such as a sock puppet; a homemade flannel board; lotto and matching games with gum seals, with geometric shapes, and with colored chips; counting books made from magazine pictures; sorting and matching activities using miscellaneous household items and an egg carton for a sorting tray; and classifying materials based upon pictures cut from furniture and clothing catalogs (see Karnes, 1968). The teachers also taught the mothers appropriate songs and finger plays, and distributed copies of them as teaching aids in the home. Books and puzzles were also made available for the mothers to take home for use with their children during the following week after each teaching session. These materials were chosen to stress useful vocabulary and basic manipulative skills. The major emphasis of all activities was on language development and was calculated to teach each child the words he needs to label the objects in his immediate environment, to abstract perceptually the characteristics of these objects, to generalize, to use the standard syntax of speech, to understand and to ask questions, and to formulate answers in his own words.

The 30 children in this study were divided into a mother-taught group and a control group. The children in the mother-taught group attended no nursery school, nor did those of the control group. Before the study began, each of the 30 children was tested in one of the classrooms by a trained examiner who was unaware of the subject's placement in the experimental or control group. At the end of the twelfth week, the children were retested. The tests included form L-M of the Stanford-Binet (1960 edition) and the experimental edition of the Illinois Test of Psycholinguistic Abilities (Kirk & McCarthy, 1961). At the beginning, the 15 children in the mother-taught group had an average Binet IQ of 91.3 (variance $= 63.42$) and the control averaged 95.5 ($v = 143.58$). After 12 weeks of mother teaching, the taught group had an average IQ of 98.8 (variance $= 71.67$) and the control a mean of 95.5 ($v = 108.08$). Thus, during these 12 weeks of mother teaching in the home, the taught children gained 7.5 points of IQ while the controls gained but .1 point. The taught group also gained significantly more on several tests of the ITPA than did the children of the control group.

In subsequent studies, Professor Karnes (1969) has compared the gains of children taught by mothers from the poverty area who received inservice training and supervision with those of children taught by a professional staff in her highly structured preschool. The gains of the mother-taught children proved to be approximately as great as those taught by professional teachers for the same duration. In another part of this project, Karnes (1969) and her staff also compared the gains of children taught by teen-agers participating in a high school work-study program and trained in the fashion described above, with the gains of children from the same socioeconomic background taught by professional teachers in her structured preschool. Again the gains made by the teen-taught children were approximately equal to those made by the children taught by professional teachers. On the basis of these results, Professor Karnes advocates a new role for teachers, one in which they teach the parents and involve the entire family in the education of preschool children.

Still further evidence of the effectiveness of mothers in the teaching of their infants has come serendipitously from a project underway in Durham, North Carolina, under the direction of Robert Spaulding and Donald Stedman (personal communication with Spaulding). This evidence comes from a longitudinal study of psychological development in infants born during a given brief period of time in a poverty-ridden ghetto of Durham. There was no intention of intervening to improve the competence of the nine children in this group. The aim was to observe the course of psychological development as measured by the Bayley scale for infants. Each child and his mother were brought monthly during the first year and bi-monthly for the next year and a half to the laboratory at Duke University for testing. The mothers observed the testing. As they observed, the why's of the various items were explained by the social worker who brought the mother to the laboratory. Several groups of 15 children aged 2.5 years had come from this ghetto to form experimental nursery school groups for especially early compensatory education. The mean IQ's of each of these several groups had ranged between the middle 70's and the lower 80's. These nine children who had visited the laboratories along with their mothers failed to show the usual progressive drop in IQ. Instead, they arrived at age 2.5 years with an average Binet

IQ of approximately 110, and with no child in the group below 100. Even so, these nine children were still somewhat retarded in language development, but in the motor domain and in the social domain they were superior. It appears that when the mothers of these children had seen the kinds of things at which they succeeded and the kinds of things at which they failed on the tests, the observation prompted them to give their children practice in the "skills" they had failed. They appear to have been exceedingly effective as teachers. This finding has suggested a genuine experiment utilizing this kind of approach for the future. From Illinois comes a combination of studies, not designed for the purpose, which suggests how important it may be to intervene educationally during the first three years. The first study in this combination is one by Genevieve Painter (1968) done in a project directed by S. A. Kirk. This study concerned 20 children who were the younger siblings of four-year-olds selected from experimental preschool classes at the University of Illinois. These four-year-olds had been selected as children exceedingly likely to fail in school from the rosters of Aid to Dependent Children, Family Care, and the authorities of the public schools because their older siblings had failed. These 20 children were divided into a group of 10 (6 male, 4 female; 8 black and 2 white) for tutoring and another group of 10 (6 male and 4 female; 6 black and 4 white) to serve as controls. These children ranged in age from 8 to 24 months of age. The tutored group received intellectual stimulation for one hour a day, five days a week, for a period of one year. The controls received only the customary regimen of their families. Each of these 20 children was given a battery of tests by trained examiners before the tutoring started. The two groups were similar; the group to be tutored had a mean Cattell (1960) IQ of 98.8 and the control group a mean Cattell IQ of 98.4. At the end of the year of tutoring, the Stanford-Binet was used. The tutored group had then a mean Binet IQ of 108.1 and the control group a mean Binet IQ of 98.8. The difference of 9.3 points was significant ($p < .05$). Other evidences of gain during the year of tutoring came from the Illinois Test of Psycholinguistic Abilities (Kirk, McCarthy, & Kirk, 1968), from some of the language tests of the Merrill-Palmer Scale, and from certain tests of conceptual development. These gains, however, were modest.

At age three the children in the tutored group entered the highly structured preschool of Merle Karnes (1969) for culturally disadvantaged three-year-olds. When these children were approximately four, after both the infant tutoring program and the period of a year in Karnes's preschool, these 10 children served as subjects in a study by G. E. Kirk (1969). Kirk was interested chiefly in whether the linguistic deficit of disadvantaged children is a matter of inability to discriminate phonemes or a matter of word-picture familiarity. In order to get an approximately equivalent group of untutored and unpreschooled children of poverty for comparison, Kirk assembled the entire list of children in families receiving Aid to Dependent Children in Champaign-Urbana who fell within the range of ages from 39 to 51 months. He found 30 black children who had not been to preschool, and from these he selected 10, matched as nearly as possible for chronological age with the children who had been tutored in the Painter study and who had participated in the Karnes preschool. The third group of the Kirk (1969) study were culturally advantaged white children in a Montessori nursery school whose performances do not concern us here.

When Kirk computed the IQ equivalents from the Peabody Picture Vocabulary Test (Dunn, 1959, 1965) for 10 tutored and preschooled younger siblings of the Bereiter-Engelmann group, the average was 99.9, whereas the average for the 10 who came from ADC families without such tutoring and preschool experience was only 60.1. This difference of nearly 40 points is startling. Those who know the community believe that these two groups are indeed comparable. On the other hand, it must be remembered that the tutored group started with a Cattell IQ of about 98. Unfortunately, we have no knowledge of what the Cattell IQ of the latter group might have been. According to the clinical lore, children of poverty get estimated IQ's from the Picture Vocabulary Test which are lower than those that they get from the Binet, and their Binet IQ's are lower than they get on the Cattell Scale.

The Kirk study brought out one more point of considerable interest. Kirk gave these children Seidel's Test of Picture Identification for Children which contains 174 nouns and 174 matching pictures in picture-word triplets differing in a single phoneme (e.g., roll, pole, bowl). In this test, children are asked to point to one of each such triplet as it is pronounced by the examiner. Kirk found the untutored and unpreschooled children with scores very much lower than those with the tutoring and preschool. This finding alone tended to support the reports of such investigators as Cynthia Deutsch (1964), Katz & Deutsch (1963), and Steen (1966) that the disadvantaged children of poverty lack the ability to hear the differences between these phonemes because they have lived in a very noisy environment while very young. It was the merit of Kirk to note that such tests confound the semantic, word-picture organizations with the auditory ability to discriminate such triplets of phonemes as the sound of *r* from the sound of *p* from the sound of *b* in "roll, pole, bowl." Kirk reassembled the picture-word triplets so that each picture appeared with two others of differing phonemic structure. Thus, the picture *roll* was placed in a triplet with *bears* and *saw*. The children were then asked again to point to each of the various objects as the examiner examined them, and the test was repeated with M&M's for getting things right. In this fashion, Kirk determined which of the 174 word-picture coordinations were unfamiliar to each child. After subtracting these unfamiliar word-picture combinations from the denominator of 174, he discovered that those children without the tutoring and preschooling answered correctly a far higher proportion of the phonemic discrimination index. This finding suggests that the linguistic disability of children of poverty may be considerably less one of auditory capacity to discriminate phonemes than one of knowledge of word-object coordinations.

Parent and Child Centers

Such results suggest a new approach to the modification of child-rearing practices which might well improve the quality of the life of the parents as well. This new approach would em-

ploy the love these poor parents have for their children to motivate them to organize, with help from professional leadership, to
foster competence in their children. The idea is to form, with
federal support, Parent and Child Centers. Each such Center
would serve several thousand families. Each should provide an
open door where the families could obtain the full range of the
services available within their communities either directly or
through informed and skilled referral. Each Center would also
provide the leadership to help those families in neighborhoods
to form day-care facilities for infants and toddlers and classes
for older preschool children. The mothers and fathers and also
the older children of the families served should take their turns
as aides in child-care and in teaching in these facilities. Various
bits of evidence suggest that the concern of poor parents for the
future of their children will motivate their participation in such
arrangements if they have a part in forming them, if their children can be assured of development-fostering care when they
cannot be on hand, and if they can gain periods of freedom for
shopping and recreation by their participation. Various reports
of adolescents within housing projects guarding the materials
used in the nursery schools for preschool children suggest that
they too can readily become involved in the conduct of such
facilities, although it may be necessary to pay them as they acquire special skills. Actual participation in these day-care and
nursery facilities under the leadership of people skilled in the
care of young children provides them with an opportunity for
observing and imitating the child-care practices of people relatively more expert than themselves. These Parent and Child
Centers should also follow the lead of Klaus and Gray in providing home visitors to demonstrate child-care practices in order
to bring them and their application into the home.

Although these Parent and Child Centers focus chiefly on the
needs of children, they seem likely to yield a general improvement in the quality of the life of the parents. The idea is to
utilize the love which these parents of poverty, like all parents,
have for their children to motivate them to organize and to work
in the facilities for day-care and early education. It is likely that
this cooperation will produce in slum neighborhoods, and in the

highly impersonal projects of public housing, neighborhood groups in which families become mutually helpful and inter-dependent.

Nuclear families in both the unreconstructed ghettos and in the sterile, new housing developments commonly live in humanly isolated households where only the children of various ages con-gregate in loose-knit gangs. During their earliest years, too many of these children develop in isolated households with an atmos-phere of frustration, anger, and fear forced upon the parents by their inability to alter their distressing situation or an atmosphere of boredom and depression that comes with giving up. In large measure, this human atmosphere is all too often found among those who have migrated in hope of better things only to have those hopes dashed. This atmosphere, combined with its result in parental models of the adult-lot as one of impotent frustra-tion or of hostile rage, makes the circumstances of the children of the poor in the inner cities even worse, perhaps, than those of the rural poor. Moreover, these families live largely apart from the work-a-day world where children come naturally and regu-larly in contact with adults other than their own parents and with adults in working roles who know them and are concerned for them. As a consequence, the children of both the inner city and the suburbs grow up with few adult models, and those models are likely to be unfortunate. It is thus that they turn to peer groups for their socialization. The social and moral standards that develop in the peer groups of unattended children and adolescents are seldom of the kind that will permit an organized society to survive. We have witnessed some of the consequences of the mob violence of the Watts neighborhood in Los Angeles, and in other cities, and we shall undoubtedly witness more ex-amples of such violence before this summer of 1967 is over.

We cannot escape such explosions merely by means of repres-sive measures. We can no more escape them by repressive measures than those parents of the middle class who have failed to foster close ties of affection and identification through con-sideration of their children's wishes, mutual communication about consequences, and mutually reached decisions, can control them with threats of punishment (Bandura & Walters, 1959; Hunt,

1961). On the other hand, those examples of aggressive, slum-reared adolescents who will fight to protect the facilities for the little children in their apartments or neighborhoods illustrate what appears to be a corrective emotional power of this interest in young children. Participating in the development and running of facilities for day-care and early childhood education promises a way of helping overcome the isolation of families in the slums, and potentially also in the sterile housing developments for families of the lower middle class. By cooperative participation in the planning of and in the conduct of this care and education with relative experts as models, the parents should gain something of a sense of constructive purpose. In the process, they should become less frustrated and should lose thereby some of their apathetic impotence or their hostility. As they become actively engaged in this community enterprise for the care and education of their young children, they can hardly help but provide better models for their young to emulate than many of them are now providing. The involvement of older children and adolescents in the enterprise should have similar effects upon them. As a result some interdependence should develop among the families in the neighborhood, and it is through such interdependence that the values necessary for constructive and organized societies are inculcated. In these ways, along with employment, better incomes, and better access to the social services of the community as a whole, these Parent and Child Centers should improve substantially the quality of life of the adults. At the same time the parents and older children should be learning, by imitation coupled with explanation and trial through the tutelage of the home visitors, those child-rearing practices which foster the development of those basic intellectual and motivational skills required to cope with school curricula and later to find a place in the economy which will permit them to participate in the mainstream of our increasingly affluent society.

I have given here only the barest outline of what promises to be a fruitful way of preventing a large share of that incompetence which comes with being born into families of poverty. In his message to Congress of 11 February 1967, President Johnson recommended such an approach, and the Office of Economic

Opportunity has been authorized to establish about 25 such Parent and Child Centers on an experimental basis. In neighborhoods of black people with de facto segregation, these Centers probably cannot be desegregated. What I believe is more important than immediate desegregation for these children during this preschool period is that they develop those abilities, motives, and values which will better enable them to hold their own in desegregated schools with children from parents of middle-class background, be they black or white.

Out of these relatively few Centers now authorized should come both a few especially successful models and the experience required to learn better how to organize them. The most successful models can be emulated elsewhere and studied to uncover the theoretical understanding of the child-rearing and social processes required for effective organization and for effective teaching of the understanding and skills required. Organizing many such Centers calls for training programs. We must have more investigators and innovators to get the theoretical understanding. We must have many more of those who can teach the theory and the required skills to foster child development, to organize and administer Centers at various levels from graduate schools, through college and junior colleges, to high schools. Spreading such Centers across the nation will call for training thousands of people for professional careers and for various kinds of paraprofessional careers in community organization and child care. These careers do not exist today.

Conclusion

If the behavioral sciences have discovered anything that begins to approach in human significance the antibiotics and contraceptive pills of the biological and medical sciences and the atomic energy of the physical sciences, it may well be the new evidence of the great plasticity in infant and early child development. This new evidence provides a basis for a justified hope that the cycle of poverty generating the incompetence that, in turn, generates poverty can ultimately be broken. No longer is it sensible to consider the incompetence of those who have grown up in poverty the inevitable consequence of their biological inheritance and nature.

On the other hand, we of the behavioral sciences still have a long way to go where early child care and education are concerned. Our stage probably corresponds to that in the development of antibiotics at which Dr. Fleming was when he found that streptococcic bacteria adjacent to penicillin mold will die. This finding ultimately led to the powerful antibiotics of medicine. We, too, have such a justified hope. If we will follow the leads of the data from our scientific experiments, and also of the data, even of the soft data, from the evaluations of those innovations which appear to be promising in early childhood education, and if we will yield up the attitudes and beliefs we learned by hearsay from those who taught us, we shall learn how to compensate the children of the poor for their lack of opportunity. We shall also learn how to help parents reared in poverty to organize their efforts to improve the quality of their lives and to learn how to develop in their own children that competence required for success in school, for later employment in the economy, and for participation in the mainstream of our society.

If our impatient society—and the reasons for this impatience are all too obvious—does not lose hope and faith too soon, and if the violence of those in poverty does not destroy confidence in a positive approach, it is conceivable that we of these United States of America could bring a major share of the children of the persistently poor into the mainstream of our society within a generation.

References

The dates following the names of the authors are those by which citations are identified in the text. They are, to the best of my knowledge, the original dates of publication. When a second date appears at the end of a reference, this is the one to which I have had access, and any pages given for quotations in the text refer to the publication of the second date.

Albizu-Miranda, C. 1966. "The successful retardate." Hato Rey, Puerto Rico: Division of Education, Commonwealth of Puerto Rico. (Mimeographed technical report.)

Allport, F. H. 1924. *Social psychology.* Boston: Houghton Mifflin.

Altman, J., & Das, G. D. 1964. Autoradiographic examination of the effects of enriched environment on the rate of glial multiplication in the adult rat brain. *Nature* 204:1161-65.

Amsel, A. 1958. The role of frustrative nonreward in non-continuous reward situations. *Psychological Bulletin* 55:102-19.

———, & Roussel, J. 1952. Motivational properties of frustration: I. Effect on running response of the addition of frustration to the motivational complex. *Journal of Experimental Psychology* 43:363-68.

Anastasi, Anne. 1936. The influence of specific experience upon mental organization. *Genetic Psychology Monographs* 18:245-355.

———. 1956. Intelligence and family size. *Psychological Bulletin* 53: 187-209.

———. 1958. *Differential psychology.* (3rd ed.) New York: Macmillan.

Anderson, J. E. 1940. The prediction of terminal intelligence from infant and preschool tests. *Yearbook, National Society for Studies in Education* 39 (I), 385-403.

Anderson, J. F., & Horsfall, W. R. 1963. Thermal stress and anomalous development of mosquitoes (Diptera: Culicidae). I.

Effect of constant temperature on dimorphism of adults of Aedes Stimulans. *Journal of Experimental Zoology* 154: 67-107.

Anderson, L. D. 1939. The predictive value of infancy tests in relation to intelligence at five years. *Child Development* 10: 203-12.

Angermeier, W. F., Phelps, J. B., & Reynolds, H. H. 1967. The effects of differential early rearing upon discrimination learning in monkeys. *Psychonomic Science* 8:379-80.

Atkinson, J. W., & Reitman, W. R. 1958. Performance as a function of motive strength and expectancy of goal-attainment. In J. W. Atkinson (Ed.), *Motives in fantasy, action, and society.* Princeton, N.J.: D. Van Nostrand.

Baldwin, A. L. 1955. *Behavior and development in childhood.* New York: Dryden Press.

————, Kalhorn, J., & Breese, F. H. 1945. Patterns of parent behavior. *Psychological Monographs* 58 (No. 3), 1-75.

Baldwin, J. M. 1895. *Mental development in the child and in the race: Methods and processes.* (3rd ed.) New York: Macmillan, 1906.

Bandura, A., & Walters, R. H. 1959. *Adolescent aggression.* New York: Ronald.

Battle, E. S., & Rotter, J. B. 1963. Children's feelings of personal control as related to social class and ethnic group. *Journal of Personality* 31:482-90.

Bayley, Nancy. 1940. Mental growth in young children. *Yearbook, National Society for Studies in Education* 39 (2), 11-47.

Beach, F. A. 1945. Current concepts of play in animals. *American Naturalist* 79:523-41.

Beilin, H., & Gotkin, L. 1964. Psychological issues in the development of mathematics curricula for socially disadvantaged children. Paper presented to the Invitational Conference on Mathematics Education, Chicago, April, 1964.

Bell, R. Q. 1965. Developmental psychology. *Annual Review of Psychology* 16:1-38.

Bennett, E. L., Diamond, M. C., Krech, D., & Rosenzweig, M. R. 1964. Chemical and anatomical plasticity of brain. *Science* 146:610-19.

Bereiter, C., & Engelmann, S. 1966. *Teaching disadvantaged children in the preschool.* New York: Prentice-Hall.

————, Engelmann, S., Osborn, Jean, & Reidford, P. A. 1966. An academically oriented pre-school for culturally deprived children. In F. M. Hechinger (Ed.), *Pre-school education today.* Garden City, N.Y.: Doubleday, Ch. 6.

Berlyne, D. E. 1960. *Conflict, arousal, and curiosity.* New York: McGraw-Hill.

Bernstein, B. 1960. Language and social class. *British Journal of Sociology* 11:271-76.

——. 1961. Social class and linguistic development: A theory of social learning. In A. H. Halsey, Jean Floud, & C. A. Anderson (Eds.), *Education, economy, and society.* New York: The Free Press of Glencoe, pp. 288-314.

Bexton, W. H., Heron, W., & Scott, T. H. 1954. Effects of decreased variation in the sensory environment. *Canadian Journal of Psychology* 8:70-76.

Binet, A. 1909. Les idées modernes sur les enfants. Paris: Ernest Flammarion (Cited from Stoddard, 1939).

——, & Henri, V. 1895. La psychologie individuelle. *Année psychologique* 2:411-63.

——, & Simon, T. 1905. Méthodes nouvelles pour le diagnostic du niveau intellectuel des anormaux. *Année psychologique* 11: 191-244.

——, & Simon, T. 1916. *The development of intelligence in children,* trans. by Elizabeth S. Kite. Baltimore: Williams & Wilkins.

Blank, Marian. 1967. Cognitive gains in "deprived" children through individual teaching of language for abstract thinking. Paper presented at the meeting of the Society for Research in Child Development, 3 March, New York City.

Bloch, H. A., & Flynn, F. T. 1956. *Delinquency: The juvenile offender in America today.* New York: Random House.

Bloom, B. S. 1964. *Stability and change in human characteristics.* New York: Wiley.

——, Davis, A., & Hess, R. 1965. *Compensatory education for cultural deprivation.* New York: Holt.

Boring, E. G. 1929. *A history of experimental psychology.* New York: Century.

Brattgård, S. O. 1952. The importance of adequate stimulation for the chemical composition of retinal ganglion cells during early post-natal development. *Acta Radiologica,* Stockholm, Suppl. 96, 1-80.

Bronfenbrenner, U. 1958. Socialization and social class through time and space. In Eleanor E. Maccoby, T. M. Newcomb, & E. L. Hartley (Eds.), *Readings in social psychology.* New York: Holt, pp. 400-425.

——. 1966. The psychological cost of quality and equality in education. In M. M. Tumin and M. Bressler (Eds.), *Quality and equality in education.* Washington, D.C.: U.S. Office of Education.

——. 1967. Early deprivation in mammals and man. In N. Grant (Ed.), *Early experience and behavior.* Springfield, Ill.: C. C Thomas.

Brookshire, K. H. 1958. An experimental analysis of the effects of infantile shock-trauma. *Dissertation Abstracts* 19:180.

———, Littman, R. A., & Stewart, C. N. 1961. Residua of shock-trauma in the white rat: A three-factor theory. *Psychological Monographs* 75: No. 10 (Whole No. 514).

Brown, J. S., & Farber, I. E. 1951. Emotions conceptualized as intervening variables—with suggestions toward a theory of frustration. *Psychological Bulletin* 48:465-95.

Bryan, W. L., & Harter, N. 1897. Studies in the physiology and psychology of the telegraphic language. *Psychological Review* 4: 27-53.

Buehr, R. F. 1965. Need achievement and dialect in lower-class adolescent Negroes. *Proceedings of the 73rd Annual Convention of the American Psychological Association*. Washington, D.C.: American Psychological Association, pp. 313-14.

Bühler, K. 1918. *Die geistige Entwicklung des Kindes*. Jena: Fischer.

———. 1928. Displeasure and pleasure in relation to activity. In M. L. Reymert (Ed.), *Feelings and emotions: The Wittenberg Symposium*. Worcester, Mass.: Clark University Press, Ch. 14.

Burks, Barbara S. 1928. The relative influence of nature and nurture upon mental development: A comparative study of foster parent–foster child resemblance and true parent–true child resemblance. *Yearbook, National Society for the Study of Education*, 27 (1), 219-316.

Burt, C. L. 1940. *The factors of the mind*. London: University of London Press. (New York: Macmillan, 1941.)

———, Jones, E., Miller, E., & Moodie, W. 1934. *How the mind works*. New York: Appleton.

Butler, R. A. 1953. Discrimination learning by rhesus monkeys to visual exploration motivation. *Journal of Comparative and Physiological Psychology* 46:95-98.

———. 1958. The differential effect of visual and auditory incentives on the performance of monkeys. *American Journal of Psychology* 71:591-93.

Cannon, W. B. 1915. *Bodily changes in pain, hunger, fear, and rage*. (2nd ed.) New York: Appleton, 1929.

Carmichael, L. 1926. The development of behavior in vertebrates experimentally removed from influence of external stimulation. *Psychological Review* 33:51-58.

———. 1927. A further study of the development of behavior in vertebrates experimentally removed from the influence of external stimulation. *Psychological Review* 34:34-47.

———. 1928. A further study of the development of behavior. *Psychological Review* 35:253-60.

Cattell, J. McK. 1890. Mental tests and measurements. *Mind* 15:373-81.

Cattell, Psyche. 1960. *The measurement of the intelligence of infants and young children.* New York: Psychological Corporation.

Cattell, R. B. 1937. *The fight for our national intelligence.* London: King.

———. 1950a. The fate of national intelligence: Test of a thirteen-year prediction. *Eugenics Review* 42:136-48.

———. 1950b. *Personality.* New York: McGraw.

———. 1952. *Factor analysis: An introduction and manual for psychologist and social scientist.* New York: Harper.

Cazden, Courtney. 1968. Subcultural differences in child language: An interdisciplinary review. *Merrill-Palmer Quarterly of Behavior and Development* 14:82-100.

Child, I. L. 1954. Socialization. In G. Lindzey (Ed.), *Handbook of social psychology.* Cambridge, Mass.: Addison-Wesley, Ch. 18.

Childers, A. T. 1936. Some notes on sex mores among Negro children. *American Journal of Orthopsychiatry* 6:442-48.

Chilman, Catherine S. 1965. Child rearing and family life patterns of the very poor. *Welfare in Review* 3:3-19.

Clark, A. D., & Richards, C. J. 1966. Auditory discrimination among economically disadvantaged and non-disadvantaged preschool children. *Exceptional Children* 33:259-62.

Cloward, R. A., & Ohlin, L. E. 1960. *Delinquency and opportunity: The theory of delinquent gangs.* Glencoe: The Free Press.

Coghill, G. E. 1929. *Anatomy and the problem of behavior.* Cambridge: Cambridge University Press. (New York: Macmillan.)

Cohen, A. K. 1955. *Delinquent boys: The culture of the gang.* Glencoe: The Free Press.

———, & Short, J. F., Jr. 1958. Research in delinquent subcultures. *Journal of Social Issues* 24:20-37.

Coleman, J. S. 1966. *Equality of educational opportunity.* Washington, D.C.: U.S. Government Printing Office.

Conant, J. B. 1947. *On understanding science.* New Haven: Yale University Press. (Also Mentor Books, No. 68, 1951.)

Cooley, C. H. 1902. *Human nature and the social order.* New York: Scribner's.

Cravioto, J. 1964. Malnutrition and behavioral development in the preschool child. (Mimeographed prepublication, presented at the International Conference on Prevention of Malnutrition in the Preschool Child, Washington, D.C., December, 1964.) To appear in N. Scrimshaw & J. E. Gordon (Eds.), *Malnutrition, learning, and behavior.* Cambridge, Mass.: M. I. T. Press.

Crowther, J. G. 1941. *The social relations of science.* New York: Macmillan.

Cruze, W. W. 1935. Maturation and learning in chicks. *Journal of Comparative Psychology* 20:371-409.

——. 1938. Maturation and learning ability. *Psychological Monographs* 50: No. 5.

Darwin, C. 1859. *On the origin of the species.* London: Murray.

——. 1872. *The expressions of the emotions in man and animals.* New York: Appleton, 1873.

Dashiell, J. F. 1928. *Fundamentals of objective psychology.* Boston: Houghton Mifflin.

Davis, W. A. 1948. *Social-class influences upon learning.* Cambridge, Mass.: Harvard University Press.

——, & Havighurst, R. J. 1946. Social class and color difference in childrearing. *American Sociological Review* 11:698-710.

Dember, W. N., Earl, R. W., & Paradise, N. 1957. Response by rats to differential stimulus complexity. *Journal of Comparative and Physiological Psychology* 50:514-18.

Denenberg, V. H. 1959. The interactive effects of infantile and adult shock levels upon learning. *Psychological Reports* 5:357-64.

——. 1962. The effects of early experience. In E. S. E. Hafez (Ed.), *The behaviour of domestic animals.* London: Baillière, Tindall, & Cox, Ch. 6.

——, & Bell, R. W. 1960. Critical periods for the effects of infantile experience on adult learning. *Science* 131:227-28.

——, & Karas, G. G. 1960. Interactive effects of age and duration of infantile experience on adult learning. *Psychological Reports* 7:313-22.

——, Morton, J. R. C., Kline, N. J., & Grota, L. J. 1962. Effects of duration of infantile stimulation upon emotionality. *Canadian Journal of Psychology* 16:72-76.

Dennis, W. 1942. The performance of Hopi Indian children on the Goodenough Draw-a-Man Test. *Journal of Comparative Psychology* 34:341-48.

——. 1960. Causes of retardation among institutional children: Iran. *Journal of Genetic Psychology* 96:47-59.

——. 1966. Goodenough scores, art experience, and modernization. *Journal of Social Psychology* 68:211-28.

——, & Dennis, Marsena G. 1935. The effect of restricted practice upon the reaching, sitting, and standing of two infants. *Journal of Genetic Psychology* 47:21-29.

——, & Dennis, Marsena G. 1938. Infant development under conditions of restricted practice and minimum social stimulation: A preliminary report. *Journal of Genetic Psychology* 53:151-56.

——, & Dennis, Marsena G. 1940. The effect of cradling practice upon the onset of walking in Hopi children. *Journal of Genetic Psychology* 56:77-86.

———, & Dennis, Marsena G. 1941. Infant development under conditions of restricted practice and minimum social stimulation. *Genetic Psychological Monographs* 23:149-55. Also appears as Development under controlled environmental conditions, W. Dennis (Ed.), *Readings in child psychology*. New York: Prentice-Hall, 1951, Ch. 3-1.

Deutsch, Cynthia P. 1964. Auditory discrimination and learning social factors. *The Merrill-Palmer Quarterly* 10:277-96.

Deutsch, M. 1965. The role of social class in language development and cognition. *American Journal of Orthopsychiatry* 35:78-88.

———, & Brown, B. 1964. Social influences in Negro-white intelligence differences. *Journal of Social Issues* 20 (2), 24-35.

Dewey, J. 1900. *The school and society*. Chicago: University of Chicago Press. (Phoenix Books, P3, 1960.)

———. 1902. *The child and the curriculum*. Chicago: University of Chicago Press. (Phoenix Books, P3, 1960.)

Diggory, James C. 1966. *Self-evaluation: Concepts and studies*. New York: Wiley.

Dollard, J., Doob, L. W., Miller, N. E., Mowrer, O. H., & Sears, R. R. 1939. *Frustration and aggression*. New Haven: Yale University Press.

Dunn, L. M. 1959. *Peabody Picture Vocabulary Test*. Minneapolis: American Guidance Service.

———. 1965. *Expanded manual for the Peabody Picture Vocabulary Test*. Minneapolis: American Guidance Service.

Ebbinghaus, H. 1885. *Über das Gedächtnis: Untersuchungen zur experimentellen Psychologie*. Leipzig: Duncker und Humblot. (Trans. as *Memory: A contribution to experimental psychology*, by H. A. Ruger & C. E. Bussenius. New York: Columbia University Teachers College, 1913.)

Eckblad, G. 1963. The attractiveness of uncertainty. *Scandinavian Journal of Psychology* 4:1-13.

Endler, N. S., & Hunt, J. McV. 1966. Sources of behavioral variance as measured by the S-R Inventory of Anxiousness. *Psychological Bulletin* 65:336-46.

———, Hunt, J. McV., & Rosenstein, A. J. 1962. An S-R Inventory of Anxiousness. *Psychological Monographs* 76:No. 17 (Whole No. 536).

Farber, I. E. 1948. Response fixation under anxiety and non-anxiety conditions. *Journal of Experimental Psychology* 38:111-31.

Fenichel, O. 1945. *The psychoanalytic theory of neurosis*. New York: Norton.

Ferguson, G. A. 1954. On learning and human ability. *Canadian Journal of Psychology* 8:95-112.

———. 1956. On transfer and the abilities of man. *Canadian Journal of Psychology* 10:121-31.

————. 1959. Learning and human ability: A theoretical approach. In P. H. DuBois, W. H. Manning, & C. J. Spies (Eds.), *Factor analysis and related techniques in the study of learning.* A report of a conference held at Washington University in St. Louis, Missouri, February, 1959. Technical Report No. 7, Office of Naval Research Contract No. Nonr 816 (02), pp. 174-82.

Festinger, L. 1957. *A theory of cognitive dissonance.* Evanston, Ill.: Row, Peterson.

Finch, F. H. 1946. Enrollment increases and changes in the mental level. *Applied Psychological Monographs,* No. 10, p. 75.

Fisher, Dorothy Canfield. 1912. *A Montessori mother.* New York: Holt.

Fiske, D. W., & Maddi, S. R. 1961. *Functions of varied experience.* Homewood, Ill.: Dorsey.

Flavel, J. H. 1963. *The developmental psychology of Jean Piaget.* New York: D. Van Nostrand.

Fleishman, E. A., & Hempel, W. E., Jr. 1954. Changes in factor structure of complex psychomotor test as a function of practice. *Psychometrika* 19:239-52.

Forgays, D. G., & Forgays, Janet W. 1952. The nature of the effect of free environmental experience in the rat. *Journal of Comparative and Physiological Psychology* 45:322-28.

Forgus, R. H. 1954. The effect of early perceptual learning on the behavioral organization of adult rats. *Journal of Comparative and Physiological Psychology* 47:331-36.

————. 1955a. Influence of early experience on maze-learning with and without visual cues. *Canadian Journal of Psychology* 9:207-14.

————. 1955b. Early visual and motor experience as determiners of complex maze-learning ability under rich and reduced stimulation. *Journal of Comparative and Physiological Psychology* 48:215-20.

Freedman, A. 1957. Drive conditioning in water deprivation. Unpublished doctoral dissertation, University of Illinois.

Freeman, G. L. 1934. *Introduction to physiological psychology.* New York: Ronald.

Freud, Anna. 1936. *The ego and the mechanisms of defence,* trans. by Cecil Bains. New York: International Universities Press, 1946.

————, & Burlingham, Dorothy. 1944. *Infants without families.* New York: International Universities Press.

Freud, S. 1900. The interpretation of dreams. In A. A. Brill (Trans. & Ed.), *The basic writings of Sigmund Freud.* New York: Modern Library, 1938, pp. 179-548.

————. 1904. The psychopathology of everyday life. In A. A. Brill (Trans. & Ed.), *The basic writings of Sigmund Freud.* New York: Modern Library, 1938, pp. 33-178.

————. 1905. Three contributions to the theory of sex. In A. A. Brill (Trans. & Ed.), *The basic writings of Sigmund Freud.* New York: Modern Library, 1938.

————. 1915. Instincts and their vicissitudes. In *Collected papers.* Vol. 4. London: Hogarth, 1950, pp. 60-83.

————. 1926. *Inhibition, symptom and anxiety,* trans. by H. A. Bunker as *The problem of anxiety.* New York: Norton.

Froebel, F. 1826. *The education of man,* trans. by W. N. Hailman. New York: Appleton, 1896.

Frostig, Marianne. 1964. *The Frostig program for the development of visual perception.* Chicago: Follett Publishing Co.

Fryer, D. 1922. Occupational intelligence standards. *School and Society* 16:273-77.

Gagné, R. M. 1966a. "Contributions of learning to human development." Vice-Presidential Address of Section I, American Association for the Advancement of Science Meeting, Washington, D.C.

————. 1966b. Elementary science: A new scheme of instruction. *Science* 151 (3706), 49-53.

————, & Paradise, N. E. 1961. Abilities and learning sets in knowledge acquisition. *Psychological Monographs* 75:No. 14 (Whole No. 518).

Galton, F. 1869. *Hereditary genius: An inquiry into its laws and consequences.* London: Macmillan.

————. 1883. *Inquiries into human faculty and its development.* London: Macmillan.

————. 1886. Regression towards mediocrity in heredity stature. *Journal of the Anthropological Institute* 15:246-63.

Gauron, E. F., & Becker, W. C. 1959. The effects of early sensory deprivation of adult rat behavior under competitive stress: An attempt at replication of a study by Alexander Wolf. *Journal of Comparative and Physiological Psychology* 52:689-93.

Gesell, A. 1945. *The embryology of behavior: The beginnings of the human mind.* New York: Harpers.

————. 1954. The ontogenesis of infant behavior. In L. Carmichael (Ed.), *Manual of child psychology.* New York: Wiley, Ch. 6.

————, Halverson, H. M., Thompson, Helen, Ilg, Frances L., Castner, B. M., & Bates, Louise. 1940. *The first five years of life.* New York: Harpers.

————, & Thompson, Helen. 1929. Learning and growth in identical twin infants. *Genetic Psychology Monographs* 6:1-124.

Gleser, G. C., Cronbach, L. J., & Rajaratnam, N. 1961. Generalizability of scores influenced by multiple sources of variance. *Psycho-metrika* 30:395-418.

Goddard, H. H. 1910. A measuring scale for intelligence. *Training School Bulletin* 6:146-55.

———. 1912. *The Kallikak family: A study in the heredity of feeble-mindedness.* New York: Macmillan.

Goldfarb, W. 1953. The effects of early institutional care on adolescent personality. *Journal of Experimental Education* 12:106-29.

———. 1955. Emotional and intellectual consequences of psychologic deprivation in infancy: A re-evaluation. In P. H. Hoch & J. Zubin (Eds.), *Psychopathology of childhood.* New York: Grune & Stratton, pp. 105-19.

Goldman, Jacquelin R. 1964. The effects of handling and shocking in infancy upon adult behavior in the albino rat. *Journal of Genetic Psychology* 104:301-10.

Goodenough, Florence L. 1926. *The measurement of intelligence by drawings.* Yonkers-on-Hudson, N.Y.: World Book Company.

———. 1939. A critique of experiments on raising the IQ. *Educational Methods* 19:73-79. Reprinted in W. Dennis (Ed.), *Readings in child psychology.* New York: Prentice-Hall, 1951, Ch. VI-1.

———, & Maurer, Katherine M. 1942. *The mental growth of children from two to fourteen years: A study of the predictive value of the Minnesota Preschool Scales.* Minneapolis: University of Minnesota Press.

Gordon, H. 1923. *Mental and scholastic tests among retarded children.* London: Board of Education Pamphlet No. 44.

Gordon, I. J. (Ed.) 1969. *Reaching the child through parent education: The Florida approach.* Gainesville: Institute for Development of Human Resources, College of Education, University of Florida.

Gray, Susan W., & Klaus, R. A. 1963. Early training for culturally deprived children. Proposed research project to run 9-63 to 8-64. George Peabody College and Murfreesboro, Tennessee, City Schools.

Greenberg, D., Uzgiris, Ina C., & Hunt, J. McV. 1968. Hastening the development of the blink-response with looking. *Journal of Genetic Psychology* 113:167-76.

Greenberg, J. W., Gerver, J. M., Chall, J., & Davidson, H. H. 1965. Attitudes of children from a deprived environment toward achievement concepts. *Journal of Educational Research* 58:57-72.

Griffin, G. A., & Harlow, H. F. 1966. Effects of three months of total social deprivation on social adjustment and learning in the rhesus monkey. *Child Development* 37:523-47.

Griffiths, W. J., Jr. 1960. Effects of isolation and stress on escape thresholds of albino rats. *Psychological Reports* 6:623-29.

Guilford, J. P. 1940. Human abilities. *Psychological Review* 47:367-94.

———. 1956. The structure of intellect. *Psychological Bulletin* 53:267-93.

———. 1957. A revised structure of intellect. *Reports of the Psychological Laboratory*, No. 19. Los Angeles: University of Southern California.

———. 1959. Three faces of intellect. *American Psychologist* 14:469-79.

Guthrie, E. R. 1938. *The psychology of human conflict: The clash of motives within the individual.* New York: Harper.

Hall, C. S. 1934. Emotional behavior in the rat: I. Defecation and urination as measures of individual differences in emotionality. *Journal of Comparative Psychology* 18:385-403.

Hall, M. 1893. *New memoire on the nervous system.* London: Proceedings of the Royal Academy.

Harlow, H. F. 1949. The formation of learning sets. *Psychological Review* 56:51-65.

———. 1950. Learning and satiation of response in intrinsically motivated complex puzzle performance by monkeys. *Journal of Comparative and Physiological Psychology* 43:289-94.

———. 1958. The nature of love. *American Psychologist* 13:673-85.

———, Harlow, Margaret K., & Meyer, D. R. 1950. Learning motivated by a manipulative drive. *Journal of Experimental Psychology* 40:228-34.

Harvey, O. J., Hunt, D. E., & Schroeder, H. M. 1961. *Conceptual systems and personality organization.* New York: Wiley.

Hayes, K. J. 1962. Genes, drives, and intellect. *Psychological Reports* 10:299-342.

Hebb, D. O. 1946a. Emotion in man and animal: An analysis of the intuitive processes of recognition. *Psychological Review* 53:88-106.

———. 1946b. On the nature of fear. *Psychological Review* 53:259-76.

———. 1947. The effects of early experience on problem-solving at maturity. *American Psychologist* 2:306-7.

———. 1949. *The organization of behavior.* New York: Wiley.

———, & Mahut, Helen. 1955. Motivation et recherche du changement perceptif chez le rat et chez l'homme. *Journal de psychologie normale et pathologique* 48:209-20.

———, & Riesen, A. H. 1943. The genesis of irrational fears. *Bulletin of the Canadian Psychological Association* 3:49-50.

———, & Thompson, W. R. 1954. The social significance of animal studies. In G. Lindzey (Ed.), *Handbook of social psychology.* Vol. I. Cambridge, Mass.: Addison-Wesley, Ch. 15.

———, & Williams, K. 1946. A method of rating animal intelligence. *Journal of Genetic Psychology* 34:59-65.

Heinroth, O. 1910. Beitrage zur Biologie, namentlich Ethnologie und Physiologie der Anatiden. *Verhandlungen des V International Ornithologische Kongress,* pp. 589-702 (Cited in Thorpe, 1956).

Helson, H. 1959. Adaptation-level theory. In S. Koch (Ed.), *Psychology: A study of a science.* Vol. 1. *Sensory, perceptual, and physiological formulations.* New York: McGraw-Hill, pp. 565-621.

Hendrick, I. 1943. The discussion of the "instinct to master." *Psychoanalytic Quarterly* 12:561-65.

Hernandez-Peon, R., Scherrer, H., & Jouvet, M. 1956. Modification of electric activity in cochlear nucleus during "attention" in unanesthetized cats. *Science* 123:331-32.

Hess, R. D., & Shipman, Virginia. 1965. Early experience and the socialization of cognitive modes in children. *Child Development* 36:869-86.

Hetzer, Hildegard, & Wolf, Käthe. 1928. Eine Testserie für das erste Lebensjahr. *Zeitschrift für Psychologie mit Zeitschrift für angewante Psychologie* 107:62-104.

Hieronymus, A. N. 1951. A study of social class motivation: Relationships between anxiety for education and certain socioeconomic and intellectual variables. *Journal of Educational Psychology* 42:193-295.

Hilgard, E. R. 1949. Human motives and the concept of self. *American Psychologist* 4:374-82.

Hilgard, Josephine R. 1932. Learning and maturation in preschool children. *Journal of Genetic Psychology* 41:36-56.

———. 1933. The effect of early and delayed practice on memory and motor performances studied by the method of co-twin control. *Genetic Psychology Monographs* 14:493-567.

Hirsch, J. 1963. Behavioral genetics and individuality understood: Behaviorism's counterfactual dogma blinded the behavioral sciences to the significance of meiosis. *Science* 142:1436-42.

———. 1967. Behavioral genetics, or "experimental," analysis: The challenge of science versus the lure of technology. *American Psychologist* 22:118-30.

Holmes, Frances B. 1935. An experimental study of children's fears. In A. T. Jersild & Frances B. Holmes (Eds.), *Children's fears.* New York: Child Development Monographs, No. 20, Columbia University Teachers College, pp. 167-296.

Holt, E. B. 1931. *Animal drive and the learning process.* New York: Holt.

Holzinger, K. J. 1937. *Student manual of factor analysis.* Chicago: University of Chicago Department of Education.

Horsfall, W. R., & Anderson, J. F. 1961. Suppression of male characteristics of mosquitos by thermal means. *Science* 133 (3467), 1830.

————, Anderson, J. F., & Burst, R. A. 1964. Thermal stress and anomalous development of mosquitoes (Diptera: Culicidae). III. Aedus Sierrensis. *The Canadian Entomologist* 96:1369-72.

Hubel, D. H., & Wiesel, T. N. 1959. Receptive fields of single neurons in the cat's striate cortex. *Journal of Physiology* (London) 148:574-91.

————, & Wiesel, T. N. 1960. Receptive fields of optic nerve fibers in the spider monkey. *Journal of Physiology* (London) 154: 572-80.

————, & Wiesel, T. N. 1961. Integrative action in the cat's lateral geniculate body. *Journal of Physiology* (London) 155:385-98.

Hull, C. L. 1931. Goal attraction and directing ideas conceived as habit phenomena. *Psychological Review* 38:487-506.

————. 1943. *Principles of behavior.* New York: Appleton.

Humphreys, L. G. 1939. Acquisition and extinction of verbal expectations in a situation analogous to conditioning. *Journal of Experimental Psychology* 25:294-301.

————. 1959. Discussion of Dr. Ferguson's paper. In P. H. DuBois, W. H. Manning, & C. J. Spies (Eds.), *Factor analysis and related techniques in the study of learning.* A report of a conference held at Washington University, St. Louis, Missouri, February, 1959. Technical Report No. 7, Office of Naval Research Contract No. Nonr 816 (02), pp. 183-87.

————. 1960. Investigations of the simplex. *Psychometrika* 25:313-23.

————. 1962a. The nature and organization of human abilities. In M. Katz (Ed.), *The 19th yearbook of the National Council on Measurement in Education.* Ames, Iowa: National Council on Measurement in Education, pp. 39-45.

————. 1962b. The organization of human abilities. *American Psychologist* 17:475-83.

Hunt, J. McV. 1941. The effects of infant feeding-frustration upon adult hoarding in the albino rat. *Journal of Abnormal and Social Psychology* 36:338-60.

————. 1945. Experimental psychoanalysis. In P. L. Harriman (Ed.), *Encyclopedia of psychology.* New York: Philosophical Library, pp. 140-56.

————. 1956. Psychosexual development: The infant disciplines. Unpublished paper, Psychological Development Laboratory, University of Illinois, Urbana.

————. 1960. Experience and the development of motivation: Some reinterpretations. *Child Development* 31:489-504.

————. 1961. *Intelligence and experience.* New York: Ronald.

————. 1963a. Motivation inherent in information processing and action. In O. J. Harvey (Ed.), *Motivation and social interaction: Cognitive determinants.* New York: Ronald, Ch. 3.

————. 1963b. Piaget's observations as a source of hypotheses concerning motivation. *Merrill-Palmer Quarterly* 9:263-75.

————. 1964a. The implications of changing ideas on how children develop intellectually. *Children* 11 (No. 3), 83-91.

————. 1964b. Revisiting Montessori. Introduction to the republication of Maria Montessori, *The Montessori method.* New York: Schocken Books.

————. 1965a. Intrinsic motivation and its role in psychological development. In D. Levine (Ed.), *Nebraska Symposium on Motivation* 13:189-282. Lincoln: University of Nebraska Press.

————. 1965b. Traditional personality theory in the light of recent evidence. *American Scientist* 53:80-96.

————. 1966. Toward a theory of guided learning in development. In R. H. Ojemann & Karen Pritchett (Eds.), *Giving emphasis to guided learning.* Cleveland, Ohio: Educational Research Council, pp. 98-160.

————. 1967a. Evolution of current concepts of intelligence and intellectual development. *American Montessori Society Bulletin* 6:No. 4.

————. 1967b. Political implications of the role of experience in the development of intelligence. Paper presented at the meeting of the Midwestern Psychological Association, Chicago, Ill., 6 May 1967.

————, & Luria, Zella. 1956. Investigations of the effects of early experience in sub-human animals. Mimeographed paper. Psychological Development Laboratory, University of Illinois, Urbana.

————, Schlosberg, H., Solomon, R. L., & Stellar, E. 1947. Studies of the effects of infantile experience on adult behavior in rats: I. Effects of infantile feeding frustration on adult hoarding. *Journal of Comparative and Physiological Psychology* 40:291-304.

————, & Uzgiris, Ina C. 1964. Cathexis from recognitive familiarity: An exploratory study. Mimeographed paper. Psychological Development Laboratory, University of Illinois, Urbana. Presented at symposium to honor J. P. Guilford at the meeting of the American Psychological Association, Los Angeles.

Hunter, W. S. 1912. The delayed reaction in animals and children. *Behavior Monographs* 2:No. 1, 1-85.

————. 1918. The temporal maze and kinaesthetic sensory processes in the white rat. *Psychobiology* 2:339-51.

Hydén, H. 1959. Biochemical changes in glial cells and nerve cells at varying activity. In F. Brücke (Ed.), *Proceedings of the 4th International Congress on Biochemistry*. Vol. 3. *Biochemistry of the central nervous system*. London: Pergamon, pp. 64-89.

————. 1960. The neuron. In J. Brachet & A. E. Mirsky (Eds.), *The cell: Biochemistry, physiology, morphology*. Vol. 4. *Specialized cells*. New York: Academic Press, Ch. 5, pp. 215-323.

————, & Egyhazi, E. 1962. Nuclear RNA changes of nerve cells during a learning experiment in rats. *Proceedings of the National Academy of Science* 48:1366-73.

Hymovitch, B. 1952. The effects of experimental variations in early experience on problem solving in the rat. *Journal of Comparative and Physiological Psychology* 45:313-21.

Irwin, O. C. 1930. The amount and nature of activities of new-born infants under constant external stimulating conditions during the first 10 days of life. *Genetic Psychology Monographs* 8:192.

Jennings, H. S. 1930. *The biological basis of human nature*. New York: Norton.

Johannsen, W. 1903. *Ueber Erblichkeit in Populationen und in reined Linien*. Jena: Fischer.

————. 1909. *Elemente der exakten Erblichkeitslehre*. Jena: Fischer.

John, Vera P. 1963. The intellectual development of slum children: Some preliminary findings. *American Journal of Orthopsychiatry* 33:813-22.

————, & Goldstein, L. S. 1964. The social context of language acquisition. *Merrill-Palmer Quarterly* 10:265-75.

Jones, H. E. 1954. The environment and mental development. In L. Carmichael (Ed.), *Handbook of child psychology*. New York: Wiley.

Jones, K. L. 1966. The language development of Head-Start children. (Doctoral dissertation, University of Arkansas.) Ann Arbor, Mich.: University Microfilms, No. 66-11, p. 609.

Kagan, J. 1965. Reflection-impulsivity and reading ability in primary grade children. *Child Development* 36:609-28.

Karnes, Merle B. 1968. *Helping young children develop language skills: A book of activities*. Washington, D.C.: Council for Exceptional Children.

————. 1969. A new role for teachers: Involving the entire family in the education of preschool disadvantaged children. Urbana: University of Illinois, College of Education (Mimeographed paper).

————, & Hodgins, Audrey. 1969. The effects of a highly structured preschool program on the measured intelligence of culturally disadvantaged four-year-old children. *Psychology in the Schools* 6:89-91.

————, Hodgins, Audrey S., Stoneburner, R. L., Studley, W. M., & Teska, J. A. 1968. Effects of a highly structured program of language development on intellectual functioning and psycholinguistic development of culturally disadvantaged three-year-olds. *Journal of Special Education* 2:405-12.

————, Studley, W. M., Wright, W. R., & Hodgins, Audrey S. 1968. An approach for working with mothers of disadvantaged preschool children. *Merrill-Palmer Quarterly of Behavior and Development* 14:173-84.

————, Teska, J. A., & Hodgins, Audrey S. 1969a. The effects of four programs of classroom intervention on the intellectual and language development of four-year-old disadvantaged children. Champaign: University of Illinois, College of Education, Institute of Research on Exceptional Children (Mimeographed paper).

————, Teska, J. A., & Hodgins, Audrey S. 1969b. A longitudinal study of disadvantaged children who participated in three different preschool programs. Champaign: University of Illinois, College of Education, Institute of Research on Exceptional Children (Mimeographed paper).

————, Wollersheim, Janet P., Stoneburner, R. L., Hodgins, Audrey, & Teska, J. A. 1968. An evaluation of two preschool programs for disadvantaged children: A traditional and a highly structured experimental preschool. *Exceptional Children* 34:667-76.

Katz, P. A., & Deutsch, M. 1963. Relation of auditory-visual shifting to reading achievement. *Perception and Motor Skills* 17:327-32.

Keller, Suzanne. 1963. The social world of the urban slum child: Some early findings. *American Journal of Orthopsychiatry* 33:823-31.

Kelley, T. L. 1928. *Crossroads in the minds of man: A study of differentiable mental abilities.* Stanford, Calif.: Stanford University Press.

Kelly, G. A. 1955. *The psychology of personal constructs.* New York: Norton, 2 vols.

Kendler, H. H., & Kendler, Tracy S. 1956. Inferential behavior in preschool children. *Journal of Experimental Psychology* 51:311-14.

Kennedy, W. A., *et al.* 1963. A normative sample of intelligence and achievement of Negro elementary school children in the south-eastern United States. *Monographs of the Society for Research in Child Development* Serial No. 90, Vol. 28.

Kirk, G. E. 1969. The performance of advantaged and disadvantaged preschool children on tests of picture-phonemic discrimination and picture-word recognition skills. Unpublished doctoral dissertation, University of Illinois.

Kirk, S. A., & McCarthy, J. J. 1961. *Illinois Test of Psycholinguistic Abilities.* Urbana: University of Illinois Press.

————, McCarthy, J. J., & Kirk, Winifred. 1968. *The Illinois Test of Psycholinguistic Abilities.* (Revised edition.) Urbana: University of Illinois Press.

Klaus, R. A., & Gray, Susan W. 1968. The early training project for disadvantaged children: A report after five years. *Monographs of the Society for Research in Child Development* 33 (No. 4), Ser. No. 120, pp. 1-66.

Klineberg, O. 1935. *Negro intelligence and selective migration.* New York: Columbia University Press.

Köhler, W. 1924. *The mentality of apes,* trans. by Ella Winter. New York: Vintage Books, 1959.

Krugman, M. 1961. The culturally deprived child in school. *National Education Journal* 50:22-23.

Kuo, Z. Y. 1932a. Ontogeny of embryonic behavior in aves: I. The chronology and general nature of the behavior in the chick embryo. *Journal of Experimental Zoology* 61:395-430.

————. 1932b. Ontogeny of embryonic behavior in aves: II. The mechanical factor in the various stages leading to hatching. *Journal of Experimental Zoology* 62:453-87.

————. 1932c. Ontogeny of embryonic behavior in aves: III. The structural and environmental factors in embryonic behavior. *Journal of Comparative Psychology* 13:245-71.

————. 1932d. Ontogeny of embryonic behavior in aves: IV. The influence of embryonic movements upon the bahavior after hatching. *Journal of Comparative Psychology* 14:109-22.

Lamarck, J. Chevalier de. 1809. *Zoological philosophy,* trans. of *Philosophie zoologique* by H. Elliot. London: Macmillan, 1914.

Leahy, Alice M. 1935. Nature-nurture and intelligence. *Genetic Psychology Monograph* 17:235-308.

LeShan, L. L. 1952. Time orientation and social class. *Journal of Abnormal and Social Psychology* 47:589-92.

Lesser, G. S., Fifer, G., & Clark, D. H. 1965. Mental abilities of children from different social-class and cultural groups. *Monographs of the Society for Research in Child Development* 30 (No. 4), Ser. No. 102.

Levine, S. 1956. A further study of infantile handling and adult avoidance learning. *Journal of Personality* 25:70-80.

————. 1957. Infantile experience and consummatory behavior in adulthood. *Journal of Comparative and Physiological Psychology* 50:609-12.

————. 1958. Effects of early deprivation and delayed weaning on avoidance learning in the albino rat. *Archives of Neurology and Psychiatry* 79:211-13.

————. 1959. The effects of differential infantile stimulation on emotionality at weaning. *Canadian Journal of Psychology* 13:243-47.

————. 1961. Psychophysiological effects of early stimulation. In E. Bliss (Ed.), *Roots of behavior.* New York: Hoeber.

————, Chevalier, J. A., & Korchin, S. J. 1956. The effects of early shock and handling on later avoidance learning. *Journal of Personality* 24:475-93.

Lewis, O. 1961. *The children of Sanchez.* New York: Random House.

————. 1966a. The culture of poverty. *Scientific American* 215 (No. 4), 19-25.

————. 1966b. *La Vida: A Puerto Rican family in the culture of poverty—San Juan and New York.* New York: Random House.

Liberman, R. 1962. Retinal cholinesterase and glycolysis in rats raised in darkness. *Science* 135:372-73.

Liebow, E. 1967. *Tally's corner: A study of Negro street-corner men.* Boston: Little, Brown.

Lindzey, G., Lykken, D. T., & Winston, H. D. 1960. Infantile trauma, genetic factors, and adult temperament. *Journal of Abnormal and Social Psychology* 61:7-14.

Long, B. H., & Henderson, E. H. 1967. Social schemata of school beginners: Some demographic correlates. *Proceedings of the 75th Annual Convention of the American Psychological Association.* Washington, D.C.: American Psychological Association, pp. 329-30.

Lorenz, K. 1935. Der Kumpan in der Umwelt des Vögels. *Journal of Ornithology* 83:137-214; 289-413. Trans. by author and republished as The companion in the bird's world. *Auk* 54 (1937):245-73.

Maclaurin, W. R. 1949. *Invention and innovation in the radio industry.* New York: Macmillan.

Maitland, S. C. 1966. The perspective, frustration-failure and delay of gratification in middle-class and lower-class children from organized and disorganized families. Unpublished doctoral dissertation, University of Minnesota, Minneapolis.

Maltzman, I., & Raskin, D. C. 1965. Effects of individual differences in the orienting reflex on conditioning and complex processes. *Journal of Experimental Research on Personality* 1:1-16.

Mannheim, K. 1936. *Ideology and utopia: An introduction to the so-*

ciology of knowledge, trans. by L. Wirth & E. Shils. New York: Harcourt.

Marx, M. H. 1952. Infantile deprivation and adult behavior in the rat: Retention of increased rate of eating. *Journal of Comparative and Physiological Psychology* 45:43-49.

Matthews, S. A., & Detwiler, S. R. 1926. The reaction of Amblystoma embryos following prolonged treatment with chloretone. *Journal of Experimental Zoology* 45:279-92.

McCandless, B. 1952. Environment and intelligence. *American Journal of Mental Deficiency* 56:674-91.

McClelland, D. C. 1958. Risk taking in children with high and low need for achievement. In J. W. Atkinson (Ed.), *Motives in fantasy, action, and society.* Princeton, N.J.: D. Van Nostrand.

———, Atkinson, J. W., Clark, R. A., & Lowell, E. L. 1953. *The achievement motive.* New York: Appleton.

McDonald, D. 1966. Our invisible poor. In L. A. Ferman, J. L. Kornbluh, & A. Haber (Eds.), *Poverty in America.* Ann Arbor: University of Michigan Press, pp. 6-23.

McDougall, W. 1908. *Social psychology.* Boston: Luce.

McGraw, Myrtle B. 1935. *Growth: A study of Johnny and Jimmy.* New York: Appleton.

McKelvey, R. K., & Marx, M. H. 1951. Effects of infantile food and water deprivation on adult hoarding in the rat. *Journal of Comparative and Physiological Psychology* 44:423-30.

McLuhan, M. 1964. *Understanding media.* New York: McGraw-Hill.

McMillan, Margaret. 1919. *The nursery school.* London: J. M. Dent & Sons, revised edition, 1930.

McNemar, Q. 1940. A critical examination of the University of Iowa studies of environmental influence upon the IQ. *Psychological Bulletin* 37:63-92.

———. 1942. *The revision of the Stanford-Binet scale.* Boston: Houghton Mifflin.

Mead, G. H. 1934. *Mind, self, and society.* C. W. Morris (Ed.). Chicago: University of Chicago Press.

Melton, A. W. 1941. Learning. In W. S. Munroe (Ed.), *Encyclopedia of educational research.* New York: Macmillan.

Mendel, G. 1865. Experiments in plant hybridization. *Proceedings of the Natural History Society of Brünn* (English trans. Harvard University Press, 1948).

Merton, R. K. 1945. Sociology of knowledge. In G. Gurvitch & W. E. Moore (Eds.), *Twentieth century sociology.* New York: Philosophical Library, Ch. 13.

Mierke, K. 1933. Über die Objectionsfähigkeit und ihre Bedeutung für die Typenlehre. *Archiv für die gesamte Psychologie* 89:1-108.

Miller, G. A., Galanter, E., & Pribram, K. H. 1960. *Plans and the structure of behavior.* New York: Holt.

Miller, J. O. 1968. Diffusion of intervention effects in disadvantaged families. University of Illinois, Urbana: Coordination Center, National Laboratory of Early Childhood Education.

————, & Mumbauer, Corrine. 1968. Intellectual functioning, learning performance, and cognitive style in advantaged and disadvantaged preschool children. Nashville, Tenn.: George Peabody College for Teachers (Mimeographed paper).

Miller, N. E., & Dollard, J. 1941. *Social learning and imitation.* New Haven: Yale University Press.

Miller, W. B. 1958. Lower class culture as a generating milieu of gang delinquency. *Journal of Social Issues* 14:5-19.

Milner, Esther. 1951. A study of the relationship between reading readiness in grade one school children and patterns of parent-child interactions. *Child Development* 22:95-122.

Mischel, W. 1961. Father-absence and delay of gratification: Cross-cultural comparisons. *Journal of Abnormal and Social Psychology* 62:116-24.

————, & Metzner, R. 1962. Preference for delayed reward as a function of age, intelligence and length of delay interval. *Journal of Abnormal and Social Psychology* 64:425-31.

Mittelmann, B. 1954. Motility in infants, children, and adults. *Psychoanalytic Study of the Child* 9:142-77.

Money-Kyrle, R. 1939. *Superstition and society.* Psycho-Analytic Epitomes No. 3. London: Hogarth Press.

Montessori, Maria. 1909. *The Montessori method: Scientific pedagogy as applied to child education in "The Children's House," with additions and revisions,* trans by Anne E. George. New York: Frederick Stokes, 1912.

Montgomery, K. C. 1952. A test of two explanations of spontaneous alternation. *Journal of Comparative and Physiological Psychology* 45:287-93.

————. 1953. Exploratory behavior as a function of "similarity" of stimulus situations. *Journal of Comparative and Physiological Psychology* 46:129-33.

————. 1955. The relation between fear induced by novel stimulation and exploratory behavior. *Journal of Comparative and Physiological Psychology* 48:254-60.

————, & Segall, M. 1955. Discrimination learning based upon the exploratory drive. *Journal of Comparative and Physiological Psychology* 48:225-28.

Moore, O. K. 1963. *Autotelic responsive environments and exceptional children.* Hamden, Conn.: Responsive Environments Foundation.

Morgan, C. L. 1894. *An introduction to comparative psychology.* (2nd ed.) London: Scott, 1909.

Mowrer, O. H. 1960. *Learning theory and behavior.* New York: Wiley.

Moynihan, D. P. 1965. *The Negro family: The case for national action.* Washington, D.C.: U.S. Government Printing Office.

Munsinger, H., & Kessen, W. 1964. Uncertainty, structure, and preference. *Psychological Monographs* 78 (No. 9), Whole No. 586, 1-24.

Murphy, Lois. 1961. Preventive implications of development in the preschool years. In G. Caplan (Ed.), *Prevention of mental disorders in children.* New York: Basic Books.

——. 1968. Assessment of young children: The concept of a vulnerability index. In L. Dittman, C. C. Chandler, & R. S. Lourie (Eds.), *New perspectives in early child care.* New York: Atherton, Ch. 6.

Needham, J. 1959. *A history of embryology.* New York: Abelard-Schuman.

Newell, A., Shaw, J. C., & Simon, H. A. 1958. Elements of a theory of human problem solving. *Psychological Review* 65:151-66.

Newman, H. H., Freeman, F. N., & Holzinger, K. J. 1937. *Twins: A study of heredity and environment.* Chicago: University of Chicago Press.

Nimnicht, G., Meier, J. H., & McAfee, Oralie. 1966. A first-year partial progress report of a project in an autotelic responsive environment nursery school for environmentally deprived Spanish-American children. *Journal of Research Services* 5 (No. 2), 3-34.

——, Meier, J. H., & McAfee, Oralie. 1967a. A summary of the evaluation of the experimental program for deprived children at the New Nursery School using some experimental measures. Greeley: Colorado State College (Mimeographed paper).

——, Meier, J., & McAfee, Oralie. 1967b. A report on the use of typewriters and related equipment with three and four-year old children at the New Nursery School. Greeley: Colorado State College (Mimeographed paper).

Nissen, H. W. 1930. A study of exploratory behavior in the white rat by means of the obstruction method. *Journal of Genetic Psychology* 37:361-76.

Nowlis, H. H. 1941. The influence of success and failure on the resumption of an interrupted task. *Journal of Experimental Psychology* 28:304-25.

O'Brien, Roslyn A. 1967. Preschool education of the disadvantaged: An evaluation of Head Start. Unpublished paper.

——, & Lopate, P. 1968. Preschool programs and the intellectual development of disadvantaged children. Urbana: ERIC Clearinghouse on Early Childhood Education.

Orlansky, H. 1949. Infant care and personality. *Psychological Bulletin* 46:1-48.

Osgood, C. E. 1952. The nature and measurement of meaning. *Psychological Bulletin* 49:197-237.

———, Suci, G. J., & Tannenbaum, P. H. 1957. *The measurement of meaning.* Urbana: University of Illinois Press.

Padilla, S. G. 1935. Further studies on the delayed pecking of chicks. *Journal of Comparative Psychology* 20:413-43.

Painter, Genevieve. 1968. *Infant education.* San Rafael, Calif.: Dimensions Publishing Co.

Pasamanick, B. 1962. Determinants of intelligence. Draft of paper presented at a symposium on Man and Civilization: Control of the Mind—II, University of California, San Francisco Medical Center, 27 January.

———, & Knobloch, Hilda. 1960. Brain damage and reproductive casualty. *American Journal of Orthopsychiatry* 30:298-305.

Pavlov, I. P. 1927. *Conditioned reflexes,* trans. by G. V. Anrep. London: Oxford University Press.

Piaget, J. 1924. *Judgment and reasoning in the child,* trans. by Marjorie Worden. New York: Harcourt, 1928.

———. 1926. *The child's conception of the world,* trans. by Joan and Andrew Tomlinson. New York: Harcourt, 1929.

———. 1927. *The child's conception of physical causality,* trans. by Marjorie Worden Gabian. New York: Harcourt, 1930.

———. 1932. *The moral judgment of the child,* trans. by Marjorie Worden Gabian. New York: Harcourt.

———. 1936. *The origins of intelligence in children,* trans. by Margaret Cook. New York: International Universities Press, 1952.

———. 1937. *The construction of reality in the child,* trans. by Margaret Cook. New York: Basic Books, 1954.

———. 1945. *Play, dreams, and imitation in childhood,* trans. by C. Gattegno & F. M. Hodgson. New York: Norton, 1951.

———. 1947. *The psychology of intelligence,* trans. by M. Piercy & D. E. Berlyne. Paterson, N.J.: Littlefield, Adams & Co., 1960.

———, & Inhelder, Bärbel. 1940. *Le développement des quantités chez l'enfant. Conservation et atomisme.* Neuchatel: Delachaux et Niestle.

———, & Inhelder, Bärbel. 1947. Diagnosis of mental operations and theory of intelligence. *American Journal of Mental Deficiency* 51 (3), 401-6.

Pinneau, S. R. 1955. The infantile disorders of hospitalism and anaclitic depression. *Psychological Bulletin* 52:429-59.

Pribram, K. H. 1960. A review of theory in physiological psychology. *Annual Review of Psychology* 11:1-40.

Pruette, Lorine. 1926. *G. Stanley Hall: A biography of a mind.* New York: Appleton.

Rainwater, L. 1966. Crucible of identity: The Negro lower-class family. *Daedalus* 95:172-216.

Rambusch, Nancy M. 1962. *Learning how to learn: An American approach to Montessori*. Baltimore: Helicon.

Rasch, Ellen R., Swift, H., Riesen, A. H., & Chow, K. L. 1961. Altered structure and composition of retinal cells in dark-reared mammals. *Experimental Cell Research* 25:348-63.

Raven, J. C. 1938. *Guide to using progressive matrices*. London: Lewis, 1952.

Razran, G. H. S. 1938a. Conditioning away social bias by the luncheon technique. *Psychological Bulletin* 35:693.

———. 1938b. Music, art, and the conditioned response. Unpublished paper, Eastern Psychological Association, 1-2 April.

———. 1961. The observable unconscious and the inferable conscious in current Soviet psychophysiology: Interoceptive conditioning, semantic conditioning, and the orienting reflex. *Psychological Review* 68:81-147.

Reid, J. H. 1966. America's forgotten children. *Parent's Magazine* 41 (No. 2), 40ff.

Riesen, A. H. 1947. The development of visual perception in man and chimpanzee. *Science* 106:107-8.

———. 1958. Plasticity of behavior: Psychological aspects. In H. F. Harlow & C. N. Woolsey (Eds.), *Biological and biochemical bases of behavior*. Madison: University of Wisconsin Press, pp. 425-50.

———. 1961. Stimulation as a requirement for growth and function in behavioral development. In D. W. Fiske & S. R. Maddi (Eds.), *Functions of varied experience*. Homewood, Ill.: Dorsey.

Ripin, Rowena. 1933. A comparative study of the development of infants in an institution with those in homes of low socioeconomic status. *Psychological Bulletin* 30:680-81.

Rogers, C. R. 1951. *Client-centered therapy*. Boston: Houghton Mifflin.

Romanes, G. J. 1882. *Animal intelligence*. New York: Appleton, 1883 (45).

———. 1883. *Mental evolution in animals*. New York: Appleton, 1884 (45).

Rose, J. E., & Woolsey, C. N. 1949. The relations of thalamic connections, cellular structure and evocable electrical activity in the auditory region of the cat. *Journal of Comparative Neurology* 91:441-66.

Rosen, B. D., & D'Andrade, R. 1959. The psycho-social origins of achievement motivation. *Sociometry* 22:182-218.

Rosenzweig, S. 1933. Preferences in the repetition of successful and unsuccessful activities as a function of age and personality. *Journal of Genetic Psychology* 42:423-41.

Rousseau, J. J. 1762. *Emile,* trans. by Barbara Foxley. New York: Everyman's Library, 1916.

Salama, A. A. 1962. Fixation in the rat as a function of infantile shocking, handling, and gentling. Unpublished doctoral dissertation, University of Illinois.

―――, & Hunt, J. McV. 1964. "Fixation" in the rat as a function of infantile shocking, handling, and gentling. *Journal of Genetic Psychology* 105:131-62.

Schneirla, T. C. 1959. An evolutionary and developmental theory of byphasic processes underlying approach and withdrawal. In M. R. Jones (Ed.), *Nebraska Symposium on Motivation.* Lincoln: University of Nebraska Press, pp. 1-42.

Schoggen, Maxine F. 1967. The imprint of low-income homes on young children. In Susan Gray & J. O. Miller (Eds.), *Research, change, and social responsibility: An illustrative model from early education. DARCEE Papers and Reports* 2, No. 3. Nashville, Tenn.: George Peabody College for Teachers.

Schoggen, P. H., & Schoggen, Maxine F. 1968. Behavior units in observational research. Papers presented as part of the symposium on Methodological Issues in Observational Research, American Psychological Association, San Francisco, Calif.

Sharpless, S., & Jasper, H. H. 1956. Habituation of the arousal reaction. *Brain* 79:655-80.

Shaw, C. R. 1929. *Delinquency areas: A study of the geographic distribution of school truants, juvenile delinquents, and adult offenders in Chicago.* Chicago: University of Chicago Press.

―――. 1931. *The natural history of a delinquent career.* Chicago: University of Chicago Press.

Sherman, M., & Key, Cora B. 1932. The intelligence of isolated mountain children. *Child Development* 3:279-90.

Sherrington, C. S. 1906. *The integrative action of the nervous system.* New York: Scribner's. (New edition, Cambridge: Cambridge University Press, 1947.)

Shirley, Mary M. 1931. A motor sequence favors the maturation theory. *Psychological Bulletin* 28:204-5.

―――. 1933. The first two years: A study of 25 babies: Vol. II, Intellectual development. *Institute of Child Welfare Monograph Series,* No. 7. Minneapolis: University of Minnesota Press, p. 513.

Short, J. F., Jr., & Strodtbeck, F. L. 1965. *Group process and gang delinquency.* Chicago: University of Chicago Press.

Simpson, B. R. 1939. The wandering IQ. *Journal of Psychology* 7:351-67.

Sinnott, E. W., Dunn, L. C., & Dobzhansky, T. 1958. *Principles of genetics.* New York: McGraw.

Skeels, H. M. 1965. Some preliminary findings of three follow-up studies on the effects of adoption on children from institutions. *Children* 12 (1), 33-34.

———. 1966. Adult status of children with contrasting early life experiences. *Monographs of the Society for Research in Child Development* 31 (3), Serial No. 105, 1-65.

———, & Dye, H. B. 1939. A study of the effects of differential stimulation of mentally retarded children. *Proceedings of the American Association on Mental Deficiency* 44:114-36.

———, Updegraff, Ruth, Wellman, Beth L., & Williams, H. M. 1938. A study of environmental stimulation: An orphanage preschool project. *University of Iowa Study of Child Welfare* 15:No. 4.

Skinner, B. F. 1938. *The behavior of organisms: An experimental analysis.* New York: Appleton.

———. 1953. *Science and human behavior.* New York: Macmillan.

Smilanski, S. 1961. Evaluation of early education. In UNESCO, *Educational Studies and Documents,* No. 42, pp. 8-17.

———. 1964. Progress report on a program to demonstrate ways to use a year of kindergarten to promote cognitive abilities, impart basic information and modify attitudes which are essential for scholastic success of culturally deprived children in their first two years of school. Paper presented to the Research Conference on the Education of the Culturally Deprived, University of Chicago (Israeli project, unpublished manuscript).

Smith, S. 1942. Language and non-verbal test performance of racial groups in Honolulu before and after a fourteen year interval. *Journal of Genetic Psychology* 26:51-93.

Sokolov, E. N. 1963. *Perception and the conditioned reflex.* Oxford, England: Pergamon.

Spearman, C. 1904. "General intelligence" objectively determined and measured. *American Journal of Psychology* 15:201-93.

———. 1923. *The nature of intelligence and the principles of cognition.* London: Macmillan.

———. 1927. *The abilities of man.* New York: Macmillan.

Spitz, R. A. 1945. Hospitalism: An inquiry into the genesis of psychiatric conditions in early childhood. *The Psychoanalytic Study of the Child* 1:53-74.

———. 1946a. Hospitalism: A follow-up report. *The Psychoanalytic Study of the Child* 2:113-17.

———. 1946b. Anaclitic depression. *The Psychoanalytic Study of the Child* 2:313-42.

———. 1946c. The smiling response: A contribution to the ontogenesis of social relations. *Genetic Psychology Monographs* 34:67-125.

Srb, A. M., & Owen, R. D. 1957. *General genetics*. San Francisco: W. H. Freeman & Co.

Standing, E. M. 1957. *Maria Montessori: Her life and work*. Fresno, Calif.: Academy Library Guild.

Steen, M. T. 1966. The effects of immediate and delayed reinforcement on the achievement behavior of Mexican-American children of low socio-economic status. Unpublished doctoral dissertation, Stanford University.

Stoddard, G. D. 1939. The IQ: Its ups and downs. *Educational Record* 20:44-57.

———, & Wellman, Beth L. 1940. Environment and the IQ. *Yearbook of National Society of Studies for Education* 39(I), 405-42.

Strauss, M. A. 1962. Deferred gratification, social class, and the achievement syndrome. *American Sociological Review* 27: 326-35.

Taylor, D. W. 1960. Toward an information processing theory of motivation. In M. R. Jones (Ed.), *Nebraska Symposium on Motivation*. Lincoln: University of Nebraska Press, pp. 51-78.

Terrel, G., Jr., Durkin, K., & Weisley, M. 1959. Social class and the nature of the incenter in discrimination learning. *Journal of Abnormal and Social Psychology* 59:270-72.

Thompson, G. H. 1939. *The factorial analysis of human ability*. Boston: Houghton Mifflin.

——— et al. of the Scottish Council for Research in Education. 1933. *The intelligence of Scottish children: A national survey of an age group*. London: University of London Press.

——— et al. of the Scottish Council for Research in Education. 1949. *The trend of Scottish intelligence*. London: University of London Press.

——— et al. of the Scottish Council for Research in Education. 1953. *Social implications of the 1947 mental survey*. London: University of London Press.

Thompson, W. R., & Heron, W. 1954. The effects of restricting early experience on the problem-solving capacity of dogs. *Canadian Journal of Psychology* 8:17-31.

Thorndike, E. L. 1898. Animal intelligence. *Psychological Review Monograph Supplement* 2:No. 8, 1-109.

———. 1913. *Educational psychology*. Vol. II. *The psychology of learning*. New York: Columbia University Teachers College.

———, & Woodworth, R. S. 1901. The influence of improvement in one mental function upon the efficiency of other functions. *Psychological Review* 8:247-61, 384-95, 553-64.

Thorpe, W. H., Jr. 1944. Some problems of animal learning. *Proceedings of the Linnean Society. London* 156:70-83.

————. 1956. *Learning and instinct in animals.* London: Methuen.

Thrasher, F. M. 1936. *The gang.* Chicago: University of Chicago Press.

Thurstone, L. L. 1935. *The vectors of the mind.* Chicago: University of Chicago Press.

————. 1938. *Primary mental abilities.* Chicago: University of Chicago Press.

Titchener, E. B. 1926. *A text-book of psychology.* New York: Macmillan.

Tryon, R. C. 1935. A theory of psychological components—an alternative to "mathematical factors." *Psychological Review* 42:425-54.

Tuddenham, R. D. 1948. Soldier intelligence in World Wars I and II. *American Psychologist* 3:149-59.

United Nations. 1953. *The determinants and consequences of population trends.* ST/SOA/ Series A. Population Studies. No. 17. New York: United Nations.

————. 1955. *Proceedings of the World Population Conference, Rome, 1954.* New York: United Nations, Department of Social Affairs.

Uzgiris, Ina C., & Hunt, J. McV. 1967. A longitudinal study of recognition learning. (Mimeographed prepublication, Psychological Development Laboratory, University of Illinois, Urbana.)

————, & Hunt, J. McV. 1969. Intentions or operants: On the development of intrinsic reinforcements. *Journal of Genetic Psychology.* In press.

————, & Hunt, J. McV. 1970. Toward ordinal scales of psychological development in infancy. In press.

Vernon, P. E. 1961. *The measurement of abilities.* New York: Philosophical Library.

Volkart, E. H. 1951. *Social behavior and personality: Contributions of W. I. Thomas to theory and social research.* New York: Social Science Research Council.

Walker, A. E., & Weaver, T. A., Jr. 1940. Ocular movements from the occipital lobe in the monkey. *Journal of Neurophysiology* 3:353-57.

Ward, L. F. 1883. *Dynamic sociology.* New York: D. Appleton & Co., 2 vols.

Warner, W. L., & Lunt, P. S. 1941. Yankee City Series, Vol. I. *The social life of a modern community.* New Haven, Conn.: Yale University Press.

————, Meeker, Marchia, & Ells, K. 1949. *Democracy in Jonesville.* New York: Harper.

Watson, J. B. 1919. *Psychology from the standpoint of a behaviorist.* Philadelphia: Lippincott.

————. 1928. *Psychological care of infant and child.* New York: Norton.

————, & Raynor, Rosalie. 1920. Conditioned emotional reactions. *Journal of Experimental Psychology* 3:1-14.

Weikart, D. P. (Ed.). 1967a. *Preschool intervention: A preliminary report of the Perry Preschool Project.* Ann Arbor, Mich.: Campus Publishers.

————. 1967b. Preschool programs: Preliminary findings. *The Journal of Special Education* 1:No. 2.

————. 1969. Comparative study of three preschool curricula. (Mimeographed paper presented at the biennial meeting of the Society for Research in Child Development, Santa Monica, Calif., March.)

————, Kamii, Constance K., & Radin, Norma L. 1967. Perry Preschool Project progress report. In David P. Weikart (Ed.), *Preschool intervention: A preliminary report of the Perry Preschool Project.* Ann Arbor, Mich.: Campus Publishers, pp. 1-38.

————, & Lambie, Dolores. 1967. Preschool intervention through a home teaching program. To appear in J. Hellmuth (Ed.), *The disadvantaged child,* Vol. 2. Seattle, Wash.: Special Child Publications.

————, & Wiegerink, R. 1968. Ypsilanti Preschool Curriculum Demonstration Project: A proposal. Ypsilanti, Mich.: Ypsilanti Public Schools.

Weiskrantz, L. 1958. Sensory deprivation and the cat's optic nervous system. *Nature* 181:1047-50.

Weizmann, F., Cohen, L., & Pratt, R. Jeanene. 1968. Developmental changes in infantile responses to novelty. (Mimeographed prepublication, Psychological Development Laboratory, University of Illinois, Urbana.)

Wheeler, L. R. 1942. A comparative study of the intelligence of East Tennessee mountain children. *Journal of Educational Psychology* 33:321-34.

White, B. L., Castle, P., & Held, R. 1964. Observations on the development of visually-directed reaching. *Child Development* 35:349-64.

————, & Held, R. 1966. Plasticity of sensorimotor development in the human infant. In Judy F. Rosenblith & W. Allinsmith (Eds.), *The causes of behavior: Readings in child development and educational psychology.* (2nd ed.) Boston: Allyn & Bacon.

White, R. W. 1959. Motivation reconsidered: The concept of competence. *Psychological Review* 66:297-333.

Whyte, W. R. 1943. *Street corner society.* Chicago: University of Chicago Press, 2nd ed., 1955.

Wiener, N. 1948. *Cybernetics*. New York: Wiley.

Williams, K. A. 1929. The reward value of a conditioned stimulus. *University of California Publications of Psychology* 4:31-55.

Williams, S. B., & Williams, E. 1943. Barrier-frustration and extinction in instrumental learning. *American Journal of Psychology* 56: 247-61.

Winterbottom, Marian R. 1958. The relation of need for achievement to learning experiences in independence and mastery. In J. W. Atkinson (Ed.), *Motives in fantasy, action, and society*. Princeton, N.J.: D. Van Nostrand.

Wohlwill, J. F. 1960. Developmental studies of perception. *Psychological Bulletin* 57:250-88.

Wolf, A. 1943. The dynamics of the selective inhibition of specific functions in neuroses. *Psychosomatic Medicine* 5:27-38. Reprinted in S. S. Tomkins (Ed.), *Contemporary psychopathology*. Cambridge: Harvard University Press, 1943, Ch. 31.

Woodrow, H. 1938. The relation between abilities and improvement with practice. *Journal of Educational Psychology* 29:215-30.

———. 1939. Factors in improvement with practice. *Journal of Psychology* 7:55-70.

Woodworth, R. S. 1941. Heredity and environment: A critical survey of recently published material on twins and foster children. *Social Science Research Council Bulletin*, No. 47.

Woolley, H. T. 1925. The validity of standards of mental measurement in young childhood. *School & Sociology* 21:476-82.

Zigler, E., & de Labry, J. 1962. Concept-switching in middle-class, lower-class, and retarded children. *Journal of Abnormal and Social Psychology* 65:267-73.

Author Index

Allen, V. L. (1969), 190
Allport, F. H. (1924), 106
Altman, J., & Das, G. D. (1964), 124, 195
Amsel, A. (1958), 143; —— & Roussel, J. (1952), 143
Anastasi, Anne (1936), 61; (1956), 71; (1958), 71, 117, 118, 136, 190, 197
Anderson, J. E. (1940), 22
Anderson, J. F., & Horsfall, W. R. (1963), 193; see also under Horsfall
Anderson, L. D. (1939), 22
Angermeier, W. F., Phelps, J. B., & Reynolds, H. H. (1967), 194
Atkinson, J. W., & Reitman, W. R. (1958), 213; see also under McClelland

Baldwin, A. L. (1955), 206; ——, Kalhorn, J., & Breese, F. H. (1945), 206
Baldwin, J. M. (1895), 100
Bandura, A., & Walters, R. H. (1959), 230

Bates, Louise. See under Gesell
Battle, E. S., & Rotter, J. B. (1963), 210, 213
Bayley, Nancy (1940), 60
Beach, F. A. (1945), 26, 81
Becker, W. C. See Gauron & Becker
Beilin, H., & Gotkin, L. (1964), 161
Bell, R. Q. (1965), 193
Bell, R. W. See under Denenberg
Bennett, E. L., Diamond, M. C., Krech, D., & Rosenzweig, M. R. (1964), 124, 150, 152, 195
Bereiter, C., & Engelmann, S. (1966), 69, 161, 162, 168, 169, 170, 175, 176, 177, 179, 227; ——, Engelmann, S., Osborn, Jean, & Reidford, P. A. (1966), 44
Berlyne, D. E. (1960), 26, 30, 36, 82, 83, 95
Bernstein, B. (1960), 136, 155, 206; (1961), 136, 155, 206
Bexton, W. H., Heron, W., & Scott, T. H. (1954), 32, 82, 84

Binet, A. (1909), 54, 115, 192; —— & Henri, V. (1895), 53; —— & Simon, T. (1905), 54; (1916), 54

Blank, Marion (1967), 167

Bloch, H. A., & Flynn, F. T. (1956), 157

Bloom, B. S. (1964), 151, 196; ——, Davis, A., & Hess, R. (1965), 203

Boring, E. G. (1929), 4

Brattgård, S. O. (1952), 11, 124, 152, 194, 195

Breese, F. H. See Baldwin, Kalhorn, & Breese

Bronfenbrenner, U. (1958), 136, 155, 156, 206, 208; (1966), see bibliography; (1967), see bibliography

Brookshire, K. H. (1958), see bibliography; ——, Littman, R. A., & Stewart, C. N. (1961), see bibliography

Brown, B. See under Deutsch, M.

Brown, J. S., & Farber, I. E. (1951), 26, 143

Bryan, W. L., & Harter, N. (1897), 132

Buehr, R. F. (1965), 213

Bühler, K. (1918), 26, 100; (1928), 26, 81, 100

Burks, Barbara S. (1928), 56

Burlingham, Dorothy. See under Freud, Anna

Burst, R. A. See Horsfall, Anderson, & Burst

Burt, C. L. (1940), 59, 60; ——, Jones, E., Miller, E., & Moodie, W. (1934), 60

Butler, R. A. (1953), 27; (1958), 27

Cannon, W. B. (1915), 81

Carmichael, L. (1926), 8, 121, 150; (1927), 8, 121, 150; (1928), 8, 121

Castle, P. See White, Castle, & Held

Castner, B. M. See under Gesell

Cattell, J. McK. (1890), 4, 116

Cattell, Psyche (1960), 226

Cattell, R. B. (1937), 59, 117, 197; (1950a), 56, 71, 118, 197; (1950b), 59; (1952), 59

Cazden, Courtney (1968), 207

Chall, J. See Greenberg, Gerver, Chall, & Davidson

Chevalier, J. A. See under Levine

Child, I. L. (1954), 86

Childers, A. T. (1936), 158, 211

Chilman, Catherine S. (1965), 136, 155, 156, 157, 206, 208

Chow, K. L. See Rasch, Swift, Riesen, & Chow

Clark, A. D., & Richards, C. J. (1966), 205

Clark, D. H. See Lesser, Fifer, & Clark

Clark, R. A. See under McClelland

Cloward, R. A., & Ohlin, L. E. (1960), 158

Coghill, G. E. (1929), 7, 121, 130

Cohen, A. K. (1955), 158, 212; —— & Short, J. F., Jr. (1958), 158

Cohen, L. See Weizmann, Cohen, & Pratt

Coleman, J. S. (1966), 213

Conant, J. B. (1947), 77

Cooley, C. H. (1902), 78

Cravioto, J. (1964), 204

Cronbach, L. J. See Gleser, Cronbach, & Rajaratnam

Crowther, J. G. (1941), see bibliography

Cruze, W. W. (1935), 9, 122, 151; (1938), 9, 122, 151

D'Andrade, R. *See* Rosen & D'Andrade
Darwin, C. (1859), 3; (1872), 13
Das, G. D. *See* Altman & Das
Dashiell, J. F. (1928), 26, 84
Davidson, H. H. *See* Greenberg, Gerver, Chall, & Davidson
Davis, A. *See* under Bloom
Davis, W. A. (1948), 75, 136, 155, 156, 208; —— & Havighurst, R. J. (1946), 75, 136, 155, 208
de Labry, J. *See* Zigler & de Labry
Dember, W. N., Earl, R. W., & Paradise, N. (1957), 34-35, 38, 105
Denenberg, V. H. (1959), *see* bibliography; (1962), 21, 22, 23, 91; —— & Bell, R. W. (1960), *see* bibliography; —— & Karas, G. G. (1960), *see* bibliography; ——, Morton, J. R. C., Kline, N. J., & Grota, L. J. (1962), *see* bibliography
Dennis, Marsena G. *See* under Dennis, W.
Dennis, W. (1942), 154, 198; (1960), 6, 25, 68, 87, 96, 125; (1966), 57, 74, 154, 198; —— & Dennis, Marsena G. (1935), 9; (1938), 9; (1940), 8, 25, 97; (1941), 9, 102
Detwiler, S. R. *See* Matthews & Detwiler
Deutsch, Cynthia P. (1964), 41, 69, 75, 135, 205
Deutsch, M. (1965), 206; —— & Brown, B. (1964), 75, 135, 160; *see also* Katz & Deutsch
Dewey, J. (1900), 34, 100; (1902), 24
Diamond, M. C. *See* Bennett, Diamond, Krech, & Rosenzweig .

Diggory, J. C. (1966), 201, 213
Dobzhansky, T. *See* Sinnott, Dunn, & Dobzhansky
Dollard, J., Doob, L. W., Miller, N. E., Mowrer, O. H., & Sears, R. R. (1939), 201; *see also* Miller & Dollard
Donahue, G. Bibliography on Montessori in Rambusch (1962), 44
Doob, L. W. *See* Dollard, Doob, Miller, Mowrer, & Sears
Dunn, L. C. *See* Sinnott, Dunn, & Dobzhansky
Dunn, L. M. (1959), 182, 227; (1965), 182, 227
Durkin, K. *See* Terrel, Durkin, & Weisley
Dye, H. B. *See* under Skeels

Earl, R. W. *See* Dember, Earl, & Paradise
Ebbinghaus, H. (1885), 132
Eckblad, G. (1963), 83
Egyhazi, E. *See* under Hydén
Ells, K. *See* under Warner
Endler, N. S., & Hunt, J. McV. (1966), 80; ——, Hunt, J. McV., & Rosenstein, A. J. (1962), 78
Engelmann, S. *See* under Bereiter

Farber, I. E. (1948), 22; *see also* Brown & Farber
Fenichel, O. (1945), 26
Ferguson, G. A. (1954), 61, 196; (1956), 61, 196; (1959), 61
Festinger, L. (1957), 83, 105, 143
Fifer, G. *See* Lesser, Fifer, & Clark
Finch, F. H. (1946), 72, 118, 197

Fisher, Dorothy Canfield (1912), 44, 108

Fiske, D. W., & Maddi, S. R. (1961), 25

Flavell, J. H. (1963), *see* bibliography

Fleishman, E. A., & Hempel, W. E., Jr. (1954), 61

Flynn, F. T. *See* Bloch & Flynn

Forgays, D. G., & Forgays, Janet W. (1952), 87, 125, 150, 193

Forgus, R. H. (1954), 87, 125, 150; (1955a), 87, 125, 150, 193; (1955b), 87, 125, 150, 193

Freedman, A. (1957), 19

Freeman, F. N. *See* Newman, Freeman, & Holzinger

Freeman, G. L. (1934), 26

Freud, Anna (1936), 84; —— & Burlingham, Dorothy (1944), 101

Freud, S. (1900), 21, 81; (1904), 37; (1905), 18, 19, 64, 86, 88, 192; (1915), 21, 26, 88; (1926), 21, 33, 84

Froebel, F. (1826), 18, 34, 100, 217

Frostig, Marianne (1964), 172, 173

Fryer, D. (1922), 202

Gagné, R. M. (1966a), 71, 196; (1966b), 134, 196; —— & Paradise, N. E. (1961), 71, 134, 196

Galanter, E. *See* Miller, Galanter, & Pribram

Galton, F. (1869), 50, 52, 202; (1883), 50, 52; (1886), 71

Gauron, E. F., & Becker, W. C. (1959), 12

Gerver, J. M. *See* Greenberg, Gerver, Chall, & Davidson

Gesell, A. (1945), 7; (1954), 7, 63; ——, Halverson, H. M.,

Thompson, Helen, Ilg, Frances L., Castner, B. M., & Bates, Louise (1940), 64, 130; —— & Thompson, Helen (1929), 8

Gleser, G. C., Cronbach, L. J., & Rajaratnam, N. (1961), 80

Goddard, H. H. (1910), 55; (1912), 4, 5

Goldfarb, W. (1953), 87; (1955), 87

Goldman, Jacquelin R. (1964), 22, 91

Goldstein, L. S. *See* under John

Goodenough, Florence L. (1926), 154, 198; (1939), 2, 148, 192; —— & Maurer, Katherine M. (1942), 122

Gordon, H. (1923), *see* bibliography

Gordon, I. J., (1969), 183, 221

Gotkin, L. *See* Beilin & Gotkin

Gray, Susan W., & Klaus, R. A. (1963), 136, 139, 157, 181, 183, 208; *see also* Klaus & Gray

Greenberg, D., Uzgiris, Ina C., & Hunt, J. McV. (1968), 74, 153, 195

Greenberg, J. W., Gerver, J. M., Chall, J., & Davidson, H. H. (1965), 214

Griffin, G. A., & Harlow, H. F. (1966), 194

Griffiths, W. J., Jr. (1960), 91

Grota, L. J. *See* under Denenberg

Guilford, J. P. (1940), 59, 62; (1956), 62; (1957), 62; (1959), 62, 71, 134

Guthrie, E. R. (1938), 26

Hall, C. S. (1934), 9, 21

Hall, G. S., 4, 6, 7, 116, 192, 217

Hall, M. (1893), 28

Halverson, H. M. *See* under Gesell

Harlow, H. F. (1949), *see* bibliography; (1950), 26, 81; (1958), 37, 88; ——, Harlow, Margaret K., & Meyer, D. R. (1950), 26, 81; *see also* Griffin & Harlow

Harlow, Margaret K. *See* under Harlow, H. F.

Harter, N. *See* Bryan & Harter

Harvey, O. J., Hunt, D. E., & Schroeder, H. M. (1961), 36

Havighurst, R. J. *See* under Davis, W. A.

Hayes, K. J. (1962), 58

Hebb, D. O. (1946a), 33, 91, 143; (1946b), 33, 82, 91, 143; (1947), 20, 87, 125, 150, 193, 194; (1949), 9, 11, 17, 20, 34, 68, 83, 104, 125; —— & Mahut, Helen (1955), 105; —— & Riesen, A. H. (1943), 33, 143; —— & Thompson, W. R. (1954), 43; —— & Williams, K. (1946), 12, 23, 87

Heinroth, O. (1910), 89

Held, R. *See* White, Castle, & Held

Helson, H. (1959), 83, 92

Hempel, W. E. *See* Fleishman & Hempel

Henderson, E. H. *See* Long & Henderson

Hendrick, I. (1943), 27, 82, 100

Henri, V. *See* under Binet

Hernandez-Peon, R., Scherrer, H., & Jouvet, M. (1956), 28

Heron, W. *See* Bexton, Heron, & Scott; Thompson & Heron

Hess, R. D., & Shipman, Virginia (1965), 75, 155, 205, 206, 213; *see also* under Bloom

Hetzer, Hildegard, & Wolf, Käthe (1928), 64

Hieronymus, A. N. (1951), 210, 214

Hilgard, E. R. (1949), 33, 85

Hilgard, Josephine R. (1932), 8; (1933), *see* bibliography

Hirsch, J. (1963), 149; (1967), 149

Hodgins, Audrey S. *See* under Karnes

Holmes, Frances B. (1935), 22, 92

Holt, E. B. (1931), 26

Holzinger, K. J. (1937), 59; *see also* Newman, Freeman, & Holzinger

Horsfall, W. R., & Anderson, J. F. (1961), 149; ——, Anderson, J. F., & Burst, R. A. (1964), 193; *see also* under Anderson, J. F.

Hubel, D. H., & Wiesel, T. N. (1959), 152; (1960), 152; (1961), 152

Hull, C. L. (1931), 15; (1943), 14, 26, 27, 37, 81, 132

Humphreys, L. G. (1939), 210; (1959), 61, 62, 119, 196; (1960), 61, 62; (1962a), 61, 62, 119; (1962b), 62, 196

Hunt, D. E. *See* Harvey, Hunt, & Schroeder

Hunt, J. McV. (1941), 19, 64, 86; (1945), 19, 86; (1956), 19; (1960), 27, 81; (1961), 4, 5, 6, 10, 34, 56, 73, 107, 117, 121, 129, 130, 137, 191, 196, 230; (1963a), 26, 28, 34, 81, 83, 95, 107, 210; (1963b), 36, 37, 38, 89, 90, 100; (1964a), 1, 110; (1964b), *see* bibliography; (1965a), 217; (1965b), 76, 129; (1966), 41, 129, 133; (1967a), *see* bibliography; (1967b), *see* bibliography; —— & Luria, Zella (1956), 20; ——, Schlosberg, H., Solomon, R. L., & Stellar, E. (1947), 19, 86; —— & Uzgiris, Ina C. (1964), 89, 100; *see also* Endler & Hunt; Greenberg, Uzgiris, & Hunt; under Salama; Uzgiris & Hunt

Hunter, W. S. (1912), 15; (1918), 15

Hydén, H. (1959), 11; (1960), 11, 124, 195; —— & Egyhazi, E. (1962), 195

Hymovitch, B. (1952), 87, 125, 150, 193

Ilg, Frances L. *See* under Gesell

Inhelder, Bärbel. *See* under Piaget

Irwin, O. C. (1930), 36

Jasper, H. H. *See* Sharpless & Jasper

Jennings, H. S. (1930), *see* bibliography

Johannsen, W. (1903), 51, 116; (1909), 51, 148, 193

John, Vera P. (1963), 69, 75, 136; —— & Goldstein, L. S. (1964), 69, 75, 136

Jones, E. *See* under Burt

Jones, H. E. (1954), 122, 193

Jones, K. L. (1966), 206

Jouvet, R. *See* Hernandez-Peon, Scherrer, & Jouvet

Kagan, J. (1965), 210

Kalhorn, J. *See* under Baldwin, A. L.

Kamii, Constance K. *See* under Weikart

Karas, G. G. *See* under Denenberg

Karnes, Merle B. (1968), 224; (1969), 224, 227; —— & Hodgins, Audrey S. (1969), 164; ——, Hodgins, Audrey S., Stoneburner, R. L., Studley, W. M., & Teska, J. A. (1968), 164; ——, Studley, W. M., Wright, W. R., & Hodgins, Audrey S. (1968), 183; ——, Teska, J. A., & Hodgins, Audrey S. (1969a), 174; (1969b), *see* bibliography; ——, Wollersheim, Janet P., Stoneburner, R. L., Hodgins, Audrey S., & Teska, J. A. (1968), 171

Katz, P. A., & Deutsch, M. (1963), *see* bibliography

Keller, Suzanne (1963), 205, 210, 213, 214

Kelley, T. L. (1928), 59

Kelly, G. A. (1955), 85

Kendler, H. H., & Kendler, Tracy S. (1956), 69

Kennedy, W. A., *et al.* (1963), *see* bibliography

Kessen, W. *See* Munsinger & Kessen

Key, Cora B. *See* Sherman & Key

Kirk, G. E. (1969), 227-228

Kirk, S. A., & McCarthy, J. J. (1961), 69, 172, 182; ——, McCarthy, J. J., & Kirk, Winifred (1968), 164, 226

Kirk, Winifred. *See* under Kirk, S. A.

Klaus, R. A., & Gray, Susan W. (1968), 136, 139, 157, 181, 183, 188, 220, 221; *see also* Gray & Klaus

Kline, N. J. *See* under Denenberg

Klineberg, O. (1935), 202

Knobloch, Hilda. *See* under Pasamanick

Kobler, R., 18, 163

Köhler, W. (1924), 33

Korchin, S. J. *See* under Levine

Krech, D. *See* Bennet, Diamond, Krech, & Rosenzweig

Krugman, M. (1961), 160, 213

Kuo, Z. Y. (1932a), 10, 121; (1932b), 10, 121; (1932c), 10, 121; (1932d), 10, 121

Lally, R., 183, 221

Lamarck, J. C. (1809), *see* bibliography

Lambie, Dolores. *See* under Weikart

Leahy, Alice M. (1935), *see* bibliography

LeShan, L. L. (1952), *see* bibliography

Lesser, G. S., Fifer, G., & Clark, D. H. (1965), 202

Levine, S. (1956), *see* bibliography; (1957), *see* bibliography; (1958), *see* bibliography; (1959), 21, 23, 91; (1961), 21, 23, 91; ——, Chevalier, J. A., & Korchin, S. J. (1956), 21, 23, 91

Lewis, O. (1961), 41, 109, 136, 156, 208; (1966a), 136, 155, 156, 208; (1966b), *see* bibliography

Liberman, R. (1962), 11, 124, 152, 194

Liebow, E. (1967), 204

Lindzey, G., Lykken, D. T., & Winston, H. D. (1960), 91

Littman, R. A. *See* under Brookshire

Long, B. H., & Henderson, E. H. (1967), 213

Lopate, P. *See* under O'Brien

Lorenz, K. (1935), 89

Lowell, E. L. *See* under McClelland

Lunt, P. S. *See* Warner & Lunt

Luria, Zella. *See* under Hunt, J. McV.

Lykken, D. T. *See* Lindzey, Lykken, & Winston

Maclaurin, W. R. (1949), *see* bibliography

Maddi, S. R. *See* Fiske & Maddi

Mahut, Helen. *See* under Hebb

Maitland, S. C. (1966), 209

Maltzman, I., & Raskin, D. C. (1965), 205

Mannheim, K. (1936), *see* bibliography

Marx, M. H. (1952), 86; *see also* McKelvey & Marx

Matthews, S. A., & Detwiler, S. R. (1926), 150

Maurer, Katherine M. *See* under Goodenough

McAfee, Oralie. *See* Nimnicht, Meier, & McAfee

McCandless, B. (1952), 205

McCarthy, J. J. *See* Kirk & McCarthy

McClelland, D. C. (1958), 214; ——, Atkinson, J. W., Clark, R. A., & Lowell, E. L. (1953), 212

McDonald, D. (1966), 204

McDougall, W. (1908), 27, 82

McGraw, Myrtle B. (1935), 6

McKelvey, R. K., & Marx, M. H. (1951), 86

McLuhan, M. (1964), *see* bibliography

McMillan, Margaret (1919), 138, 159, 216

McNemar, Q. (1940), 122, 148, 192; (1942), 202

Mead, G. H. (1934), 78

Meeker, Marchia. *See* under Warner

Meier, J. H. *See* Nimnicht, Meier, & McAfee

Melton, A. W. (1941), 26

Mendel, G. (1865), 51, 193

Merton, R. K. (1945), *see* bibliography

Metzner, R. *See* under Mischel

Meyer, D. R. *See* under Harlow, H. F.

Mierke, K. (1933), 88

Miller, E. *See* under Burt

Miller, G. A., Galanter, E., & Pribram, K. H. (1960), 27, 29, 30, 102

Miller, J. O. (1968), 183, 222;
—— & Mumbauer, Corrine (1968), *see* bibliography

Miller, N. E., & Dollard, J. (1941), 15, 26, 37, 81, 103, 119; *see also* Dollard, Doob, Miller, Mowrer, & Sears

Miller, W. B. (1958), 158, 212

Milner, Esther (1951), 205

Mischel, W. (1961), 209; —— & Metzner, R. (1962), 209

Mittlemann, B. (1954), 100

Money-Kryle, R. (1939), 64

Montessori, Maria (1909), 3, 44-46, 100, 138, 159, 216

Montgomery, K. C. (1952), 26, 105; (1953), 27, 82, 105; (1955), 27, 82; —— & Segall, M. (1955), 27, 82

Moodie, W. *See* under Burt

Moore, O. K. (1963), 163

Morgan, C. L. (1894), 14, 132

Morton, J. R. C. *See* under Denenberg

Mowrer, O. H. (1960), 26, 81, 88; *see also* Dollard, Doob, Miller, Mowrer, & Sears

Moynihan, D. P. (1965), 215

Mumbauer, Corrine. *See* under Miller, J. O.

Munsinger, H., & Kessen, W. (1964), 83

Murphy, Lois (1961), 204; (1968), 204

Needham, J. (1959), 49

Newell, A., Shaw, J. C., & Simon, H. A. (1958), 16

Newman, H. H., Freeman, F. N., & Holzinger, K. J. (1937), 60

Nimnicht, G., Meier, J. H., & McAfee, Oralie (1966), 163; (1967a), 163; (1967b), 163

Nissen, H. W. (1930), 31, 82, 84, 105

Nowlis, H. H. (1941), 88

O'Brien, Roslyn A. (1967), 171; —— & Lopate, P. (1968), 171

Ohlin, L. E. *See* Cloward & Ohlin

O'Kelly, L. I., 27, 82

Orlansky, H. (1949), 19, 86

Osborn, Jean. *See* under Bereiter

Osgood, C. E. (1952), 15, 24; ——, Suci, G. J., & Tannenbaum, P. H. (1957), 81

Owen, R. D. *See* Srb & Owen

Padilla, S. G. (1935), 122, 151

Painter, Genevieve (1968), 226

Paradise, N. E. *See* Dember, Earl, & Paradise; Gagné & Paradise

Pasamanick, B. (1962), 204; —— & Knobloch, Hilda (1960), 193

Pavlov, I. P. (1927), 95, 132

Pestalozzi, J. H., 18

Phelps, J. B. *See* Angermeier, Phelps, & Reynolds

Piaget, J. (1924), *see* bibliography; (1926), *see* bibliography; (1927), *see* bibliography; (1932), *see* bibliography; (1936), 24, 30, 34, 36, 37, 38, 42, 50, 60, 89, 100, 103, 104, 124, 134, 196; (1937), 50, 103, 134; (1945), 38, 42; (1947), *see* bibliography; —— Inhelder, Bärbel (1940), *see* bibliography; (1947), 31, 66, 134

Pinneau, S. R. (1955), 65

Plutarch, 18

Pratt, R. Jeanene. *See* Weizmann, Cohen, & Pratt

Pribram, K. H. (1960), 16; *see also* Miller, Galanter, & Pribram

Pruette, Lorine (1926), 6, 24

Radin, Norma L. *See* under Weikart

Rainwater, L. (1966), 215

Rajaratnam, N. *See* Gleser, Cronbach, & Rajaratnam

Rambusch, Nancy M. (1962), 44

Rasch, Ellen R., Swift, H., Riesen, A. H., & Chow, K. L. (1961), 11, 124, 152, 194

Raskin, D. C. *See* Maltzman & Raskin

Raven, J. C. (1938), 59

Raynor, Rosalie. *See* under Watson

Razran, G. H. S. (1938a), 88; (1938b), 88; (1961), 30, 36, 95

Reid, J. H. (1966), 211

Reidford, P. A. *See* under Bereiter

Reitman, W. R. *See* Atkinson & Reitman

Reynolds, H. H. *See* Angermeier, Phelps, & Reynolds

Richards, C. J. *See* Clark & Richards

Riesen, A. H. (1947), *see* bibliography; (1958), 11, 24, 151; (1961), *see* bibliography; *see also* under Hebb; Rasch, Swift, Riesen, & Chow

Ripin, Rowena (1933), 122

Rogers, C. R. (1951), 85

Romanes, G. J. (1882), 14; (1883), 14

Rose, J. E., & Woolsey, C. N. (1949), 17

Rosen, B. D., & D'Andrade, R. (1959), 212

Rosenstein, A. J. *See* under Endler

Rosenzweig, S. (1933), 88

Rotter, J. B. *See* Battle & Rotter

Rousseau, J. J. (1762), 18

Roussel, J. *See* Amsel & Roussel

Salama, A. A. (1962), 92; —— & Hunt, J. McV. (1964), 22, 91

Scherrer, H. *See* Hernandez-Peon, Scherrer, & Jouvet

Schlosberg, H. *See* under Hunt, J. McV.

Schneirla, T. C. (1959), 31

Schoggen, Maxine F. (1967), 211; *see also* Schoggen & Schoggen

Schoggen, P. H., & Schoggen, Maxine F. (1968), 156, 207

Schroeder, H. M. *See* Harvey, Hunt, & Schroeder

Scott, T. H. *See* Bexton, Heron, & Scott

Sears, R. R. *See* Dollard, Doob, Miller, Mowrer, & Sears

Segall, M. *See* under Montgomery

Sharpless, S., & Jasper, H. H. (1956), 205

Shaw, C. R. (1929), 158, 211; (1931), 158

Shaw, J. C. *See* Newell, Shaw, & Simon

Sherman, M., & Key, Cora B. (1932), 202

Sherrington, C. S. (1906), 28

Shirley, Mary M. (1931), 63; (1933), 63

Short, J. F., Jr., & Strodtbeck, F. L. (1965), 158, 211, 272; see also Cohen & Short

Simpson, B. R. (1939), 2

Simon, H. A. See Newell, Shaw, & Simon

Simon, T. See under Binet

Sinnott, E. W., Dunn, L. C., & Dobzhansky, T. (1958), 51

Skeels, H. M. (1965), see bibliography; (1966), see bibliography; —— & Dye, H. B. (1939), 2, 39, 64, 122, 148, 192; ——, Updegraff, Ruth, Wellman, Beth L., & Williams, H. M. (1938), 122

Skinner, B. F. (1938), 132; (1953), 133, 162

Smedslund, J., 44

Smilanski, S. (1961), 155; (1964), 155

Smith, S. (1942), 72, 118, 197

Smock, C. D., 48

Sokolov, E. N. (1963), 95

Solomon, R. L. See under Hunt, J. McV.

Spearman, C. (1904), 58; (1923), 58; (1927), 58

Spitz, R. A. (1945), 64, 96; (1946a), 64, 96; (1946b), 64, 96; (1946c), 37, 90

Srb, A. M., & Owen, R. D. (1957), 51

Standing, E. M. (1957), 44

Steen, M. T. (1966), 209

Stellar, E. See under Hunt, J. McV.

Stewart, C. N. See under Brookshire

Stoddard, G. D. (1939), see bibliography; —— Wellman, Beth L. (1940), 2

Stoneburner, R. L. See under Karnes

Strauss, M. A. (1962), 209, 213

Strodtbeck, F. L. See Short & Strodtbeck

Studley, W. M. See under Karnes

Suci, G. J. See under Osgood

Swift, H. See Rasch, Swift, Riesen, & Chow

Tannenbaum, P. H. See under Osgood

Taylor, D. W. (1960), 27

Terrel, G., Jr., Durkin, K., & Weisley, M. (1959), 209

Teska, J. A. See under Karnes

Thomas, W. I. Volkart (1951), on, 78

Thompson, G. H. (1939), 59; ——, et al. (1933), 72, 118; ——, et al. (1949), 72, 188; ——, et al. (1953), 72, 118

Thompson, Helen. See under Gesell

Thompson, W. R., & Heron, W. (1954), 12, 87, 125, 150, 194; see also under Hebb

Thorndike, E. L. (1898), 132; (1913), 14; —— & Woodworth, R. S. (1901), 14

Thorpe, W. H., Jr. (1944), 89; (1956), see bibliography

Thrasher, F. M. (1936), 158

Thurstone, L. L. (1935), 59; (1938), 59

Titchener, E. B. (1926), 104

Tryon, R. C. (1935), 59

Tuddenham, R. D. (1948), 197

United Nations (1953), 71; (1955), 71

Updegraff, Ruth. See under Skeels

Uzgiris, Ina C., & Hunt, J. McV. (1967), see bibliography; (1969), 100; (1970), 42, 67, 130; see also Greenberg, Uzgiris, & Hunt; under Hunt

Vernon, P. E. (1961), 59, 62
Volkart, E. H. (1951), 78

Walker, A. E., & Weaver, T. A., Jr. (1940), 28
Walters, R. H. *See* Bandura & Walters
Ward, L. F. (1883), 192
Warner, W. L., & Lunt, P. S. (1941), 158; ——, Meeker, Marchia, & Ells, K. (1949), *see* bibliography
Watson, J. B. (1919), 24; (1928), 9; —— & Raynor, Rosalie (1920), 33
Weaver, T. A., Jr. *See* Walker & Weaver
Weikart, D. P. (1967a), 160, 176, 221; (1967b), 160, 171, 173, 176; (1969), 175, 176; ——, Kamii, Constance K., & Radin, Norma L. (1967), *see* bibliography; —— & Lambie, Dolores (1967), 176; —— & Wiegerink, R. (1968), 176
Weir, M. W., 100
Weiskrantz, L. (1958), 11, 124, 152, 194
Weisley, M. *See* Terrel, Durkin, & Weisley
Weizmann, F., Cohen, L., & Pratt, R. Jeanene (1968), 100
Wellman, Beth. *See* under Skeels; under Stoddard
Wetzel, R., 162
Wheeler, L. R. (1942), 72, 118, 197
White, B. L., Castle, P., & Held, R. (1964), 126; —— & Held,

R. (1966), 67, 74, 126, 127, 129, 133, 152, 195
White, R. W. (1959), 27, 82
Whyte, W. R. (1943), 158
Wiegerink, R. *See* under Weikart
Wiener, N. (1948), 16
Wiesel, T. N. *See* Hubel & Wiesel
Wilkins, R., 145
Williams, E. *See* Williams, S. B., & Williams
Williams, H. M. *See* under Skeels
Williams, K. *See* under Hebb
Williams, K. A. (1929), 88
Williams, S. B., & Williams, E. (1943), 88
Winston, H. D. *See* Lindzey, Lykken, & Winston
Winterbottom, Marian R. (1958), 212
Wohlwill, J. F. (1960), *see* bibliography
Wolf, A. (1943), 12
Wollersheim, Janet P. *See* under Karnes
Woodrow, H. (1938), *see* bibliography; (1939), *see* bibliography
Woodworth, R. S. (1941), 5; *see also* Thorndike & Woodworth
Woolley, H. T. (1925), *see* bibliography
Woolsey, C. N. *See* Rose and Woolsey
Wright, W. R. *See* under Karnes

Zigler, E., & de Labry, J. (1962), 209

Subject Index

Abilities: Diagnosing children's, 70. Factor analysis of, 58-62; transfer of training and, 61-62. Primary mental, 59.

Ability: Early experience and adult problem-solving, 20, 86.

Accommodation, 132; Assimilation and, 132.

Achievement: Poverty and opportunity for, 213.

Achievement, tests of: Intelligence-test similarities to, 118-119.

ANXIETY (*see also* Anxiousness) Association with pain and, 91. Dissonance-incongruity theory of, 84-85. Indicators of, 90-92; defecation and urination as, 91; infant pain experience and, 91-92. Lower- vs. middle-class children's, 92. Self-concept and, 85. Separation: dissonance-incongruity and, 37, 85, 105; object permanence in, 101. Trauma theory of, 90-92; adaption level for pain and, 92; infantile pain experience and, 91-92.

Anxiousness: S-R inventory of, 78-80; sources of variance in, 79-80. Trait theory of, 77; S-R inventory and, 79.

Aristotle: Divisions of mind by, 147.

Arousal: "Collative variables" and, 105. Incongruity and, 105.

A/S ratio, 9; Early experience and, 12, 87, 125.

Assimilation, 132; Accommodation and, 132.

Attention: Habituation and lack of, 205.

Attentional preference: Incongruity optimal and, 105. Novelty and, 104-106. Recognitive familiarity and early, 89, 100.

Behavior: Anatomic maturation and development of, 62. Chaining theory of complex, 14. Early experience and adult eating and hoarding, 19, 86; and adult problem-solving, 20, 87. Fixative effect of shock on, 91; infantile pain experience and, 22, 92.

Behavioral sciences: Findings of great human significance in, 232.

Blink-response: Looking and age of, 153, 195-196.

Brain: Early experience and the anatomical development of, 123-124, 151-152, 194-195. Intrinsic and extrinsic portions of, 17; A/S ratio and, 17; experience as programmer of, 17.

Brain function: Computer conception of, 16. Static vs. active conceptions of, 14-17. Telephone switchboard theory of, 13. Transcortical vs. center-peripheral, 16.

Calvin: Reading schools and, 146.

Casa di Bambini, 108.

Cathexis (see Emotional attachment).

Centers: Parent and Child, 187-190, 228-232.

Child-rearing practices: Diffusion of, 140, 221. Improving parental: curriculum for, 226; failure of professional talk in, 181, 219; home visitors in, 181, 220; maternal imitation in, 181-183, 220-222; Parent and Child Centers in, 187-189, 228-232; preschool observation in, 181-183, 220-222; utilizing love of children in, 229.

Cities: Migration from farms to, 144. Technological advances and problems in, 114, 144.

Community mental-health service, 142; Incompetence as disease for, 143.

Comparative psychology: Darwin as originator of, 14.

COMPENSATORY EDUCATION

Bereiter-Engelmann program of, 168; motivation in the, 168; results from the, 169-170.

Comparative evaluative studies of, 171-180; tests used in, 172.

Defects in traditional preschool for, 138, 160.

Head Start, defects in, 138, 160.

History of, 138, 159.

Hughes and Karnes programs, 175.

Language in, 44, 46, 160, 168; English as a foreign, 168; Hughes's approach to, 165; sensorimotor experience and, 175, 177.

Materials-centered: Montessori Schools as, 162; New Nursery School as, 163; talking typewriter in, 163.

McMillan, Margaret, and, 138, 159, 216.

Montessori's effort in, 137.

Mothers as teachers in, 183-184, 224-225; curriculum for, 226.

Nursery schools invented as, 137.

One-to-one tutorial, 167.

Parents involved in, 176, 181-183, 184-185, 220-221, 222, 231.

Preventive programs vs., 180.

Project planning in, 166.

Remedial nature of, 171.

Research and development needed, 138, 141, 218.

Success from varieties of, 161-171.

Support needed, 141.

Teacher-centered: Bereiter-Engelmann programs, 161;

teacher-student ratio and success with, 162.

Teacher-planned games for, 163; Karnes's, 164; materials used in, 164.

Test-gains from, 164, 176.

Token-reward technique in, 162.

Traditional preschool curricular inadequacies for, 138, 216.

Varieties or continua of, 161-168; comparative evaluations of, 171-180; one-to-one tutorial, 167; teacher-centered vs. teacher-planned, 163-166; teacher- vs. materials-centered, 161-162.

COMPETENCE

Changing beliefs about, 1, 2, 112-121; politics and the, 112.

Cortical chemistry in animals and, 152, 194-195.

Circumstances in development of, 144-154; animal studies of early, 12, 87, 123-126, 144-152; A/S ratio and early, 12, 87, 125; class differences in the, 135, 149, 155-159; cumulative effect of, 153; early perceptual, 125; equality of opportunity for, 155, 215; importance of preverbal, 20; poverty and the, 155-159.

Development of: desegregation without compensatory education in the, 201; divisions of mind hampers the, 147; equality of opportunity for the, 215, 228; perceptual vs. motor factors in, 125-126. Fostering early childhood: challenges which demand, 1, 114-115; Parent and Child Centers in, 187-189, 228; political dangers in haste in, 113; problem of the match

in, 129. Linguistic: class differences in fostering, 135, 155-156. Motivational: class differences in fostering, 156-157. Negro's lack of: history of slavery and poverty in, 145. Plasticity in development of: ethical implications of, 199. Poverty and lack of, 145. Societal importance of: technological advances and the, 1, 145. Standards of conduct in: class differences and, 157.

Control: Poverty and locus of, 213.

Cortex: Acetylcholinesterase activity of, 152, 194-195. Thickness of, 152, 194-195.

Cultural deprivation, 2, 39; Counteracting: curricula for, 69, 139-141, 159, 175, 224-228; danger of too-high hopes for, 136-140; language vs. sensorimotor experience in, 43, 175; Parent and Child Centers in, 187-189, 228-232; parents involved in, 139, 140, 182-183, 221-228; preschool enrichment for, 42-44, 159; therapeutic counseling in, 139. Deficit from, 40-42, 109-110, 155-159, 204-214; early reversibility of, 39, 110; experiences accounting for, 155-159, 202-214; habituation to voices in, 41; maximal between ages 18 and 36 months, 109.

Desegregation: Supreme Court decision of 1954, 145.

DEVELOPMENT

Achievement tests and, 151, 196.

Behavioral: anatomic maturation and, 62; cephalocaudal

progression in, 63; emotional vs. cognitive factors in, 86-88; experience and infant, 152; ordinal scales of infant, 42, 67, 130; orphanage rearing and retardation of, 123, 125-126, 148; sequential order in, 62-68; use and rate of, 67, 74, 153, 195.

Belief in predetermination of, 6, 62; accommodation-assimilation and, 132; animal studies of early experience and, 11-13, 65, 87, 125; A/S ratio of Hebb and, 9, 12, 65, 87, 125; cephalocaudal principle and, 130; effects of pet-rearing and, 12; embryology of chick behavior and, 10, 131; equality and, 191; evidence consonant with, 7-9, 62-64; evidence dissonant with, 11-13, 64-68, 121-127, 150-154; evolutionary increase in uterine control and, 10; Freud's influence on, 64; Gesell vs. Piaget and the, 66; G. Stanley Hall's influence on the, 6, 50, 121; Hebb's work and, 9, 11, 65, 68, 83, 123, 143; historical origins of, 6-7, 49-51, 121; Hunt's studies of infantile experience and, 19, 64, 86; influence of visual experience on retinal maturation for, 11; inherited patterns of growth and, 122; interactionism and, 193; Piaget's work and, 65-66; proximodistal principle and, 130; recapitulation theory and, 121; self-fulfilling prophecy in, 128; sequential order and, 63, 66, 130-131; Spitz's studies and, 64-65.

Beliefs untenable about, 113.

Conceptions of, 49-52; interac-

tionism among, 51; predeterminism among, 50; preformationism among, 49.

Coordination of reflexive schemata in, 99; S-S conditioning as, 99.

Dangers from pushing early, 129.

Diagnostic testing of, 69.

Duration of circumstances and change in, 150, 196.

Early cognitive, 96ff; interest a function of experience in, 101; intentions in, 102; intrinsic motivation in, 94; perceptual vs. motor factors in, 97; variety of redundant changes of input and, 98.

Eye-hand coordination in: experience and, 126-127.

Fate of early instinctual needs and, 86.

Fostering early cognitive, 94ff; combining language and sensorimotor experience in, 177; freedom of infant choice in, 107; incongruity or novelty in, 107; interest and surprise in, 129; mothers as teachers in, 183-184; problem of the match in, 108; variety of recognition and, 101.

Fostering values in: poverty and experiences, 157-159.

Infantile experience in, 64.

Infantile instinctual experience and, 86.

Infantile perceptual experience and, 86-88; A/S ratio and effects of, 87.

Inherited patterns of growth in, 122.

IQ as rate of: predeterminism and constancy of, 55.

Language: ITPA as diagnostic of, 69; poverty and, 135.

Locomotor: scooting not creeping in, 68; sequential order in, 63.

Motivational: class differences in, 135-136; epigenesis of intrinsic, 36; poverty and, 156-157.

Neuroanatomical: early experience and, 98, 124, 151-152, 194-195.

Of pecking chicks, 122.

Plasticity of: age and decreasing, 196; ethical implications of, 199-200; longitudinal prediction and, 128; school readiness and, 129.

Poverty and intrauterine, 204.

Practice effects on: implications of epigenesis for, 134; temporary nature of, 8, 13.

Psychosexual theory of, 86; evidence and, 86.

Rate of infantile: plasticity in the, 126-27, 133, 195-196.

Theoretical conceptions of, 49-52.

Diffusion: Klaus-Gray demonstration of, 139-140. Vertical and horizontal, 140.

Dimension: Semantic consequences of, 119.

Disease: Incompetence and, 144.

Drive: Homeostatic need as, 81. Painful stimulation as, 81. Sex as, 81. Uselessness of drive naming, 27.

Early experience: A/S ratio and, 12. Competence and, 20. Effects of infantile shock as, 21-22. Emotional vs. intellectual effects in, 19. Hebb's neuropsychologizing and, 20. Plato on, 18. Political implications of role of, 112. Rousseau's

Emile and, 18. Sensory vs. motor, 24-25.

Early Training Project, 181.

Education: Calvin and Luther and, 146. Compensatory (*see* Compensatory education). Early childhood: Arizona Center for, 165; Bereiter-Engelmann program for, 168-171; Mexican-Americans and, 165; New Nursery School at Greeley for, 163; Peabody Center for, 162; interactionism and individualization of, 149. Emotion and motivation in, 146. Mental health vs., 146.

Emotional attachment: A/S ratio and encounters needed for, 90. Food reward in, 88. Freud's theory of, 88. Gratification theory of, 88-90; Harlow's work and the, 88. Recognition pleasure and, 90. Recognitive familiarity in, 89, 101; imprinting as, 89, 101.

Empty organism: S-R and theory of, 15.

Environment: Effect of stability and time in an, 150.

"Environmental force units," 207; Poor and professional families compared in, 207-208.

Epigenesis, 35, 36, 94, 96, 99, 104; Of intrinsic motivation, 94, 111.

Equality of men: Ethical concern of forefathers in, 191.

Equality of opportunity: Developmental plasticity of the ethics of, 199-200.

Ethics: Developmental plasticity and, 199-200.

Eugenics vs. euthenics, 4, 191.

Eye-hand coordination: Experience and the age of landmarks in, 126, 133, 195.

Factor analysis: Abilities as modes of transfer in, 61. Group factors in intelligence from, 58-59. Meaning of factors, 59-60. Practice and the stability of factors from, 61. Primary mental abilities from, 59. Simplex pattern from repeated testings, 61. Spearman's *g* and *s* from, 58. Unlimited number of factors from, 62.

Faculty psychology: Evidence against, 14.

Farming: Industrial revolution in, 114.

Fate: Self vs. circumstances in, 213.

Fear, 33, 85, 105; Dissonance-incongruity basis for, 33, 85, 105. Hebb's theory of, 33, 85, 105.

Feeding-frustration: Effects of infantile, 19, 64, 86.

Fixation: Reduction from infantile shock, 22.

Gangs: Value acquisition in slum, 211-212.

Genotype: Defined, 51, 148, 193. Phenotype and, 51, 148, 193.

Genotypic potential: Tests as indices of, 68-69.

Grief: Separation, 37.

Group factors, 58-60.

Habituation: Poverty and auditory, 41, 205.

Head Start: Curriculum not compensatory in, 137-139, 216. Danger of discouragement from failure of, 141. Evaluative studies of, 160. Governmental locus of, 159. Laudable purpose of, 137, 159.

Limitations of, 137. No harm from, 217.

Human nature: Changing beliefs about, 2; brain as static switchboard, 13-17; conception of trauma among, 21; drive theory of motivation among, 25-39; fixed intelligence among, 3; motor vs. perceptual experiences, 24; predetermination of development, 6; preverbal experience unimportant, 17-25; theory of psychosexual development, 18.

Illinois Test of Psycholinguistic Abilities (ITPA), 69, 164.

Images: Language as signs for, 106.

Imitation: Interest in novelty and, 38, 106. Intrinsic motivation of, 38, 103. Language acquisition by, 38, 106-107. Miller-Dollard theory of, 103. Recognitive familiarity and pseudo, 38, 102-103.

Imprinting: Following keeps perceptual contact, 101. Recognitive conception of, 89, 101.

INCOMPETENCE

Belief in inborn, predetermined, 147, 190; evidence dissonant with, 148-155; interactionism and the, 148-149, 193; plasticity of infant development and the, 74, 153, 195. Compensatory education for early, 159-180.

Conditions of poverty fostering, 155-159, 202-215; biological, 204; failure to acquire cognitive skills, 155-156, 204-208; failure to acquire motivation, 156-157, 208-211; failure to develop standards of conduct, 157-159, 211-214;

plasticity of early development and the, 232-233; violence and, 158.
Diet and, 193.
Emotional stress during gestation and, 193.
Hope of preventing, 147, 189,
232-233.
Infantile isolation of monkeys
and their, 194.
Premature delivery and, 193.
Preventing development of
early, 180-187; hope of, 140;
diffusion in, 182-183; home
visitors in, 181; involving parents in, 181, 185-186, 219;
mothers as teachers in, 183;
need for research and development for, 141, 181, 189;
Parent and Child Centers in,
187-189, 228-232.
INCONGRUITY, 29, 30, 31, 34, 83,
105
Aesthetic standards and, 30.
Approach behavior and, 32,
34. Attractiveness of optimal,
34, 83, 105. Arousal potential
and, 105. Collative variables
and, 105. Cortical organization and, 105. Direction-
hedonic question and, 31-35.
Dissonance and, 105. Fear
and, 33, 83, 105. Intrinsic
motivation and, 28-31, 96.
Orienting reflex and, 30, 36,
96; developmental progress
dependent on, 96. Uncertainty
and, 83, 105. Variety of standards for, 30, 85. Withdrawal
behavior and, 32-34, 85.
Infantile experience (see Early
experience).
Initiative: Poverty and opportunities to learn, 208.
INTELLIGENCE (see also IQ)
Belief in fixed, 3-6, 54, 56-57,
60, 88, 115, 192; constancy
of IQ and the, 5, 55, 117;
disgenic factors and, 117-119;
early questioning of, 192; effects of early experience and,
193-194; evidence dissonant
with, 5-6, 61-62, 117-118,
148-155, 193-199; Galton's
role in, 116; genetic evidence
dissonant with, 193; historical
basis for, 3-5, 50-57, 116; interactionism and the, 116-117;
rising average IQ and the,
117-118.
Beliefs about now untenable,
113.
Class differences in, 135, 202;
child-rearing and, 135-136.
Concrete operations of: sequence in development of,
66-67.
Correlational analysis of: heredity vs. environment and
the, 56-61.
Development of academic:
longitudinal evidence on the,
151, 196.
Differential fertility and, 71-
73; causal direction in, 72;
rising average IQ and, 71-72.
Dimensional concept of: semantic consequences of, 55,
120.
Draw-a-Man measures of: cultural variation in, 74, 154, 198.
Factor analysis of, 58-62; abilities as modes of transfer in,
61; heredity vs. environment
and, 60-62; meaning of factors
in, 59; transfer of training and,
196-197.
Genotypic vs. phenotypic potential, 68.
Heredity vs. environment in:
cultural variations in Draw-a-
Man IQ and, 57, 74, 154, 198;

interactionism and, 57; proper question re, 57-58; proportionality question of, 57. Hierarchical organization of, 61-62, 134; detour problems and, 194; experience and the, 196-197; factor analytic evidence of, 134; infantile isolation, learning-sets, and, 194; Piaget's observations and the, 196-197; problem-solving evidence of, 134; sensorimotor evidence of, 134.
Impulsivity-reflectivity and, 210.
Infant tests of: longitudinal prediction with, 60, 70; reliability and validity of, 60; remedial procedures and, 69.
Plasticity of tested, 198.
Predicted drop vs. upward trend in, 72, 197.
Sensorimotor: hierarchical organization of, 134.
Structural nature of, 52-62; Burt's inborn capacity and, 54; complex faculty of Binet and, 54; effects of practice on factor, 61; ethnic variations in, 203; faculty of fixed quantity and, 54; Galton's sensorimotor tests and, 53; group factors in the, 58-60; Guilford's factor theory of the, 62; socioeconomic status and, 203; Spearman's g and s, 58; tests to diagnose the, 70; Thurstone's primary abilities as the, 59; transfer of training and, 61.
Terms: dimension and scale for, 55, 119.
Tested level of: industrial development and, 197-198.
Testing of: achievement-testing and the, 118-119; changes

in practice of, 68; contemporary vs. longitudinal validity in the, 70; genotypic potential and, 68; hierarchical organization and the, 73; longitudinal validity in the, 70.
Tests of: American development of Binet, 53-55; genotypic potential and, 68, 115-118; longitudinal prediction with, 199.
Interaction: Poverty and verbal, 207.
Interactionism, 51-52, 116, 148, 193; Jennings and, 52. Johannsen's genotype and phenotype in, 51-52, 116. Johannsen's origination of, 51. Johannsen vs. Mendel and, 193. Order in development and, 133. Sex of mosquitoes and, 149.
IQ: As a predetermined rate of development, 55. Constancy of, 5-7, 55, 116-117, 152-153. Cultural variations in Draw-a-Man, 57, 74, 154, 198. Increases in average: change of circumstances and, 123, 197-198. Plasticity of infant, 7, 55, 74, 127, 153-154, 193, 195. Predicted drop vs. average rise in, 117-118. Proportion of variance fixed by age four, 151. Proportions of variance in: hereditary vs. environmental, 56-57. Reliability of infant, 60. Studies of twins and, 5, 6. Validity of: longitudinal vs. cross-sectional, 127. "Wandering," 2.

Kallikak family, 5.

Labor: Automation and demand for, 144.

Language: Class differences in, 135-136, 155-156, 206. Poverty and, 206.

Learning: Accommodation-assimilation and, 66, 132-133. Conceptual separation from maturation, 51. Piaget's theory and, 66, 132. Traditional rubrics of, 132; limitations of, 133.

Learning-sets: And infantile isolation, 194.

Luther, Martin: Reading schools and, 146.

Match (see Problem of the match).

Maturation: Early experience and, 11-12, 125-128, 151-152, 194-196. Visual experience and neuroanatomical, 125-128, 151-152, 194-196.

Mediation: Conception of in S-R theory, 15. Receptor function in developing, 24.

Mental health: Education vs., 143, 146-147. Unconcern for competence in, 146-147.

Mind: Aristotle's three divisions of, 144; governmental institutions and, 147.

Mosquitoes: Sex and embryo temperature in, 149, 193.

MOTIVATION
Behavior without drive, 26-27.
Development of: poverty and, 136, 208-210.
Direction-hedonic question of: incongruity and the, 31-35.
Drive theory of, 26, 81; drive naming and, 27, 82; evidence against, 26-27, 81-82.
Fear as: dissonance and incongruity in, 31-33, 85, 105.
Impulsivity vs. reflectivity in, 210.

Incongruity and approach, 31.
Incongruity and fear, 33.
Incongruity and withdrawal, 32.
Interest in the familiar, 37, 89, 100-101; babbling and, 38; hand watching and, 38.
Interest in increasing complexity, 34-35, 38, 105.
Interest in the novel as, 38, 83, 106.
Intrinsic in information processing and action, 28-29, 82-83, 94-111; adaptation level and, 83; apathy from monotony in, 104; attentional preference for recognitive familiarity in, 37, 101; babbling and, 102; cognitive dissonance as, 83; conception of, 95; epigenesis in development of, 35-39, 94-111; fear of the dark as, 33; feedback loop in, 28; hand watching and, 102; imitation and, 106; imprinting and, 101; incongruity and complexity in, 34; incongruity with standards as, 29, 82; interest in novelty as, 105-106; joy from spontaneous activity in, 99; Montessori's use of, 45, 162; optimal incongruity and, 83; orienting response in, 30, 36, 95-96; Piaget's observations and, 36; pseudoimitation and recognitive familiarity, 103; recognitive familiarity in, 100; stages in the development of, 96-107; stimulus deprivation and, 84; TOTE unit in, 29; varieties of standards in, 29-31.
Need for achievement in, 211-213; maternal role in, 212; paternal behavior and, 212; performance and, 213; pov-

erty and opportunity to learn, 212-213.

Poverty and opportunities to learn, 208.

Poverty and future goals in, 208.

Poverty and persistence of, 209-210.

Poverty, the welfare laws, and, 215.

Psychodynamic theory of: incongruity and, 84.

Reinforcement in: concrete vs. social, 209; poverty and immediate, 209.

Self-concept in: competitive schools and the, 201.

Spatial and temporal organization in, 210, 211.

Spontaneous activity and, 27.

Stimulus deprivation and, 32.

Urge to mastery in, 82.

Negroes: History of incompetence, 145.

Novelty: Informational incongruity as, 105.

Nursery schools: New Nursery School (Greeley, Colorado), 163. Variations in traditional curricula of, 166.

Opportunity: Competence and economic, 200.

Optic disc: Dark-rearing and pallor of, 151.

Orienting response: Attentional aspects, 95. Emotional aspects, 95.

Parent and Child Centers, 187, 228; Compensatory education in: day-care for, 187, 229. Correction of family isolation in, 189, 230. Educational requirements of deploying, 189,

232. Improving quality of adult life in, 189, 231. Mutual interdependence of families in, 189, 229-230. President's recommendation of, 189, 231.

Parents: And preventing early incompetence, 180-189, 220-228. Centers for children and, 187, 228.

Pecking: Accuracy and experience in, 122.

Peer gangs: Values developed in, 158, 211-214.

Perception: Repeated encounters and loss of meaning in, 104.

Personality: Individual differences in: sources of anxiousness in, 78; traits as static dimensions of, 78.

Personality theory: All behavior is motivated in, 81. Concepts making observations surprising in, 77. Personologists vs. social psychologists in, 78. Recent evidence and, 76. Thomas, W. I., and, 78. Traits as source of behavioral variance, 77.

Personnel selection: Testing genotypic potential and, 68.

Phenotype: Defined, 51. Genotype and, 148, 193.

Phonemes: Auditory discrimination of, 69, 75, 136; object familiarity and, 228.

Poor (see Poverty).

POVERTY

Children of: auditory discrimination in, 69, 75, 136, 228; auditory-vocal habituation in, 41, 205; chronic illnesses of, 204; cognitive development of, 204; concrete vs. social re-

ward in, 209; control of fate in, 213; defective uterine development in, 204; "environmental force units" for, 207; goal-setting reality in, 214; habituation and inattention of, 206; immediate vs. delayed reinforcement in, 209; impulsivity-reflectivity in, 210; incompetence and heredity of, 203; IQs of black, 202; IQs of mountain, 202; language-learning opportunities of, 205; lack of motivational persistence in, 213; lack of self-esteem in, 213-214; low IQs of, 190; motivational opportunities of, 208, 211; motivational persistence in, 209; need for achievement in, 212-213; neonatal vulnerability in, 204; nutritional deficiencies in, 204; opportunities to acquire values in, 211; opportunities missing for, 202; reinforcement experiences of, 210; risk-taking in, 214; scholastic ability of, 203; spatial organization in homes of, 211; syntactical models for, 206; temporal organization in homes of, 211; temporal orientations of, 210-211; "tuning out" of voices in, 205; welfare laws and, 215; what to do about, 215.
Families of: lack of democratic atmosphere in, 206.
Hope of breaking the cycle of: plasticity of early development and, 232.
Incompetence of those in: early experience and the, 190-191.
Parents of: authoritarian child-rearing of, 206; lack of conceptual communication in, 205, 206; love of children in, 208; syntactical models in, 206.
Natural-incompetence view of, 190.
Predeterminism, 50-51; Constancy of IQ as, 55. Evidence for: cephalocaudal progression as, 63. Freud's psychosexual theory and, 64. Galton's contribution to, 3, 50, 192. Gesell's norms and, 63. Hall's use of recapitulation as, 51. Mendel and, 52.
Prediction: Improvement with age of longitudinal, 128.
Preformationism, 49-50; Predeterminism and, 50.
Prematurity: Poverty and, 204.
Preschool: Montessori's contributions to, 44-46.
Pride: Poverty and sense of, 213.
Problem of the match: Interest and surprise in, 129. Nature of, 42. Preschool enrichment and the, 42-44.
Problem-solving ability: Cage- vs. pet-rearing and, 20. Early experience and adult, 20, 86. Early experience in animals and their, 193-194.
Pseudoimitation: Recognitive motivation of, 103.
Psychodynamics: Cognitive dissonance and, 84-85. Incongruity theory and, 84.
Psychosexual development: relative unimportance of, 18-19.
Public mental health service: Compensatory education as, 142-143.
Pure stimulus act, 15.

Reaching and grasping: Recognitive motivation of, 103.

Readiness: Problem of the match and, 129.

Reformation: Education and the, 146.

Reinforcement: Concrete vs. social: class differences in, 209. Drive-reduction theory of, 81. Social status and delay of, 209.

Retina: Dark-rearing and development of, 151. Dark-rearing and histology of, 152. Glial and neural cells in ganglion of: early visual experience and, 194-195.

Ribonucleic acid (*see* RNA).

Risk-taking: Poverty and, 214.

RNA: Capacity to synthesize: early experience and, 98. Dark-rearing and retinal, 152. Early experience and production of, 124. Retinal-ganglion production of: early visual experience and, 194.

Scale: Semantic implications of, 119-120.

School readiness: Changing conceptions of, 73-75. Hierarchical organization of abilities and, 73. Mental age as, 73. Predetermination by age, 73; evidence against, 74. Testing and, 68.

Scholastic achievement: Pride and, 213.

Science: Knowledge or process, 77. Of persons and conduct, 76.

Semantic differential, 81.

Separation anxiety, 37.

Slums (*see also* Poverty): Violence in, 230.

Smiling: Delight from recognition and, 90. Recognitive familiarity and, 101.

Standards of conduct (*see* Values).

Stimulus deprivation, 32, 83.

Supreme Court: Desegregation decision of the, 145.

Talking typewriter, 43; Kobler, Richard, and the, 163.

Technological culture: Competence needed in, 1, 200.

Test: Illinois Test of Psycholinguistic Abilities (ITPA), 182. Mental as Goddard's term, 55. Peabody Picture Vocabulary, 182.

Test - Operate - Test - Exit (TOTE) unit, 29.

Tewksbury State Hospital, 133.

Top-level reaching: Experience and age of, 134.

TOTE unit, 29, 3.

Traits: Age and increase in stability of, 196. Duration of circumstances and stability of, 150, 196.

Trauma: Effect of infantile shock, 22. Freud's conception of, 21. Infantile handling and shock, 21-23. Infantile pain experience as, 90-91. Strain differences in, 91. Strong homeostatic need as, 90-91.

Validity: Longitudinal vs. cross-sectional, 127.

Values: Imitation and, 158. Opportunities to acquire: peer groups of slums and, 211-212; poverty and, 211-214. Poverty and achievement, 213. Poverty and acquisition of, 157-159. Violence and acquiring, 158.

Violence: Failure of repression to control, 230. Poverty and, 158-159.

Vision: Blink-response in: looking and development of, 153. Dark-rearing and development of, 151.

ILLINI BOOKS

IB-1	Grierson's Raid: A Cavalry Adventure of the Civil War	D. Alexander Brown	$1.75
IB-2	The Mars Project	Wernher von Braun	$ .95
IB-3	The New Exploration: A Philosophy of Regional Planning	Benton MacKaye, with an introduction by Lewis Mumford	$1.75
IB-4	Tragicomedy: Its Origin and Development in Italy, France, and England	Marvin T. Herrick	$1.95
IB-5	Themes in Greek and Latin Epitaphs	Richmond Lattimore	$1.95
IB-6	The Doctrine of Responsible Party Government: Its Origins and Present State	Austin Ranney	$1.25
IB-7	An Alternative to War or Surrender	Charles E. Osgood	$1.45
IB-8	Reference Books in the Mass Media	Eleanor Blum	$1.50
IB-9	Life in a Mexican Village: Tepoztlán Restudied	Oscar Lewis	$2.95
IB-10	*Three Presidents and Their Books: The Reading of Jefferson, Lincoln, and Franklin D. Roosevelt	Arthur E. Bestor, David C. Mearns, and Jonathan Daniels	$ .95
IB-11	Cultural Sciences: Their Origin and Development	Florian Znaniecki	$2.25
IB-12	The Legend of Noah: Renaissance Rationalism in Art, Science, and Letters	Don Cameron Allen	$1.45
IB-13	*The Mathematical Theory of Communication	Claude E. Shannon and Warren Weaver	$1.45
IB-14	Philosophy and Ordinary Language	Charles E. Caton, ed.	$1.95
IB-15	Four Theories of the Press	Fred S. Siebert, Theodore Peterson, and Wilbur Schramm	$1.45
IB-16	Constitutional Problems Under Lincoln	James G. Randall	$2.95
IB-17	Viva Mexicol	Charles Macomb Flandrau, edited and with an introduction by C. Harvey Gardiner	$1.95
IB-18	Comic Theory in the Sixteenth Century	Marvin T. Herrick	$1.75

Also available in clothbound editions.

IB-19	Black Hawk: An Autobiography	Donald Jackson, ed.	$1.75
IB-20	Mexican Government in Transition	Robert E. Scott	$2.25
IB-21	John Locke and the Doctrine of Majority-Rule	Willmoore Kendall	$1.25
IB-22	The Framing of the Fourteenth Amendment	Joseph B. James	$1.45
IB-23	The Mind and Spirit of John Peter Altgeld: Selected Writings and Addresses	Henry M. Christman, ed.	$1.25
IB-24	A History of the United States Weather Bureau	Donald R. Whitnah	$1.75
IB-25	Freedom of the Press in England, 1476-1776: The Rise and Decline of Government Controls	Fredrick Seaton Siebert	$2.25
IB-26	Freedom and Communications	Dan Lacy	$1.50
IB-27	The Early Development of Henry James	Cornelia Pulsifer Kelley, with an introduction by Lyon N. Richardson	$1.95
IB-28	*Law in the Soviet Society	Wayne R. LaFave, ed.	$1.95
IB-29	Beyond the Mountains of the Moon: The Lives of Four Africans	Edward H. Winter	$1.75
IB-30	The History of Doctor Johann Faustus	H. G. Haile	$1.45
IB-31	One World	Wendell L. Willkie, with an introduction by Donald Bruce Johnson	$1.75
IB-32	William Makepeace Thackeray: Contributions to the Morning Chronicle	Gordon N. Ray, ed.	$1.45
IB-33	Italian Comedy in the Renaissance	Marvin T. Herrick	$1.75
IB-34	Death in the Literature of Unamuno	Mario J. Valdés	$1.25
IB-35	*Port of New York: Essays on Fourteen American Moderns	Paul Rosenfeld, with an introductory essay by Sherman Paul	$2.25
IB-36	*How to Do Library Research	Robert B. Downs	$1.45
IB-37	Henry James: Representative Selections, with Introduction, Bibliography, and Notes	Lyon N. Richardson	$3.50

* Also available in clothbound editions.

IB-38	Symbolic Crusade: Status Politics and the American Temperance Movement	Joseph R. Gusfield	$1.75
IB-39	*Genesis and Structure of Society	Giovanni Gentile, translated by H. S. Harris	$1.95
IB-40	The Social Philosophy of Giovanni Gentile	H. S. Harris	$2.45
IB-41	*As We Saw the Thirties: Essays on Social and Political Movements of a Decade	Rita James Simon, ed.	$2.45
IB-42	The Symbolic Uses of Politics	Murray Edelman	$2.45
IB-43	White-Collar Trade Unions: Contemporary Developments in Industrialized Societies	Adolf Sturmthal, ed.	$3.50
IB-44	*The Labor Arbitration Process	R. W. Fleming	$2.45
IB-45	*Edmund Wilson: A Study of Literary Vocation in Our Time	Sherman Paul	$2.45
IB-46	*George Santayana's America: Essays on Literature and Culture	James Ballowe, ed.	$2.25
IB-47	The Measurement of Meaning	Charles E. Osgood, George J. Suci, and Percy H. Tannenbaum	$3.45
IB-48	*The Miracle of Growth	Foreword by Arnold Gesell	$1.75
IB-49	*Information Theory and Esthetic Perception	Abraham Moles	$2.45
IB-50	Outlawing the Spoils: A History of the Civil Service Reform Movement, 1865-1883	Ari Hoogenboom	$2.95
IB-51	*Community Colleges: A President's View	Thomas E. O'Connell	$1.95
IB-52	*The Joys and Sorrows of Recent American Art	Allen S. Weller	$3.95
IB-53	*Dimensions of Academic Freedom	Walter P. Metzger, Sanford H. Kadish, Arthur DeBardeleben, and Edward J. Bloustein	$ .95
IB-54	*Essays on Frege	E. D. Klemke, ed.	$3.95
IB-55	The Fine Hammered Steel of Herman Melville	Milton R. Stern	$2.95

* Also available in clothbound editions.

IB-56	*The Challenge of Incompetence and Poverty: Papers on the Role of Early Education	J. McVicker Hunt	$3.45
IB-57	*Mission Overseas: A Handbook for U.S. Families in Developing Countries	Harold D. Guither and W. N. Thompson	$2.95
IB-58	*Teaching and Learning	Donald Vandenberg, ed.	$3.45
IB-59	*Theory of Knowledge and Problems of Education	Donald Vandenberg, ed.	$3.45
IB-60	*The Art of William Carlos Williams: A Discovery and Possession of America	James Guimond	$2.45
IB-61	*Psychological Tests and Personnel Decisions (Second Edition)	Lee J. Cronbach and Goldine C. Gleser	$2.95
IB-62	*Mass Communications (Second Edition)	Wilbur Schramm, ed.	$4.50

* Also available in clothbound editions.

University of Illinois Press Urbana, Chicago, and London